COMPOSITION: Discovery and Communication

Ray Kytle

CENTRAL MICHIGAN UNIVERSITY

COMPOSITION:

Discovery

and

Communication

RANDOM HOUSE NEW YORK

for Annette

PREFACE

The premise underlying the form and content of *Composition: Discovery and Communication* is that the production of an expository-argumentative essay involves a process. The two major aspects of this process are analysis, the stage of discovery, and composition, the stage of communication.

Through analysis, the student explores his subject in order to discover the content that he wishes to communicate and establishes the classifications, which structure and order that content. Only after having performed these "prewriting" preliminaries is the student in a position to formulate his thesis and move on to the second aspect of composition: written communication. Section One, "Preliminaries to Composition," is devoted to that portion of composition that must precede the writing of the first word of the first sentence of the introductory paragraph of an essay.

In Section Two, "Composition," I have concentrated on a strictly limited number of basic principles. In stating, elaborating, and exemplifying these principles I was constantly aware of minor exceptions and effective alternatives. But I was much more painfully aware of the general composition student's intense desire (if not blessed rage) for some recognizable order—some embraceable structure to serve him as a solid and trustworthy base. The student can more readily venture beyond the confines of these principles for knowing that he can fall back on them with confidence should his writing venture turn misadventure.

Sections One and Two represent the "compositional center" of the text. They are intended to provide the basic competencies. Sections Three and Five are more ambitious. They aim to refine the quality of discovery and the quality of communication. Taken together, they aim to encourage richness of thought precisely and pleasingly expressed.

Often, in the skillful and experienced writer, the stages in the process of composition are not distinguishable. Discovery, communication, and refinement of thought and expression coalesce in the ongoing process of creation. However, most freshmen have yet to achieve the skill and experience which produce that intuitive self-critical voice that guides the practiced writer. To help the student become conscious of and adept at the process of composition is the purpose of *Composition: Discovery and Communication.* For, with few exceptions, it is only after he has made the transition from the unconscious and the uncritical to the conscious and the critical that the writer can progress to that final stage where discovery–communication–refinement, thought-writing-style become one.

December, 1969   R. K.

Acknowledgments

Greg Cowan and Elisabeth McPherson have my heartfelt thanks for their invaluable editorial assistance and advice. Tom Davis read large portions of the manuscript and made helpful comments. I am indebted to John Ostrom's *Better Paragraphs* for the concept of "unity words."

Contents

Section Five: Clear Thinking for Composition   167

Section Six: The Research Paper   253

Section One

PRELIMINARIES
TO
COMPOSITION

Composition of an essay does not begin when you put pen to paper to write the first word of the first sentence of your introduction paragraph. An essential part of the total process of composition takes place before that first word is written. For before you can begin to write on a subject, you must dis-cover what you want to say about it. Discovering *what you want to say about a subject is quite different from* recovering *(through systematic recall) what you already think about it, what the popular views about it are, and so forth.* Discovery *is an active investigation of the subject in which you examine it from dif-ferent points of view, recognize its complexity, and gain new and deeper insight into it.*

The focus of this section is on the nature and uses of analysis—a technique of discovery.

1

Analysis

Objectivity: The Prerequisite

You cannot competently practice analysis until you can achieve and maintain an open mind and an *objective attitude* toward your subject. In the dialogues that illustrate analysis we will note those reasoning habits that most blatantly interfere with objectivity. Later, in the section "Clear Thinking for Composition," we will examine some of the more insidious forces that undermine objectivity.

Insight: The Goal

Once you have learned to achieve and maintain an open mind when analyzing a subject, you will not feel compelled to prove the accuracy of certain preconceptions about it. Instead, your attitude will be: "I want to *understand* as much as possible about the subject. And I won't know what I'm going to say about the subject until I have gained as much *insight* into it as possible." The problem becomes, then, how to achieve insight.

Analysis: The Method

The way to achieve insight is through *analysis*. Analysis is the method by which you explore your subject and discover its richness and diversity. You will not know what you are going to say about the subject; you will not formulate your thesis assertion about the subject, until *after* you have *analyzed* it. Three principles govern analysis, and you should have them firmly in mind whenever you undertake exploration through analysis. The first two principles are:

1. Examine the subject from various points of view.
2. Classify these points of view.

It is impossible to overemphasize the importance of these two steps, because it is looking at the subject from various points of view that will lead you to insight, and it is classifying these points of view that will give an order and structure to your paper. Let's take some examples:

Subject: Fraternities

POINTS OF VIEW	CLASSIFICATION
1. What do fraternities do?	Function
2. What do fraternities achieve?	Achievements
3. Who is invited to join fraternities?	Membership
4. How much does it cost to belong to a fraternity?	Expense
5. Are there any drawbacks to having fraternities on campus?	Disadvantages

Notice that when you analyze a subject by looking at it from different points of view, you break it down into its parts, you examine various aspects of the subject.

Subject: Punishment of Criminals

POINTS OF VIEW	CLASSIFICATION
1. What kind of punishment is used?	Type
2. What is the purpose of punishment?	Purpose
3. What does punishment achieve?	Effect
4. What does punishment cost?	Expense

In this case it is obvious that any *one* of the *classifications* derived from a preliminary analysis of "Punishment of Criminals" is broad enough to serve as a subject for a full-length theme. So, instead of writing on the subject "Punishment of Criminals," which is too *broad* a subject, you should *limit your subject* by writing on one of the classifications. But, of course, before you can write on it, you must analyze it. For example:

Limited Subject: The Purpose of Punishment of Criminals

POINTS OF VIEW	CLASSIFICATION
1. What is meant by "punishment" and "criminals"?	Definition of key terms
2. What are the commonly stated purposes?	Avowed purposes
3. Are there any unstated, hidden purposes?	Unavowed purposes

This subject obviously requires that you *inform yourself* before you can begin to answer these questions. After informing yourself, you might come up with a topic outline similar to that below:

The Purpose of Punishment of Criminals

   I. Definition of Key Terms
      A. Punishment: imprisonment
      B. Criminals: adult felons

  II. Avowed Purposes
      A. To deter potential criminals
      B. To rehabilitate criminals

 III. Unavowed Purposes
      A. To satisfy vindictive needs
      B. To encourage social solidarity

When you look at a subject from as many points of view as possible, you will automatically adhere to the third principle of analysis, which is:

3. Recognize the complexity of the subject.

When you look at a given subject from as many points of view as possible, you will probably realize that the matter is more complex than you may have thought at first. And in many cases the subject will turn out to be so complex that you will have to acknowledge that no *general* law or principle concerning it can be laid down. This is especially true of broad subjects which, when concretized, turn out to be composed of almost infinite variables. When you encounter such subjects, you must beware of making any categorical assertions about them. (A categorical assertion is an assertion without any qualification or condition: "Love is good," "Freedom must be defended.")
Some examples of this type of subject are:

Love	Beauty
Communism	Liberty
Honor	Protest

The point is that no single unqualified assertion about any of these subjects can possibly be valid because the subjects denote too many variables. Instead of making a categorical assertion about the subject, you must content yourself with an analysis of it (or of some aspect of it). To illustrate:

Subject: Love

POINTS OF VIEW	CLASSIFICATION
1. What kind of love?	Type
2. Love for whom?	Object
3. Love for what purpose?	Motive

Limited Subject: Object of Love

POINTS OF VIEW	CLASSIFICATION
1. Love of mother for son	Maternal love
2. Love of father for son	Paternal love
3. Love of son for parent	Filial love
4. Love of brother for sister	Brotherly love
5. Love of sister for brother	Sisterly love
6. Love of man for his country	Patriotic love
7. Love of man for his fellow man	Humanitarian love
8. Love of man for the ill and weak	Compassionate love
9. Love of man for God	Religious love

At this point we realize that when we classify love by the *object* of love, we come up with a *type* of love. For example, love of mother for son (object) is classified as maternal love (type). But each type of love can be further subdivided according to the *motives* or *needs* of the person loving. For instance, we speak of *exploitative* maternal love, *possessive* maternal love, *selfish* maternal love, *self-sacrificing* maternal love, and so forth. So, as is obvious, no generalization about "Love," no statement that "Love is . . . ," can possibly be accurate, because any such categorical assertion *ignores the complexity of the subject.*

You may sometimes find yourself with a subject that is simply too complex to work with. The tip-off is that when you begin to analyze it, it just keeps on breaking down into smaller and smaller pieces, like a clod of dry earth. The more you handle it, the more it crumbles. In this case, you should work with one of the little pieces that crumbles off, not with the whole subject. For example, we found that maternal love broke down, when it was looked at from different points of view, into such types as "exploitative," "possessive," and so forth. Take *one* of these subdivisions of a subdivision and work with it:

Limited Subject: Possessive Maternal Love

POINTS OF VIEW	CLASSIFICATION
1. What are the characteristics of possessive maternal love?	Characteristics
2. What causes a mother to love in this way?	Causes
3. What are the effects of this type of love on the children?	Effects

SUMMARY

Analysis requires that you approach your subject with an open mind—with objectivity. The goal of analysis is insight and understanding. To analyze a subject, you look at it from as many points of view as possible and then classify these various points of view. You must always recognize and respect the complexity of the subject, because failure to recognize its complexity will lead to oversimplification and, hence, to inaccuracy.

With these general remarks in mind, let us turn to some dialogues that show the process of analysis in action.

2

Analysis in Action

☞ YVONNE AND THE DIRTY-MINDED INSTRUCTOR:
An Exciting Dialogue—With a Moral

Yvonne is a pretty, blond-haired, sexy freshman of eighteen. She could be the girl sitting next to you or in front of you, provided, of course, that that girl is pretty, blond-haired, and sexy. When Yvonne left home for college, her mother took her aside and warned her to watch out for dirty-minded young college instructors who would try to put wrong ideas into her head.

Yvonne didn't really pay much attention, even though she promised to watch out; but sure enough, the very first day she walked into her freshman composition class, there was the young instructor her mother had warned her about. And sure enough, after he checked the role, he assigned a theme on the subject, of all things, "premarital sex"! As soon as the other students had begun writing, Yvonne rushed to the front of the classroom, and the thrilling dialogue that follows began:

YVONNE (*incredulously*): By premarital sexual relations do you mean having sex with a man before you're married to him?
INSTRUCTOR: Yes.
YVONNE (*impulsively*): Oh! That's bad! Everbody knows that.
INSTRUCTOR: What do you mean, "bad"?
YVONNE (*with conviction*): Wrong.
INSTRUCTOR: What do you mean, "wrong"?
YVONNE: You shouldn't do it.

INSTRUCTOR: Why not?

YVONNE (*becoming exasperated*): Because it's *wrong!*

INSTRUCTOR: You mean that *you* don't believe in having premarital relationships?

YVONNE: What kind of girl do you think I am?

INSTRUCTOR: In other words, you feel that if you could be convinced that there were some advantages to premarital sex relations, you would engage in them. And you don't want to?

YVONNE: Yes.

INSTRUCTOR: It's the same sort of thing as losing your belief in God. Then there would be nothing to keep you from going out and doing all sorts of horrible things.

YVONNE (*delighted at finally being understood*): That's it, exactly.

INSTRUCTOR: Do you see any advantages or good points about being a social worker?

YVONNE (*suspiciously*): What's that got to do with anything?

INSTRUCTOR: Do you?

YVONNE: Of course. There're lots of good points. Help people, do your part, all sorts of things.

INSTRUCTOR: Do you want to be a social worker?

YVONNE: Ugh! Icky people!

INSTRUCTOR: Social workers?

YVONNE: No, of course not. The people social workers work with.

INSTRUCTOR: Well then?

YVONNE: Well then, what? You're trying to trap me.

INSTRUCTOR: Well then, you can see the advantages and rewards of being a social worker, but you don't feel that recognizing them means you have to become one.

YVONNE: Of course not.

INSTRUCTOR: Then why do you feel that if you discover some advantages to premarital sexual relations you will have to become your boyfriend's lover?

YVONNE (*disgustedly*): I just don't understand you. They're not the same thing at all. Having sex with your boyfriend is *wrong.*

At this point let's interrupt and try to figure out what's going through Yvonne's pretty blond head.

Objectivity

In the first place, we can perceive the *lack of objectivity* which is one of the major blocks to logical thinking.

She feels *personally involved* in the question of premarital sexual relationships. Yvonne is no psychotic; we're not going to throw her into a mental institution, but she is, nevertheless, displaying here a form of a common paranoid reaction which is called "delusion of reference." If a paranoid person sees two people whispering together, he may immediately deduce that they are whispering about him—perhaps plotting how best to kill him. In a similar way, a hypochondriac will read of the symptoms of some disease or illness and immediately discover those symptoms in himself.

Yvonne, here, is taking the subject personally. She feels that somehow the question of whether or not *she* should have premarital experiences is tied up with the subject.

Either–Or Thinking

Secondly, Yvonne feels that if an act is not, to use her word, "wrong," then it must be "right." This is *either-or* thinking, and we will, in Section Five, look at several of the causes of it. She feels that premarital sex must be *either all* bad, *or* it must be *all* right, *all* good. But, of course, this doesn't follow.

And, finally, Yvonne is scared. She is afraid to find anything "good" about the subject because that will mean, to her mind, that she must jump into bed with her boyfriend, and, the fact is, she doesn't want to. This is that old and false fear we have of the mystical connection between thought and deed. To think it is to do it, and the one will lead to the other.

So, she is really thinking like this, although she doesn't realize it:

If I find anything at all desirable or pleasant about premarital sex, that means it's not bad but good, and then I'll have to do it; but I don't want to, so I'm not going to look at the good side or even think about the subject at all, because then I'd become a bad girl and would be ashamed of myself and contemptible to my parents.

Once Yvonne realizes that to think is not to do and that an act can be both "right" and "wrong" from different points of view, she can achieve the intellectual detachment, the *objectivity*, which will allow her to move to the second phase in dealing with a subject, which is analysis.

Analysis

If you recall, we left Yvonne stamping her feet in anger at the stupidity of her instructor. He had suggested that if she could see advantages in being a social worker and not want to be one, she could safely see advantages to premarital sex and yet not engage in it. But she only shook her head and cried, "Having sex with your boyfriend is *wrong!*" This intriguing exchange continues:

INSTRUCTOR: But you feel that being a social worker is wrong, too.

YVONNE: No, wrong for me, but not *wrong*. They're not the same thing at *all*.

INSTRUCTOR: Oh. And is premarital sex wrong for you?

YVONNE: Of course. But it's also *wrong* wrong.

INSTRUCTOR: *Wrong* wrong?

YVONNE (*with conviction*): *Wrong* wrong.

INSTRUCTOR: Do you mean *morally* wrong?

YVONNE: What else do you think I could have meant?

INSTRUCTOR: But being a social worker is not morally wrong?

YVONNE: No.

INSTRUCTOR: It's wrong for you. *Personally* wrong?

YVONNE: Yes.

INSTRUCTOR: So you are objecting to social work for *personal* reasons and to premarital sex for *moral* reasons.

YVONNE (*happily*): Exactly! You're not as stupid as I thought.

INSTRUCTOR: Thank you.

YVONNE: You're welcome.

INSTRUCTOR: May we return to the point?

YVONNE: Let's do.

INSTRUCTOR: You are objecting to premarital sex on the grounds of *morality*. What do you mean by *moral* reasons?

YVONNE: Moral is moral. Right and wrong.

INSTRUCTOR: Are we going to start this again?

YVONNE: God, I hope not.

INSTRUCTOR: Exactly—God!

YVONNE: What?

INSTRUCTOR: When you refer to moral reasons, don't you actually have in mind *religious* sanctions against premarital sex?

YVONNE: Of course. "Thou shalt not commit adultery."

INSTRUCTOR: (*patiently*): That refers to extramarital sex, not premarital.

YVONNE (*crestfallen*): Oh.

INSTRUCTOR: So you are objecting to premarital sex on *religious* grounds.

YVONNE: Yes.

INSTRUCTOR: We could call this a *point of view*. You are citing an argument against premarital sex from a *religious* point of view.

YVONNE: Yes.

INSTRUCTOR: Can you think of any other points of view from which objections can be found?

YVONNE (*brightly*): Sure!

INSTRUCTOR: For example?

YVONNE: The *social* point of view.

INSTRUCTOR: Yes?

YVONNE: Well, what do you think my neighbors at home would do if they found out?

INSTRUCTOR: What?

YVONNE: They would die!

INSTRUCTOR: Really? How sad.

YVONNE: Not die. *Die!*

INSTRUCTOR: Die?

YVONNE: *Die!*

INSTRUCTOR: This again?

YVONNE: They would be shocked and talk about me.

INSTRUCTOR: Yes?

YVONNE: And it would get around.

INSTRUCTOR: Yes?

YVONNE: And the girls at church would whisper behind my back.

INSTRUCTOR: Yes?

YVONNE: And people would look at me funny.

INSTRUCTOR: Yes?

YVONNE (*bursting into tears*): Oh! I just couldn't stand it!

INSTRUCTOR (*handing Yvonne his handkerchief*): You're losing your detachment again.

YVONNE (*sniffling*): Sorry.

INSTRUCTOR: In other words, you could also argue against premarital sex from the point of view of the *social consequences of detection.*

YVONNE: Oh boy!

INSTRUCTOR: You could show that, from a *social* point of view, the couple might suffer the consequences of gossip, condemnation, and ostracism.

YVONNE: Oh!

Once again, we must break into this emotion-charged scene with the cold voice of reason.

Yvonne, after achieving the necessary detachment, has been able to begin *analyzing* the topic. She is still against premarital sex, but she has progressed from an emotion-laden cry that it is "wrong," which blocked rational thought about the subject. She has come to realize that there are different *points of view* from which one can look at the matter.

Points of View

Imagine yourself trying to view a mansion surrounded by a high, dense hedge. The hedge has holes in it here and there, and you peer through one and then another and another. Each opening allows you to see only a small portion of the mansion. But by the time you have looked through all of the holes, or *points of view,* you will have an accurate conception of the nature and appearance of the mansion. But if you were asked to describe the mansion and looked through only one or two holes, you would probably be able to give only a very incomplete, or even inaccurate, description. For example, what if the hole you looked through only allowed you to see the servants' quarters? In that case you might even deny that there was a mansion at all.

The first step that Yvonne took was to realize that by "wrong," she was referring to the viewpoint labeled "religion"— she found that she could argue against premarital sex from the *religious* point of view.

After that, she moved on to another vantage point, the "social" point of view, and realized that there were a number of reasons to refrain from premarital sex because of *society's* reaction to such behavior.

So far, then, the points of view from which Yvonne has looked at the subject have allowed her to see only its *unfavorable* aspects (like ugly parts of the mansion). But if she continues to move along the hedge searching for additional openings, she may find one or two points of view from which the scene is attractive. Let us return:

INSTRUCTOR: Earlier, if you recall, you mentioned that social work wasn't for you, not because it was wrong, but just because you weren't interested in it.

YVONNE: Yes.

INSTRUCTOR: It was not for you, *personally.*

YVONNE: Yes.

INSTRUCTOR: You were rejecting it from a *personal* point of view.

YVONNE (*impatiently*): Yes.

INSTRUCTOR: You are also rejecting premarital sex from a *personal* point of view, and this view is largely determined by the *religious sanctions* against it and the *social consequences* of it.

YVONNE (*with a despairing sigh*): Yes.

INSTRUCTOR: But some people do not accept these religious sanctions and are not disturbed by the thought of the social consequences you mention.

YVONNE: Oh! I hate people like that!

INSTRUCTOR: Really?

YVONNE: Ugh! Hippies. Yippies. Flower people. Pot heads. Speed freaks. They don't wash. They smell. They have long stringy hair. Oh! they give me goose bumps!

INSTRUCTOR: You're not being objective.

YVONNE (*rubbing the goose bumps on her arms*): Icky people!

Moral Judgment

Yvonne is here manifesting another common block to logical thinking—*moral judgment*. The purpose of analysis is *understanding*. Hasty moral judgment substitutes a judgmental label for understanding.

Condemnation by Association

Furthermore, she is committing another error. She is letting her personal reaction to the type of *person* she associates with a form of activity (premarital sex) determine her reaction to that activity. She dislikes the type of person she associates with the act; therefore, she condemns the act. When one is analyzing aspects of a form of behavior (premarital sex, pot smoking, churchgoing) or an abstraction (democracy, freedom, black power) or whatever, he must not let his personal and subjective reaction to the type of person popularly associated with the subject color his analysis of that subject. Not only does such a reaction destroy one's *objectivity* and lead to *moral judgment,* but it also puts one on *very* shaky logical ground. For, over a period of time, the type of person associated with, for example, a form of behavior, may change drastically. And if one has built an argument based on the type of person associated with the form of behavior, he will find himself robbed of his reasons. An example of such a change is the case of women smoking cigarettes in public. Earlier in the century, if a woman was seen smoking in public, it was an almost sure sign that she was a prostitute. Many people argued that a lady should not smoke in public because only prostitutes did so. If, today, one based an argument against women smoking in public on such grounds, he would either be laughed at or slapped in the face.

It is a block to logical thinking to base an attack on a concept on one's personal, or even society's, reaction to those who are associated with it.

But let us return to Yvonne.

INSTRUCTOR: Forget the type of people you associate with premarital relations and be objective.

YVONNE (*agreeably*): OK.

INSTRUCTOR: Can you discover any favorable aspects of premarital sex from a *personal* point of view by putting yourself in the place of those people who give little or no weight to the religious sanctions against or the social consequences of such behavior?

YVONNE: This country is going to the dogs.

INSTRUCTOR: Is that relevant?

YVONNE: No.

INSTRUCTOR: Try.

YVONNE (*blushes*): Well . . .

INSTRUCTOR: Yes?

YVONNE (*giggles*): Well . . .

INSTRUCTOR: Yes?

YVONNE (*looking at the floor to avoid the eyes of her instructor*): Well . . . It might be *fun!* Oh! I just hate icky people like that!

INSTRUCTOR: You're losing your objectivity again.

YVONNE: Yes.

INSTRUCTOR: What do you mean by "fun"?

YVONNE (*blushing*): You know what I mean.

INSTRUCTOR: From a personal point of view, premarital relations might be a source of *pleasure.*

YVONNE: Yes, I guess.

INSTRUCTOR: Anything else?

YVONNE: Well. They might *have to.*

INSTRUCTOR: Have to?

YVONNE: I mean . . . Well, what if the fellow was going to school, or something, and they couldn't get married because neither had enough money. But they really loved each other. Oh! It would be horrible if they had to wait and wait until they were old and sick and ugly. Oh! I'd just die! (*Yvonne collapses in tears again.*)

INSTRUCTOR: Here, take my handkerchief.

YVONNE (*blowing her nose*): Thank you.

Empathy

Even though Yvonne is getting emotional again, she has taken a valuable step. She has looked at the subject from a *different point of view.* She has put herself in the place of someone who holds a personal point of view opposite her own and has tried to understand *that person's* situation and view of the subject. This has allowed her to achieve a *broader perspective,* a more complete view of the subject. This has also enabled her to realize the *complexity* of the subject. She now sees that a simple right or wrong response is inadequate.

INSTRUCTOR: Are you OK now?

YVONNE: Yes, but I feel sorry for those poor people.

INSTRUCTOR: Would you say that they are in a *special situation?*

YVONNE: Yes.

INSTRUCTOR: Caused by *economic* factors?

YVONNE: Yes.

INSTRUCTOR: Can you think of anything else in favor of premarital sex from a personal point of view?

YVONNE: Well, they're not hurting anybody. It's their own business. It's something private done between two people which doesn't interfere with the life of anybody else.

INSTRUCTOR: In other words, it's their right as adults to choose how to conduct their private lives.

YVONNE: Yes.

INSTRUCTOR: So, from a *personal* point of view, we could say that there are at least three considerations in favor of premarital sex: It may give the couple *pleasure,* it may be necessary because of the couple's *special situation,* and it is *their right* to choose it.

YVONNE: Yes.

SUMMARY

Thinking back over this scene, we can perceive the steps which Yvonne took:

1. Confronted with the subject, she had first to achieve *objectivity.*
2. Then, she was able to begin *analysis* of the subject in order to gain *insight.*
3. This analysis involved:
   a. looking at the subject from different *points of view;*
   b. *classifying* these points of view;
   c. recognizing the *complexity* of the subject.

Throughout her analysis, she had to fight against the intrusion of such blocks to logical thinking as moral judgment, either-or thinking, and condemnation by association. All of these blocks interfere with insight, which is the goal of analysis.

To understand a personal point of view on the subject which differed from her own personal point of view, Yvonne found it helpful to *empathize* with those people who held that point of view, in order to *broaden her perspective* on the subject and to *recognize its complexity.*

It is only at this point, *after* thoroughly analyzing the subject, that Yvonne is in a position to state a *meaningful* opinion on the subject.

An "opinion" stated before analysis of a subject, even if it is defensible, is a mere prejudice, for a prejudice is any *irrationally held belief,* whether accurate or inaccurate. A prejudice differs from an opinion in this element of irrationality. The way a prejudiced person thinks might be summed up by the statement: "My mind's made up; don't confuse me with the facts."

Yvonne's feeling at the beginning of the scene that "premarital sex is bad" was a prejudice. By the end of the scene Yvonne has developed a rationally held *opinion* concerning premarital sex. She still feels that it is not for her, but now she knows why.

Represented in the form of a topic outline, her analysis looks like this:

  I. Religious Sanctions Against Premarital Sex
 II. Social Consequences of Detection
    A. Gossip
    B. Condemnation
    C. Ostracism
III. Personal Considerations Justifying Premarital Sex
    A. Pleasure
    B. Special situation
    C. Right of couple

Now Yvonne is in a position to formulate her thesis statement. Her findings on the subject can be classified as negative and positive, depending on the point of view taken. The *religious* and *social* points of view reveal negative aspects. The *personal* point of view reveals positive aspects. Thus Yvonne's thesis statement should be phrased in such a way that it accurately reflects these different points of view. She might write:

Thesis Statement A—One may regard premarital sexual relations as morally wrong because of the sanctions in the Christian religion against such behavior. Furthermore, the social consequences of one's engaging in premarital sex are almost certain to be unpleasant. However, if two people do not accept these sanctions and do not fear the probable social consequences, their engaging in premarital sexual relations can be defended from a strictly personal point of view.

Thesis Statement A gives approximately the same weight to each of the three points of view. It does this by allotting each point of view its own independent clause. Hence each point of view is grammatically "independent," like a nation, and stands on equal footing with the other points of view. Yvonne is, in this statement, being neutral.

She might, however, wish to indicate her own personal bias, or feeling, which happens not to favor premarital sexual relations. She can do this, *while at the same time recognizing a point of view different from her own* (which she must do if she is to give a full and balanced picture of the subject), by putting the *personal* point of view in a *subordinate clause*. This has the effect of throwing the emphasis on the negative aspects of premarital sexual relations. She might then phrase her thesis statement in the following manner:

Thesis Statement B—Although premarital sexual relations may be defended from a personal point of view, the social consequences of one's engaging in such behavior are almost certain to be extremely unpleasant. Furthermore, the Christian religion strongly condemns such relations.

Finally, although Yvonne would obviously not wish to do so, the thesis could be phrased to emphasize the personal considerations justifying premarital relations. Again, however, the thesis must reflect the complexity of the subject. It cannot ignore the "negative" considerations discovered through analysis. Such a thesis might read:

Thesis Statement C—It cannot be denied that the couple engaging in premarital sexual relations must brave lingering religious sanctions against such behavior and the possible condemnation of society. Nevertheless, such relations are justified because one's sexual behavior is a private and personal matter.

☛ YVONNE AND THE TENDER TRAP:
A Tale of Innocence Enlightened—With a Moral

Yvonne, as you already know, is not at her beautiful best when it comes to analyzing an assigned subject prior to writing a theme. Some time after the scene we have just witnessed, her instructor assigned an essay on the subject of "marriage." At first, Yvonne didn't think she would have any trouble. She sat down and dashed off a paragraph in no time at all. But, then, her mind stopped. So, she called up her boyfriend and asked if she could come over to his apartment. Since she didn't tell him that she had a theme to write, he said, "Sure, come on over."

Before we focus in on them, we should take a brief look at her boyfriend. His name is C. S. Rott, which stands for College Student who has Read This Text. His last name is appropriate, as we shall see, because after reading this text he got a bit carried away. He now regards the opinions of anyone who hasn't read it as so much rot.

C. S. is a good-looking fellow. Not outstanding, but good-looking. Some envious male students who don't know him well wonder how he ever managed to get a girl like Yvonne. But not his good friends, for he is essentially good-hearted; his only vice, one he picked up after reading this text, is his habit of telling people that their ideas are rot.

When we join them, Yvonne, who is wearing tight slacks and a clinging sweater and looking her sexy best, is standing before the couch in the living room of C. S.'s apartment, reading her paragraph to her boyfriend. C. S. is looking glum and frustrated as he sits cross-legged on the couch, for she has just told him about her theme.

YVONNE (*with expressive gestures as she reads*): Marriage is a noble union made in heaven, blessed by God, and hallowed by man. It takes two lonely, separate persons and makes them one and indivisible, for better or for worse, in sickness and in health, forever. It provides a warm, peaceful, happy, loving nest in which to raise the young which are its natural offspring. Yes, marriage leads to the joys of family life. It provides a happy home in which can be heard the joyful lilt of children's voices, the light patter of little feet, the excited laughter of little angels at play. Marriage is a wonderful thing.

YVONNE (*with a beatific smile*): What do you think?

C. S. ROTT: I think you want to get married.

YVONNE (*blushing*): I mean about the paragraph?

C. S. ROTT: I think it's rot.

YVONNE (*in a hurt voice*): C. S., how could you?

C. S. ROTT (*with feigned despair*): The influence of my name. I can't help it.

YVONNE: But "rot" in what way?

C. S. ROTT: I'll show you. (*He picks up her paper and pretends to read.*) Marriage is a clever snare conceived in hell, hexed by the devil, and perpetrated on unsuspecting man by conniving woman. It takes two separate, happy persons and chains them together, one and indivisible—until they get divorced —in a misery of boredom. It provides a steaming, tension-ridden, hate-filled cauldron in which to boil the unfortunate children who are its accidental by-product. It provides a one-bedroom furnished cage in which to be tormented by the howls of colicky infants, the stench of wet diapers, and the screaming, tearful quarrels of selfish offspring. Yes, marriage is a wonderful thing.

YVONNE (*crying*): Oh, C. S.! How could you?

C. S. ROTT (*holding Yvonne and looking at the dandruff in the part of her hair*): I don't know, I just did it.

YVONNE: Oh!

C. S. ROTT (*relenting*): If it's any help, my paragraph is just as much rot as yours.

YVONNE (*beginning to brighten*): Really?

C. S. ROTT: Yes, neither one actually says a thing.

YVONNE: How come?

C. S. ROTT: Both are simply *reactions* to the subject. Both are *subjective* responses, both are full of *moral judgment* and *either-or* thinking, both contain *hidden assertions*. Neither one is a meaningful *analysis* of the subject.

YVONNE (*admiringly, gazing up into Rott's eyes*): My hero! (*She kisses him.*) You analyze it for me; I'll listen.

C. S. ROTT: Whose assignment is this, anyway?

YVONNE (*caressing him*): But you're so smart. Please?

C. S. ROTT (*secretly flattered, but with pretended reluctance*): Well, OK. (*Yvonne happily kisses him again and curls up on the couch.*) Now the subject you are writing on is "Marriage." So, you must first of all:

1. Avoid getting *personally involved*. You must be *objective*.
2. Avoid *either-or thinking*.
3. Avoid *moral judgment*.

YVONNE (*contentedly, filing her finger nails*): Yes, darling.

C. S. ROTT: Then you can begin to *analyze* the subject. The purpose of analysis is understanding. To understand, you have to *recognize the complexity* of the subject, To recognize the complexity of the subject, you must look at it from various *points of view.*

YVONNE (*sleepily*): Yes, darling.

C. S. ROTT: All right, then. What's one point of view from which we can look at marriage?

YVONNE (*dreamily*): Love! Love and marriage go together like a horse and carriage.

C. S. ROTT: False analogy.

YVONNE: What?

C. S. ROTT: Hidden assertion.

YVONNE: Huh?

C. S. ROTT: Through your comparison of love and marriage to a horse and carriage, you are really asserting that there is a necessary connection between the two.

YVONNE (*indignantly*): But there is. Ask any girl. If she loves a man, she wants to marry him.

C. S. ROTT (*with conviction*): Cultural conditioning and economic dependency plus maternal instinct.

YVONNE (*hopelessly*): I'm lost.

C. S. ROTT (*patiently*): When you say "love," you are describing a *reason* why people get married, right?

YVONNE: Of course.

C. S. ROTT: So, you are looking at marriage from the point of view of why people get married, from the point of view of *motives* for marriage.

YVONNE: Yes.

C. S. ROTT: But, from this point of view, are there any other common or possible motives besides love?

YVONNE (*turning to C. S., who is sitting beside her on the couch, and tickling him under his chin*): Coochy, coochy, coo!

C. S. ROTT (*scratching*): Ugh, little monsters. But that's right; a couple could marry in order to raise children.

YVONNE (*with visions of an appliance-stuffed house*): Or to get economic security.

C. S. ROTT: Or emotional security.

YVONNE: Or because it was expected.

C. S. ROTT: Or because they wanted to live together and didn't dare without being married.

YVONNE (*pleased with herself*): I get the idea!

C. S. ROTT: Bravo! So, from the point of view of *motivation*, we have six reasons why people may marry: because they love each other, because they want children, because they want economic security, because they want emotional security, because it is expected, because they want to live together.

YVONNE (*losing interest*): Yes.

C. S. ROTT: Is there any other point of view from which marriage can be considered?

YVONNE (*removing her shoes and wiggling her toes*): I don't know.

C. S. ROTT: Well, think.

YVONNE (*starting to get up*): Let's go to a movie. There's a double feature at the Center—*King Kong* and *King Kong Meets Godzilla.*

C. S. ROTT: Sit down!

YVONNE (*subsiding with a sigh*): Yes, darling.

C. S. ROTT: We call marriage an "institution," don't we?

YVONNE (*subdued*): Yes, darling.

C. S. ROTT: Is the Democratic party an institution?

YVONNE: Yes, darling.

C. S. ROTT: Classify it.

YVONNE (*blinking her eyes*): What?

C. S. ROTT: Put it into the class or group of institutions to which it belongs. What *type* of institution is it?

YVONNE: A *political* institution.

C. S. ROTT: And the Catholic Church?

YVONNE: A *religious* institution.

C. S. ROTT: And the World Bank?

YVONNE: An *economic* institution.

C. S. ROTT: And marriage?

YVONNE: A *social* institution.

C. S. ROTT: Good girl. So we can look at marriage from the point of view of a social institution. The Democratic party, the Catholic Church, and the World Bank have certain *functions* as institutions. Marriage, too, has certain functions as a *social* institution.

YVONNE: Name one.

C. S. ROTT: You name one.

YVONNE: I can't.

C. S. ROTT: Think.

YVONNE (*after a moment, tentatively*): Well, just imagine what might happen without the institution of marriage.

C. S. ROTT: What?

YVONNE (*getting more and more excited as she talks*): Oh, it's terrible. The world would be full of unwed mothers carrying their poor babies from door to door, looking for a home. A woman might give a man the best years of her life and then he could just kick her out into a dark, cold winter night and slam the door. And she couldn't do a thing. She might starve or have to go to work as a washerwoman to feed her children. A man could leave all his money to any young flirt he wanted to and leave his children to suffer. And no one would be responsible for raising the children and clothing them and feeding them. Oh, it's terrible!

C. S. ROTT (*holding and comforting Yvonne, who has collapsed in tears*): Come on, darling, get hold of yourself.

YVONNE (*sniffling*): Sorry, darling.

C. S. ROTT: So, we can look at marriage from the point of view of its social functions.

YVONNE (*drying her eyes*): Yes, darling.

C. S. ROTT: One of the social functions of the institution of marriage, then, is to provide for children. The institution of marriage assures that someone will be responsible for the feeding, clothing, and rearing of the young.

YVONNE: Yes.

C. S. ROTT: Marriage as a social institution is also, as you suggest, a means of providing the woman with the emotional security she needs to best perform her role as a mother.

YVONNE: Yes.

C. S. ROTT: OK. Is there still another point of view from which you can look at marriage?

YVONNE (*sitting up and giggling*): Well, when you sign the marriage license and say "I do," you're hooked!

C. S. ROTT (*trying to keep from shuddering*): I can feel the barb in my guts, like a fish. But what exactly do you mean, "hooked"?

YVONNE (*laughing*): You can't get away, brother!

C. S. ROTT: Why not?

YVONNE (*smugly*): You can't break the contract.

C. S. ROTT: Exactly. A contract. From what point of view are you looking at marriage now?

YVONNE: From the *legal* point of view. If you try anything, I'll call daddy's lawyer.

C. S. ROTT: Unfortunately, you are right. Marriage is, from a legal point of view, a contract between two people in which both are bound to fulfill certain obligations in respect to each other and the offspring of the marriage. Thus, a man or woman may be lawfully punished for failure to meet the obligations of the contract. They may be punished for child neglect, cruelty, desertion, adultery, etc.

YVONNE (*gleefully rubbing her hands*): And don't forget that the man may be required to pay child support and alimony if he ever tries to weasel out of the deal!

C. S. ROTT: What a lovely thought.

YVONNE: But true! But true!

C. S. ROTT: I think I'd like to get back to your essay.

YVONNE (*smugly*): I want to look at the legal point of view some more!

C. S. ROTT (*ignoring her*): We have now looked at marriage from a personal, a social, and a legal point of view. Or, to put it another way, from the point of view of:

1. The *motives* of the couple who marry.
2. The *social functions* of the institution of marriage.
3. The *legal* aspects of marriage.

YVONNE: Yes, darling.

C. S. ROTT: To sum up, then, we have found that there are at least six motives for marriage: love, a desire for children, a desire for economic security, a desire for emotional security, a desire to conform, and a desire to live together. Marriage as a social institution has at least two functions: to provide for the rearing and socialization of children and to provide the woman with the emotional security she needs to best perform her role as a mother. Finally, marriage is a legal contract between the marriage partners in which both undertake certain responsibilities and which provides for penalties if these responsibilities are not met.

YVONNE (*climbing on to C. S.'s lap and embracing him*): You're great!

C. S. ROTT: Yes, darling.

SUMMARY

Yvonne doesn't seem to have benefited very much from the exciting exchange with her instructor in the earlier dialogue. Once again, however, reason prevails in the end, so there's cause for hope.

In outline form C. S. and Yvonne's analysis of "marriage" looks like this:

I. Motives for Marriage
   A. Love
   B. Desire for children
   C. Desire for economic security
   D. Desire for emotional security
   E. Desire to conform
   F. Desire to live together

II. Social Functions of the Institution of Marriage
   A. To provide for the rearing and socialization of children
   B. To provide the woman with the emotional security she needs to best perform her role as mother

III. Legal Aspects of Marriage
   A. Contract in which both parties agree to fulfill certain obligations
   B. Contract providing for penalties if obligations are not fulfilled

Full development of all these aspects of marriage would probably be impossible in a standard 500-word theme. Yvonne might choose to restrict her discussion to any one of the three major points of view. However, if she did decide to write on the subject as analyzed, without limiting it, her thesis should reflect all three major points of view from which she examined the subject. And her thesis should be carefully formulated to indicate the order and emphasis of the whole essay:

Thesis Statement A—Although marriage is both a legally binding contract and an institution with significant social functions, it is most often entered into because of the personal needs of the two people involved. (This thesis statement puts the emphasis of the essay on the personal motives that cause people to marry.)

Thesis Statement B—Marriage is a legally binding contract which is often entered into because of the personal needs of the marriage partners. However, it is as a social institution that it is most significant. (This thesis statement obviously throws the emphasis on marriage as a social institution.)

Thesis Statement C—People tend to regard marriage as a means of satisfying personal needs, or as a socially important institution. However, it should not be forgotten that marriage is, also, a legal contract between two parties involving mutual obligations and responsibilities. (This thesis statement emphasizes marriage as a legally binding contract.)

3

From Analysis to Thesis

As the two dialogues illustrate, analyzing, outlining the analysis, and formulating the thesis statement constitute a natural unit. They are the necessary preliminaries to written composition. So before we turn to the matter of writing, let's examine in more detail these three preliminaries and the manner in which they are interrelated.

THE TOPIC OUTLINE

As we have seen in "Yvonne and the Dirty-Minded Instructor" and "Yvonne and the Tender Trap," extraneous matters have a way of slipping into analysis of a subject. And if you're not careful, they will also slip into your composition. This tendency of the irrelevant to intrude is what makes an outline desirable. However thoughtful and complete your analysis of a subject prior to writing on it, it is difficult to get that thoughtfulness and completeness down on paper without some thoughtless and irrelevant ideas creeping in—unless you are writing from an outline of your analysis. Furthermore, writing from an outline guarantees that you really have analyzed your subject before you begin to write on it. Man is his own greatest enemy in composition as much as in any other sphere. There's a tendency to start writing after you've only "half analyzed" the subject; but a complete outline necessitates a complete analysis.

So, as you analyze a subject, it's wise to systematize your findings in a topic outline. As you outline your analysis:

1. Identify your major points of view with roman numerals.
2. Identify the elements in each major point of view with capital letters.
3. Identify the elements in each capital letter point of view with arabic numerals.

Your topic outline evolves as your analysis progresses, as in the following "dialogue of the mind with itself."

Analysis—The Dialogue of the Mind with Itself

ASSIGNMENT: Write a theme on the subject "Discipline."

STEP ONE: Preliminary analysis to determine if the subject should be limited.

MIND: Discipline covers a very wide range. You can discipline cats or rats, Pomeranians or pre-adolescents. Discipline of what or whom?

STUDENT: Discipline of children, then.

Limitation of *object* of discipline

MIND: By whom—parents or priests, policemen or school authorities?

STUDENT: Discipline of children by parents.

Limitation of *administrator* of discipline

MIND: Discipline by what means? Whip, switch, belt, fist? After all, what you say won't apply to all methods equally.

STUDENT: Parental discipline of children by spanking.

Limitation of *nature* or *method* of discipline

STEP TWO: Analysis of limited subject.

MIND: What are some points of view from which you can examine the subject?

STUDENT: The most obvious are *reasons* for it and *effects* of it. Why parents discipline their children by spanking and how such discipline affects the child.

MIND: OK. Take reasons. What are some reasons parents give?

STUDENT: They claim it's necessary in order to punish the child for bad behavior. They also claim it will reform the child.

MIND: You better classify these two reasons.

STUDENT: They are commonly stated reasons for disciplining a child.

MIND: Are there any unstated reasons then?

STUDENT: Well, I can remember plenty of times I got spanked for nothing. I think parents sometimes enjoy it.

MIND: That's pretty strong. It seems to suggest they're sadistic. What do you mean, "enjoy it"?

Limited subject: Parental discipline of children by spanking

I. *Reasons* for spanking as a means of disciplining children
II. *Effects* of such discipline

I. Reasons for spanking as a means of disciplining children
  A. Stated reasons
    1. To punish the child
    2. To reform the child

  B. Unstated reasons

STUDENT: Well, it kind of lets them get rid of hostility. When you live constantly with other people, there's bound to be friction. I think parents sometimes swat their kids because the kids have gotten on their nerves, and spanking relieves this built-up hostility.

MIND: Can you think of another unstated reason?

STUDENT: I'm not sure. Why do most parents spank their kids if they use an obscene word, or if they tell their parents to "go to hell," or if they get caught playing "doctor"?

MIND: It sounds like cultural conditioning to me. Maybe discipline is used to help create conformity to a culturally conditioned ideal of behavior.

STUDENT: I'll buy that.

MIND: OK. What about the effects of such discipline on the child?

STUDENT: Well, it generally affects his behavior, all right.

MIND: In what way?

STUDENT: Well, it may achieve a couple of the goals we've already talked about. It may lead him to reform, and it may also lead him to conform.

1. To relieve the parents' hostility toward the child

2. To create conformity to a culturally conditioned ideal of behavior

II. Effects of such discipline

A. On behavior

  1. Reform
  2. Conformity

MIND: Are you sure these are really two different effects on his behavior, rather than one?

STUDENT: In a way. It can cause him to reform, and renounce the particular behavior he was punished for. But over a long period, it may also teach him the need to conform in general. In other words, he may learn to suppress such general traits as aggressiveness and assertiveness, and sexual impulses, and spontaneity—traits which were responsible for *particular* acts he was punished for.

MIND: OK. But what else? Does such discipline only affect the child's behavior?

STUDENT: No. It's obviously going to have psychological effects, too.

MIND: Such as?

STUDENT: It may create fear, and anger, and, especially if the child feels he has been unjustly punished, resentment.

B. Effects on the mind of the child

    1. Fear
    2. Anger
    3. Resentment

COMPLETED OUTLINE

Limited Subject: Parental Discipline of Children by Spanking

I. Reasons for Spanking as a Means of Disciplining Children
   A. Stated reasons
      1. To punish the child
      2. To reform the child
   B. Unstated reasons
      1. To relieve parental hostility toward the child
      2. To create conformity to a culturally conditioned ideal of behavior
II. Effects of Such Discipline
   A. On behavior
      1. Reform
      2. Conformity
   B. On the mind of the child
      1. Fear
      2. Anger
      3. Resentment

Order and Mutual Exclusiveness

After you've constructed a topic outline of your analysis, you can run a couple of quick tests on it, tests that take a good deal longer in the telling than in the doing.

ORDER

First, you should look over the outline to see if it reflects the order in which you want to develop your points. If some of the points you wish to make are less important than others, it's well to get these minor points out of the way first. If you intend to devote more space to one or two points than to others, save these major points for last.

But, above all else, *have a reason for the order you choose.* Carlyle condemned self-consciousness as sickness. In composition, self-consciousness is health. The cardinal rule of composition is know *what* you are doing and *why* you are doing it. If you *consciously* order your points for a deliberate reason, your order will almost certainly be effective.

MUTUAL EXCLUSIVENESS OF POINTS OF VIEW

After you have established the order in which you wish to develop your ideas, check your outline to be sure that the various classifications are mutually exclusive.

1. All roman numeral points of view should be mutually exclusive.
2. All capital letter points of view stated under a particular roman numeral should be mutually exclusive.
3. All arabic numeral points of view stated under a particular capital letter should be mutually exclusive.

Points of view are *mutually exclusive* when they do not overlap. "Love" and "hate" are mutually exclusive points of view. Although one person may love and hate another at the same time, as *points of view,* "love" and "hate" are mutually exclusive. "Sexual love" and "platonic love" are mutually exclusive points of view, although a particular person may love another in both ways. But "love" and "platonic love" are *not* mutually exclusive points of view. "Love" overlaps and includes "platonic love."

Each *type* of symbol in an outline (roman numeral, capital letter, arabic numeral) properly designates *separate* and *equal* points of view. Hence if you were writing a theme on "mercy killing," you might want to distinguish among:

I. Personal Considerations
II. Moral Considerations
III. Legal Considerations

The three points of view—personal, moral, legal—are *separate* (mutually exclusive), and they are *equal* (each lies on the same level of specificity).

In the "Discipline" outline:

I. *Reasons*
   are distinguished from
II. *Effects*
   A. Effects on *behavior*
      are distinguished from
   B. Effects on the *mind*
      1. *Fear*
         is distinguished from
      2. *Anger*
         is distinguished from
      3. *Resentment*

Each type of symbol designates *separate* and *equal* points of view.

You can think of your various points of view in terms of circles: if it is possible to overlap two circles, or include one in another, you *do not* have mutually exclusive points of view.

Hence:

But not:

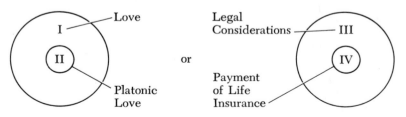

Exercise: Mutual Exclusiveness of Points of View

Following are some pairs. Represent each element by a circle. If you can either *overlap* two circles, or *include* one circle in another, the two elements are not mutually exclusive. To illustrate:

I. American
II. Communist

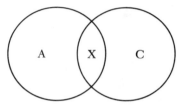

The overlap indicates that there are some Americans who are communists (and vice versa). Hence the two categories are not mutually exclusive.

I. Disorder
II. Riot

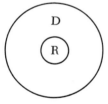

The inclusion of "riot" within the larger circle "disorder" indicates that the two elements lack mutual exclusiveness because a riot is simply one type of disorder out of many types.

1. Educational—informative
2. Comedy—drama
3. Young marrieds—progressives
4. Hippies—intellectuals
5. Childishness—selfishness
6. Pot smokers—middle class
7. Virgins—passionate women
8. Freedom—communism
9. Capitalism—free enterprise
10. Freedom-loving Americans—agitators
11. Nudists—normal people
12. Black militants—responsible Negroes
13. Real love—sexual love
14. Fun—work
15. Intellectual types—people in touch with reality
16. Queers—decent citizens
17. Welfare recipients—those willing to work
18. Making money—being true to yourself
19. Adulterer—good husband
20. Entertaining—educational

THE THESIS STATEMENT

After arranging your outline to reflect the order in which you wish to develop your points and checking it for mutual exclusiveness of classifications, you are ready to formulate your thesis statement. The purpose of your thesis is twofold:

1. To inform the reader of the *main points* of your essay
2. To inform the reader of the *order* in which you are going to expand on these points

Two Types of Thesis Statements

We can distinguish between two types of thesis statements: *open* and *closed*.

An open thesis statement is often unsatisfactory. It does not adequately inform your reader of the main points of your essay or of the order in which you will develop the main points. The following are *open* thesis statements:

The freshman faces many problems.

Censorship is undesirable.

It is wiser to buy a VW than to buy a Ford.

Dorm hours for coeds are necessary.

An open thesis statement not only fails to indicate sequence but is difficult to support. Even if you show, for example, that a VW is cheaper to purchase, gets better mileage, is easier to drive in town, and has a higher resale value than a Ford, you still haven't *necessarily* convinced the reader of the truth of your thesis. For he can counter each desirable quality you discuss with a desirable quality which a Ford has but a VW lacks. Furthermore, an open thesis statement is frequently symptomatic. It often indicates that you have failed to analyze your subject in a thorough manner.

A *closed* thesis statement is one which sets forth the main points of your essay and indicates the order in which you are going to develop these points. Such a thesis makes your job of convincing the reader easier. If in your body paragraphs you adequately support each point in the thesis, your reader is forced to accept your thesis, like it or not. Such a thesis also guarantees that you have indeed analyzed your subject. The open theses listed above can easily be converted into closed theses:

The freshman must avoid homesickness, he must learn to make new friends, and he must cope with the academic demands of college.

Censorship endangers the freedoms of speech and press.

A VW is cheaper to purchase, gets better mileage, is easier to drive in town, and has a higher resale value than a Ford.

Dorm hours for coeds reassure parents and assure that the coed will have enough time to study.

A precise, exact thesis convinces the reader that you know what you're doing and, thus, prejudices him in your favor. Further, a precise thesis, derived from your topic outline, reveals the scope of your essay to you; it tells you what your job is: where to begin and when to stop. And, as you develop your thesis in the body paragraphs, a process we'll examine closely, your thesis serves as a touchstone for every topic sentence. It enforces unity on the entire composition because every topic sentence must be clearly related to some part of the thesis statement. If the relation of a particular topic sentence to the thesis assertion is not clear, it is a sign that you are getting off the track.

☞ NOTE: The point to remember is that in composition you *never* write *on* a subject. When you are assigned a subject on which to write a theme, you analyze that subject and systematize your analysis in a topic outline. On the basis of that outline, you formulate a thesis statement. The thesis must be an *assertion* about your subject. Your job in the body paragraphs of your essay is to convince the reader that your thesis assertion is valid.

Exercise: Thesis Statements

Formulate a closed thesis statement for each of the following sentence outlines.

1. *Limited Subject: Different Types of Television Commercials*

I. Some television commercials are in the form of cartoons.
  A. The Plymouth commercial is a cartoon.
  B. The General Electric commercial is a cartoon.
II. Some television commercials are based on jingles.
  A. The Salem commercial is based on a jingle.
  B. The Winston commercial is based on a jingle.
III. Some television commercials are demonstrations.
  A. A commercial for a patented knife sharpener is a demonstration.
  B. The Shell mileage commercial is a demonstration.
IV. Some television commercials are lectures.
  A. Commercials sponsored by the American Cancer Society are lectures.
  B. Some milk commercials are lectures.

2. *Limited Subject: Advantages of Living in a Dorm*

I. Living in a dorm allows one to meet other students.
  A. One meets other students in the dining hall.
  B. One gets to know the students on his floor.
II. Living in a dorm is fun.
  A. People play pranks on each other.
  B. One can participate in bull sessions.
III. Dorm living is a source of social knowledge.
  A. One learns to adjust.
  B. One learns to mix with others.

3. *Limited Subject: Depression and the Fresh-*
man

I. A freshman is vulnerable to a feeling of depression.
   A. He is away from home for a long period, perhaps for the first time.
   B. He is responsible for his own success or failure.
   C. He may find himself without a feeling of purpose and direction.

II. Such a feeling of depression is self-perpetuating.
   A. It is difficult to study when one is depressed.
   B. When one doesn't study, his grades suffer.
   C. Falling grades generate more depression.

III. Depression can be conquered.
   A. Making new friends to replace those left at home helps.
   B. Joining campus organizations helps.
   C. Forcing oneself to study, instead of brooding, helps.

4. *Limited Subject: Problems That Face the*
Divorced Woman

I. The divorcée will find it difficult to begin a "new life."
   A. She is not as young and probably not as physically attractive as she was at the time of her marriage.
   B. Fewer marriageable men of her age are available.
   C. She bears an inevitable stigma.

II. The divorcée faces sexual conflicts.
   A. Many men regard a divorced woman as "fast" and, hence, legitimate prey.
   B. Many women regard a divorced woman as a "she-wolf on the prowl" and see acts of friendliness as attempts to seduce their husbands or boyfriends.

III. The divorcée is likely to be very lonely.
   A. Accustomed to living with a man, she now finds herself living without male companionship.
   B. She loses most of the friends she had while married.

5. *Limited Subject: Two Types of Fear*

I. One type of fear has an object and can be overcome by action.

    A. It is aroused in us by a specific, concrete, external situation.

        1. It comes with footsteps that echo our own along a deserted street at night, stopping when we stop to listen, starting again when we start.

        2. It comes with a physical threat by an animal or a man.

        3. It comes with the sudden onrush of a train as we approach a blind railroad crossing.

    B. It can be overcome by action.

        1. We can fight.

        2. We can flee.

II. The other type of fear has no object and can be only temporarily overcome by action.

    A. It is not aroused by specific external danger.

        1. It comes in the night as we lie in bed unable to sleep.

        2. It comes when we are alone on an empty, darkened street.

    B. It is a feeling of oppressive dread.

        1. Something terrible is going to happen, but we don't know when.

        2. Something terrible is going to happen, but we don't know what.

    C. It can be only temporarily overcome by action.

        1. It returns when we are in bed again.

        2. It returns when we are again alone in a deserted place.

III. The second type of fear is actually a fear of ourselves.

    A. It is a fear of forbidden thoughts buried in our unconscious.

    B. It is a fear of forbidden emotions buried in our unconscious.

    C. It is a fear aroused by our feeling that we should be punished in some dreadful manner for these awful thoughts and emotions.

Exercise: Preliminaries to Composition

This is the first of five exercises designed to let you implement in a sequential manner the three basic stages in composition:

I. Preliminaries to Composition
II. Composition
   A. Introduction Paragraphs
   B. Body Paragraphs
   C. Conclusion Paragraphs
III. Polishing Composition

When this exercise is returned to you, you should retain it for further development later.

Directions: Analyze two of the subjects listed below and construct a topic outline of each analysis. (If you limit the subject, be sure to state that limited subject above your outline.) Then formulate a closed thesis statement for each subject, based on your topic outline.

COLLEGE LIFE
College
Dormitories
Study habits
Roommates
Required courses
Liberal education
Specialization
Grades
Examinations
Student power

SOCIAL LIFE
Dating
Drinking
Popularity

SOCIAL LIFE
Conformity
Romance
Friends
Fads
Parties

GENERAL
Advertising
Travel
Health
Automobiles
Divorce
Religion
Girdles
Hit tunes

GENERAL
Crash diets
Hobbies
Mercy killing
Pets
Highway safety
Police
Parents
Relatives
In-laws
Styles
Movies
TV
Morals
Graffiti

Section Two

COMPOSITION

The ability to write an effective essay is neither an innate aptitude possessed by a lucky few nor an inalienable right guaranteed to all by the Constitution. It is a skill. Acquiring any skill necessitates self-discipline, patience, attention to basic principles, and practice. If you have mastered the preliminaries to composition—the ability to achieve objectivity, analyze your subject, systematize your analysis in a topic outline, and formulate a precise thesis statement—writing an effective essay poses no insuperable difficulties.

In the chapters that follow we will analyze the essay from three major points of view:

1. Introduction paragraphs
2. Body paragraphs
3. Conclusion paragraphs

1
Introduction Paragraphs

You've probably had the experience of being shaken out of a sound sleep by someone who just couldn't wait to tell you something, and who rushed into his story as soon as he saw your eyelids flicker open. Unless you're more alert than most, your reaction was probably of this order: "Huh? What time is it? What's happening?" And the person who awakened you had to go back and start his story all over again.

To understand, we need a *context*. We need to know the larger issue or consideration of which a particular subject is one aspect. The function of the *first part* of your introduction paragraph is to establish this context. You should familiarize the reader with the surroundings so that, by the time he comes to your thesis at the end of the introduction paragraph, he will be oriented and paying attention to what you are saying instead of looking around trying to figure out where he is and what is happening.

To discover the context in which you should place your subject, practice "reverse analysis." Determine the larger classification of which your subject is a part by asking yourself:

1. What larger issue is my subject a part of?
2. What broader subject or area or concept is my subject associated with?

Next put your subject in the context you've established. You can determine the relation between context and subject by asking yourself:

1. How is my subject related to this broader issue?
2. How are the two connected?
3. How is my subject a part of this larger concern?

After you've put your subject in the context you've established, you can then state your thesis about your subject.

In your introduction paragraph, then, you should:

1. Establish the context of your subject.
2. Put your subject in the context you've established.
3. State your thesis about your subject.

Let's look at this three-step process in action:

Limited Subject: Parental Discipline of Children by Spanking

Thesis Statement—The reasons parents give for disciplining their children by spanking are partially discredited by unacknowledged motives. Similarly, though such discipline may bring about desired changes in the behavior of the child, it may produce undesirable emotional reactions.

Developing the Introduction Paragraph

1. Establishing the context

Most agree that a child must be subject to discipline. But about the proper administrator of discipline and the form it should take there is less unanimity. Some say it should be left to school authorities; others claim it is solely the responsibility of the family. To some, discipline is a mild verbal reproof; to others it is a beating.

☞ NOTE: Your limited subject is "parental discipline of children by spanking." Spanking of the child by his parents is one form of *discipline of the child,* which is the larger classification of which your subject is a part. The four sentences above establish the context by considering the larger matter of *discipline of the child.*

2. Putting your subject in the context you've established

Parental discipline of children by spanking, however, arouses little controversy. It lies in a neutral zone between a permissive and an authoritarian approach to discipline.

☞ NOTE: Here you put your subject, "spanking of the child by his parents," in the context you've established. You show its relation to the more general matter of discipline of the child.

3. Stating your thesis

But spanking as a means of disciplining children is not as innocent as it may appear. The reasons parents give for such discipline are partially discredited by unacknowledged motives. Similarly, though such discipline may bring about desired changes in the behavior of the child, it may produce undesirable emotional reactions.

☞ NOTE: You should not just dump in your thesis without regard to the sentences that have gone before. Here a transitional sentence helps smooth the way from the second part of your introduction paragraph to the statement of your thesis.

The completed introduction paragraph

Most agree that a child must be subject to discipline. But about the proper administrator of discipline and the form it should take there is less unanimity. Some say it should be left to school authorities; others claim it is solely the responsibility of the family. To some, discipline is a mild verbal reproof; to others it is a beating. Parental discipline of children by spanking, however, arouses little controversy. It lies in a neutral zone between a permissive and an authoritarian approach to discipline. But spanking as a means of disciplining children is not as innocent as it may appear. The reasons parents give for such discipline are partially discredited by unacknowledged motives. Similarly, though such discipline may bring about desired changes in the behavior of the child, it may produce undesirable emotional reactions.

Limited Subject: Racial Intermarriage Between
Negroes and Whites in America

Thesis Statement—The racially intermarried couple will find life easier if both are college graduates and if they have an income that puts them in the upper middle class.

Developing the Introduction Paragraph

1. Establishing the context

Prejudice dies slowly. Anti-Semitism lingers on in Germany and flourishes in the Arab world. Britain acted to halt the influx of Asians and Australia has not yet repealed her discriminatory immigration laws.

☞ NOTE: Racial intermarriage is controversial because it arouses the *prejudice* many feel against blacks. Therefore, prejudice is that larger classification within which racial intermarriage falls, and it provides the context we need in order to understand the difficulties facing the racially intermarried couple.

2. Putting your subject in the context you've established

In America prejudice manifests itself most blatantly in the attitudes of many whites toward the Negro. Even those who claim to be free of prejudice toward the Negro often "draw the line" at interracial marriage.

☞ NOTE: Your subject is "interracial marriage between Negro and white." The context you've established is "prejudice." The first of the two sentences above shows that the Negro in America is the object of prejudice. The second shows that interracial marriage between Negro and white arouses prejudice.

3. Stating your thesis

The racially intermarried couple will find it easier to combat the prejudice many will feel toward them if both are college graduates and if they have an income that puts them in the upper middle class.

☞ NOTE: After you have established the context of your subject and have put your subject in that context, you will often find that your thesis can be more precisely phrased in terms of the context you've established. After all, having college degrees and a high level of income "makes life easier" for just about any couple. The modified thesis points these two accomplishments toward combating prejudice, the particular difficulty facing the racially intermarried couple.

The completed introduction paragraph

Prejudice dies slowly. Anti-Semitism lingers on in Germany and flourishes in the Arab world. Britain acted to halt the influx of Asians and Australia has not yet repealed her discriminatory immigration laws. In America prejudice manifests itself most blatantly in the attitudes of many whites toward the Negro. Even those who claim to be free of prejudice toward the Negro often "draw the line" at interracial marriage. The racially intermarried couple will find it easier to combat the prejudice many will feel toward them if both are college graduates and if they have an income that puts them in the upper middle class.

Exercises: Introduction Paragraphs

A. Return to the sentence outlines on pages 43–45 for which you have already formulated thesis statements. Write an introduction paragraph for each outline in which you successively:

1. Establish the context of your subject.
2. Show the place of your subject in this larger context.
3. State your thesis about your subject.

B. For the exercise on page 46 you analyzed two subjects, outlined your analyses, and formulated appropriate thesis statements. Write an introduction paragraph for each outline in which you successively:

1. Establish the context of your subject.
2. Show the place of your subject in the context you've established.
3. State your thesis about your subject.

When this exercise is returned to you, you should retain it for further development.

2

Effective Body Paragraphs

If you've read Christopher Marlowe's *Faustus* you'll remember the two angels, one good, one bad, who torment Faustus with contradictory advice:

GOOD ANGEL: Sweet Faustus, think of heaven and heavenly things.
BAD ANGEL: No, Faustus, think of honor and wealth.

BAD ANGEL: Too late.
GOOD ANGEL: Never too late, if Faustus will repent.

If Faustus had only paid attention to the Good Angel he would have gone blissfully to heaven instead of being dragged miserably shrieking off to hell.

Alas, life isn't as simple as it once was, as so many are fond of saying. Ambivalence and ambiguity rule and have even invaded the good and bad angel market. On your shoulder squats a reader who may appear evil but who is really a good angel in disguise. He squats there and whispers "I don't believe you," "You haven't supported that assertion," "I'm not convinced," "Give me an example." And the only way to silence him is to do as he demands.

When this squatting reader we've mentioned comes to your thesis at the end of your introduction paragraph, his reaction is, "Oh yeah? Prove it." Convincing a skeptical reader of the validity of your thesis assertion is your job in the body paragraphs of your essay.* In order to convince him, you must generally devote at least one paragraph to each major aspect of your thesis assertion.† To illustrate:

Thesis—Although marriage is both a legally binding contract and an institution with significant social functions, it is most often entered into because of the personal needs of the couple involved.

☞ NOTE: This thesis necessitates a minimum of three body paragraphs: one which explains why and how marriage is a legally binding contract; one which proves that marriage as an institution has significant social functions; one which shows that the personal needs of the couple are generally the main motive for marriage.

Thesis—But spanking as a means of disciplining children is not as innocent as it may appear. The reasons parents give for such discipline are partially discredited by unacknowledged motives. Similarly, though such discipline may bring about desired changes in the behavior of the child, it may produce unfavorable emotional reactions.

☞ NOTE: This thesis necessitates a minimum of four body paragraphs: one which sets forth the reasons parents give for spanking; one which explains discreditable unacknowledged motives; one which sets forth the desired changes in behavior which spanking may bring about; one which shows the unfavorable emotional reactions spanking may create.

---

* Instead of using the cumbersome phrase "body paragraph" throughout, we will simply speak of the "paragraph." When we mean a paragraph that has some function other than supporting a topic sentence assertion (whether stated or implied), we will distinguish it with the appropriate label: introduction, transitional, conclusion, and so forth.

† As you gain proficiency in composition, you may find that you wish to treat more than one aspect of your thesis in a single paragraph. This is certainly acceptable. However, it is helpful to think in terms of "one aspect of thesis assertion, one paragraph." Thinking in this way will prevent you from sliding over aspects of your thesis without supporting and developing them adequately.

An argumentative paragraph is not just a few lines on a piece of paper, the first of which is indented. It is a miniature essay. The essay supports and develops a thesis assertion; the paragraph supports and develops a topic sentence assertion. In the essay, the various aspects of the thesis assertion are examined; in the paragraph the various aspects of the topic sentence assertion are examined. The theme displays full and progressive development; so should the paragraph. Substitute "thesis" for "topic sentence" and "introduction" for "transition," and all of the principles of effective paragraphs that we are going to examine apply with equal validity to the whole essay. For this reason, if you can write successful paragraphs, you can write successful essays.

PRINCIPLES OF EFFECTIVE PARAGRAPHS

Principle 1: An Effective Paragraph Acknowledges the Opposition

To say that an effective paragraph acknowledges the opposition is simply to say that in your writing as well as in your analysis you should recognize and respect the complexity of your subject. Whenever you take a "pro" or "con" position on some aspect of a controversial question, you must acknowledge that you are aware of the other position but are rejecting if for considered reasons. If you don't acknowledge your opposition, the reader may well say to himself: "All this is very well, my friend, but I can think of an objection to every point you make. Since you're obviously afraid to acknowledge my objections, your argument doesn't convince me one bit."

Say that after carefully considering the matter of police response to criminal behavior, you decide that a "get tough" policy is actually needed. Now, obviously, you don't want your calm and considered opinion to be mistaken for the outraged outcry of a prejudiced, sadistic, neurotic, scapegoat-seeking bigot! So you must demonstrate to your potentially hostile reader in a tone of sweet reasonableness that, though you are aware of his position, you find it in error. Your paragraph, then, might read like this:

Many people today feel that the cry for stronger police action against criminals and criminal acts is actually a disguised cry for suppression of disaffected minority groups in America—especially blacks and youthful white dissenters. Perhaps there is some justice in this charge. However, the unworthy motives of some of those who urge "law and order" should not be allowed to discredit law and order themselves. It is certainly true that every citizen should be free of the fear of personal violence. Stronger police action, including more numerous arrests and stiffer sentences, against those who have threatened to use or have actually used force against others might well reduce the incidence of crimes against persons and property. Though man may not be wholly rational, neither is he entirely irrational. If a potential criminal were convinced that his committing a crime would almost certainly result in his arrest, and that, once arrested, he would face a lengthy incarceration, his reason would have stronger arguments with which to counsel against lawbreaking.

☞ NOTE: When you take a position on a controversial subject that necessitates acknowledging the opposition, do so in the first part of your paragraph. Then come on with your views. Since, in both the paragraph and the theme, the reader remembers best what he reads last, it is your argument, not the opposition's, that he will carry away.

Principle 2: An Effective Paragraph Exhibits a Clear, Precise, and Limited Topic Sentence

A paragraph without a topic sentence is a ship without a rudder, a car without a steering wheel, a train without a track. It's a paragraph potentially out of control, running wild, a menace to clear thinking. Like a rudder or a steering wheel, the topic sentence is a means of control—through the topic sentence you control the direction of your paragraph. And, like the tracks on which a train runs, the topic sentence forces you to go in a particular direction and ensures that, with a little elementary caution, you will arrive at your destination.

A. The topic sentence should be *clear.* This is primarily a matter of sentence style and structure, and you'll be better able to distinguish between a clear and unclear sentence after reading the chapter, "Principles of Precise Expression." However, the prerequisite for clarity in the topic sentence (as in the thesis) is that it be stated as an *assertion.* Never formulate your topic sentence in the form of a *question,* for a question gives no direction. Whenever you feel tempted to state your topic sentence as a question, state instead your *answer* to the question:

Not: What's wrong with the system of grading?
But: Receiving low grades discourages rather than motivates many students.

or

Many students feel threatened by the never-ending evaluation of their capacities entailed by the practice of grading.

or

The practice of grading makes close rapport between instructor and student difficult.

B. The topic sentence should be *precise.* Vague words, fuzzy words if you like, words that have no distinct boundaries, deprive your topic sentence of precision.

Imprecise: The entering freshman faces many problems.

☞ NOTE: Deciding whether you should take an eight o'clock class is a *problem.* So is deciding whether to marry the girl back home before some other guy gets her. The term covers such a wide range of possibilities that it gives neither you nor the reader direction.

Precise: In his first days on campus the entering freshman must decide where to live, what courses to take, and whether or not he should go Greek.

C. The topic sentence should be *limited*. In a paragraph you develop one main idea or major assertion. If your topic sentence is insufficiently limited, it is impossible to do an adequate job of developing it in the restricted space of a single paragraph. You can limit your topic sentence by limiting the subject about which you are making an assertion or by limiting the assertion you make about the subject, or by limiting both subject and assertion about it. For example:

Too Broad: Material possessions are status symbols.

☞ NOTE: What material possessions? *All* material possessions? Down-at-the-heel shoes, horn-rimmed glasses?

Limitation of Subject: A private airplane is a status symbol.

Too Broad: The study of history reveals a lot about man's nature.

☞ NOTE: Obviously, that which the study of history reveals about man's nature is far too extensive to be brought within the compass of a single paragraph.

Limitation of Assertion About Subject: The study of history reveals that man does not always learn from experience.

Too Broad: America's educational system is outmoded.

☞ NOTE: America's public educational system alone embraces primary schools, secondary schools, and state junior colleges, colleges and universities. The nature of these schools differs among various regions of the country and among various sized cities. The ways in which the system could be said to be outmoded are far too numerous even to list, much less develop, in a single paragraph. Furthermore, it is unlikely that an assertion about a particular deficiency would apply with equal validity to all levels of the system, all geographical areas, etc.

Limitation of Subject and Assertion: The large state universities tend to stifle creativity and spontaneity in the student.

or

The faculty of large state universities seem to feel that their purpose is to exclude as many students as possible rather than include as many as possible (one way in which, some argue, one part of America's educational system is outmoded).

Principle 3: An Effective Paragraph Displays Full and Progressive Development of the Topic Sentence Assertion

Now we are really coming to the heart of the matter. Here are three paragraphs. Judge each one "satisfactory" or "unsatisfactory" as soon as you finish reading it.

1. Communism as a political system is democratic. It encourages freedom of the press. Similarly, it is tolerant of dissent and criticism, whether written or in the form of demonstrations. Finally, it guarantees free and open elections of government officials on all levels.

2. The principal's office was a shambles. All the windows were shattered. Water stood in puddles on the floor and stained the once handsome drapes. The large desk which had stood in the center of the office was upended in one corner, its drawers open, and their contents scattered about the floor. Obscene scrawls from colored crayons disfigured the walls.

3. Communism as a political system is opposed to democratic values. It restricts the freedoms of the press. Similarly, it is intolerant of dissent and criticism, whether written or in the form of demonstrations. Finally, it does not allow those free and open elections of government officials on all levels that are an essential aspect of a democracy.

Only paragraph 2 is satisfactory. Paragraphs 1 and 3 are equally unsatisfactory, and for identical reasons. They are both unsatisfactory because they rely on *unsupported assertions*. Unsupported assertions do not support a conclusion. Let's look at this matter more closely.

TWO TYPES OF TOPIC SENTENCES: TWO TYPES OF DEVELOPMENT

For our purposes, we need to distinguish between only two types of topic sentences:

1. Those which can be adequately supported by details, illustrations, and examples alone.
2. Those which can only be adequately supported by reasons *and* details, illustrations, examples, or verifiable explanations.

In a paragraph with a topic sentence of the first sort, the details, illustrations, and examples *add up* to support the topic sentence assertion. The principal's office was not a shambles *because* his desk was upended; it takes more than an upended desk to make a room a shambles. But all the details in the paragraph add up to form, in aggregate, a shambles.

In a paragraph with a topic sentence of the second sort, each *reason* has a direct causal relation to the topic sentence assertion. Communism as a political system *is opposed to democratic values* BECAUSE it *is intolerant of dissent and criticism*. But unsupported assertions *alone,* even a hundred, will *never* add up to support the topic sentence assertion.

They will not add up to support your topic sentence assertion because the reader, a perverse and hard-to-convince fellow at best, can completely negate your argument with four little words: "I don't believe you." The *reasons* you give in support of a conclusion (topic sentence assertion) will not convince the reader of the validity of that conclusion unless he is convinced that they, the *reasons,* are true. This is what development of an argumentative paragraph is all about—convincing your reader that the *reasons* that you give in support of a *conclusion* are, indeed, *true.*

How do you convince the skeptical reader of the truth of your reasons? You convince him by moving toward the specific. By getting down to concretes. By giving him examples or explanations that can be verified. Let's illustrate this process:

Topic Sentence: Communism as a political system *is opposed to democratic values.*

BECAUSE: It *restricts the freedom of the press and censors literature.*

For instance: All newspapers are operated by the state and are subject to censorship by the state.

For instance: The state supervises and restricts the importation and distribution of the literature of other countries.

BECAUSE: It *is intolerant of dissent, whether written or in the form of demonstrations.*

For instance: In the aftermath of the invasion of Czechoslovakia, five young men were arrested and jailed for having tried to send a letter of support to Czechoslovak party leader, Alexander Dubcek.

For instance: Five persons who staged a demonstration in Red Square protesting the Soviet invasion of Czechoslovakia were tried and sentenced to exile.

BECAUSE: It *does not allow free and open elections of government officials.*

For instance: A private citizen is not free to file for an office, pay a fee, and have his name put on the ballot.

For instance: Only one slate of candidates appears on the ballot, so the voter is given no meaningful freedom of choice.

    This is now a satisfactory paragraph. Each of the three "reasons" why communism as a political system is opposed to democratic values has been supported by verifiable explanation. Without example or specific explanation a "reason" is simply an *unsupported assertion,* and unsupported assertions do not support a conclusion. Let's take another example:

Heavy petting between two people with a strong relationship is morally acceptable. It doesn't violate the girl's chastity. Furthermore, it doesn't involve promiscuous behavior.

    This is *not* a paragraph. It is a conclusion (first sentence) and two *unsupported assertions.* All the skeptical reader has to say is, "That's what you say. To me it's unchaste and promiscuous." Again, if you are to convince the reader of the validity of your conclusion, you must convince him of the truth of your reasons in support of it. In this case, your reasons involve assertions about two unconcretized abstractions: *chastity* and *promiscuity.* Therefore, you must concretize the abstractions in terms of your assertions about them:

Topic Sentence: Heavy petting between two people with a strong relationship *is morally acceptable.*

BECAUSE: Such petting *does not violate the girl's chastity.*

Because: By very definition petting, of whatever degree, is sexual behavior that stops short of actual intercourse. Since virginity is usually the primary criterion for chastity, and petting does not cause a loss of virginity, the girl remains chaste.

BECAUSE: The girl who engages in this behavior in the context of a strong relationship *is not being promiscuous.*

Because: She is seriously involved with one man. She dates this man regularly and does not engage in heavy petting with others. In some respects it is as if the couple were married. They probably see each other daily. They engage in numerous nonsexual activities together. In no way is the girl behaving in a "loose" or promiscuous fashion.

You must always move toward the specific. You must get down to statements that are verifiable. Only statements of this sort will convince the reader of the truth of your reasons. After all, you cannot validly ask a girl to answer "true" or "false" to the question, "Are you chaste?" It is not an either-or situation. She might respond, "Do you mean chaste in spirit or chaste in body? If you mean chaste in body, do you mean chastity as virginity or chastity as sleeping only with men I love?" and so forth.

But once you have concretized the abstraction "chastity" to mean virginity, you can validly ask for a "true" or "false" response to the question, "Are you a virgin?"

Similarly, when you assert that "heavy petting between two people who have a strong relationship *does not involve promiscuity,*" you are not yet down to a verifiable situation because "promiscuity" has different meanings for different people. But the assertion that a girl in such a relationship sees her man daily or almost daily *is* verifiable. Your reader (if he has enough gall), can go out and ask people who have a strong relationship and who engage in heavy petting whether or not they see each other daily or almost daily.

One more example, this time from a student theme:

Competition is an advantage to the consumer since it tends to bring him desirable prices, quality, and variety. This situation occurs when businesses in competition must produce more favorable products than their competitors in order to get the consumer's business.

The student has completely ignored the whispered admonitions of the good angel on his shoulder. Note, first of all, the sloppy phrasing of the topic sentence. "Competition" *among whom, for what?* What are "desirable prices?" How do you "bring" someone quality? The student means that "Free competition among producers for the consumer dollar promotes the production of a large variety of goods of high quality at low prices." This is enough. The writer has *three* classifications he must develop, three "hows" and "whys" he must answer, three "I don't believe you's" to confound:

1. Free competition promotes *variety* of goods.
2. Free competition promotes *high quality* of goods.
3. Free competition promotes *low price* of goods.

But these responsibilities don't sway this writer. He ignores the legitimate demands of the reader. Instead of giving reasons and examples in support of each of the three assertions he has already made, he immediately trots out *another* big assertion:

This situation occurs ["Oh yeah?" says the squatting reader] when businesses in competition must produce more favorable products than their competitors in order to get the consumer's business. [End "paragraph."]

When you write an argumentative essay, your position is analogous to that of the prosecuting attorney in a courtroom. The burden of proof is on *you*. No matter how widely accepted your position, you must still give evidence in support of it. The prosecuting attorney cannot go into the courtroom and say, "The defendant is guilty. Since everybody in his right mind agrees, the prosecution rests." He must produce convincing evidence in support of his conclusion. Similarly, you must present reasonable and persuasive evidence in support of your topic sentence assertion. But the prosecuting attorney will not convince the jury if he contents himself with *unsupported* assertions in support of his conclusion: "The defendant is guilty because he broke into the house, tied up the old lady, and stole her life's savings." He must convince the jury of the truth of *each* of these assertions before they will agree with him that his conclusion follows. Similarly, you must convince the reader of the truth of each reason you give in support of your topic sentence assertion.

If you state that "Free competition among producers for the consumer dollar promotes the production of a large variety of goods of high quality at low prices," you must convince the reader of the truth of *each* of these three assertions before moving on.

SUMMARY

Your goal in developing a body paragraph is to convince your reader of the truth or tenability of your topic sentence *assertion*. To convince him, you must move toward the specific and the verifiable. Whenever you give a reason in support of the topic sentence, ask yourself if your reader can reasonably query, "Why?" or "How?" If he can, you must give specific explanation or example before moving on to the next reason. If you ignore the demands of the skeptical reader, he will ignore your argument.

A topic sentence represents an opinion, a judgment, a conclusion. Hopefully, you were led to this conclusion by experiences: facts read, reasons discussed, persons known, examples recalled, details amassed, etc. When you "develop" the topic sentence assertion, you recreate for the reader the experiences that led you to the conclusion that the topic sentence assertion represents. You convince your reader, in short, by setting before him the reasons, details, facts, examples that convinced you.

The process of paragraph development is as natural as breathing. As we go through life, experiencing and learning, we "inhale" experiences and knowledge which lead us to form the many opinions which we hold. After we express one of our opinions in a topic sentence, we must then "exhale" into the paragraph the experiences and knowledge which led us to form this opinion.

Exercise: Paragraph Development

Below are some fully developed student paragraphs. Outline each paragraph to reveal its structure. In parentheses indicate the function of each sentence with the appropriate label: "topic sentence," "reason," "example," "illustration," "clarification," "qualification," "restatement," "conclusion," and so forth. To illustrate:

Television advertisements for cigarettes are deceiving. First of all, they are biased in their presentation of cigarette smoking. These advertisements show beautiful women and handsome men who are contentedly smoking cigarettes. What they don't show are the nicotine stains on the hands and teeth of smokers, the coughing and sore throats which can result from smoking, and the constant smell of tobacco smoke which accompanies the smoker. Another ploy of cigarette advertisements is their emphasis on the masculinity of males and the femininity of females who smoke. One of the advertisements shows a big rancher of the West riding a horse and caring for his herd of cattle. The immediate thought of the male viewer is that this is a *real* man and that if he smokes this particular brand of cigarettes, he will also be a real man. The same holds true in another advertisement which shows a sexy, daring woman who has fought for her rights. Again, the implied assertion is that if the female viewer smokes this particular brand of cigarettes, she too will be sexy, daring, and a real woman. By making cigarette smoking appear glamourous and by exploiting people's desire to appear masculine or feminine, television advertisements for cigarettes have presented a deceptive picture of the results of cigarette smoking.

I. Television advertisements for cigarettes are deceiving. (topic sentence)
   A. First of all, they are biased in their presentation of cigarette smoking. (reason)
      1. These advertisements show beautiful women and handsome men who are contentedly smoking cigarettes. (reason)
      2. What they don't show are the nicotine stains on the hands and teeth of the smoker, the coughing and sore throats

which can result from smoking, and the constant smell of tobacco smoke which accompanies the smoker. (reason)

B. Another ploy of cigarette advertisements is their emphasis on the masculinity of males and the femininity of females who smoke. (reason)

    1. One of the advertisements shows a big rancher of the West riding a horse and caring for his herd of cattle. (example)

        a. The immediate thought of the male viewer is that this is a *real* man and that if he smokes this particular brand of cigarettes he will also be a real man. (clarification)

    2. The same holds true in another advertisement which shows a sexy, daring woman who has fought for her rights. (example)

        a. Again, the implied assertion is that if the female viewer smokes this particular brand of cigarettes, she too will be sexy, daring, and a real woman. (clarification)

I. By making cigarette smoking appear glamourous and by exploiting people's desire to appear masculine or feminine, television advertisements for cigarettes have presented a deceptive picture of the results of cigarette smoking. (restatement)

1. Examinations are not a valid test of a student's general knowledge. The test may be given on a day when a particular student is emotionally upset or physically below par. The exam may be too minute; in other words, the instructor may cover a lot of material and what the student thought most important may be left out and minute details asked for instead. The test may not be the kind a student is best at. An essay test, for example, favors the student who is verbally proficient and penalizes the student who "knows the facts" but doesn't write well. Furthermore, many students cram the night before a test and forget the material as soon as they leave the classroom and the test is over. For such students, the examination tests memory, not general knowledge.

2. Dormitory life is educational. One lesson to be learned while living in a dormitory is how to get along with other people. When so many people live in one relatively small area, it becomes necessary to give in a little to the wishes of other people, to share with one another,

and to be considerate of the other dormitory residents. A wide variety of views on many different subjects and issues is also learned. Dormitory residents come from different cultural backgrounds which have formed different views and attitudes in each of these people. When these various views and attitudes are compared, one can see the complexity of the different subjects and issues and can make his own judgments. Another lesson that a student learns while living in a dormitory is to take on greater responsibility. Before entering college a person does have to take on some of the responsibility of making his own decisions and caring for his own well-being, but his parents are still carrying the greater part of these responsibilities and are there to guide him. However, when a person enters college he must make his own decisions and care for his own needs without his parents' constant supervision and help. Each of these things—learning to get along with others, learning the different views on subjects and issues, and learning to take on greater responsibility—is an educational aspect of dormitory life.

3. Summer jobs for students are educational. The student acquires one or even several skills. The nature of these skills depends upon the type of job; in order to do a job satisfactorily, one must learn the skills involved. In other words, he must learn the procedure for doing the work which his job creates. A summer job also teaches the student how to get along with other people. While working the student comes in contact with many people, which include the boss, fellow employees, customers, and business associates. The student must be able to please these people; and from his experiences in doing so, or even sometimes not doing so, he learns that he cannot be selfish and that he must see other people's points of view and do as they wish even though he doesn't agree with them. A summer job also teaches the student to take on responsibility. Getting the job done and doing it correctly is up to the student and no one else. He finds that he has to make the right decisions on his own and that he can't ask someone else what to do whenever he needs an answer. Acquiring new skills, learning to get along with other people, and learning to accept responsibility are all educational aspects of summer jobs.

4. Halloween is not only a time of innocent fun and excitement, but is also a time of danger. In recent years many young children have been seriously injured by sadistic practical jokers. On Halloween night thousands of costumed little kids run from door to door shouting "Trick or Treat." They stand with sacks open, eagerly anticipating "goodies"; but instead of receiving the innocent treats they expect,

some are handed "treats" which are harmful, poisonous, and even deadly. Drugs, razor blades and pins have been found in candy bars, popcorn balls and other sweets. Unsuspecting children may easily slash their tongues or consume poison. Last year in Essex Ville, Michigan a boy bit into a candy bar and his tongue was almost slashed off by a hidden razor blade. *The Detroit Free Press* printed an account of another little boy who died as a result of the LSD in a piece of his Halloween candy. In Mt. Pleasant last year a girl ate some candy with poison in it and had to be rushed to the hospital. Halloween is no longer just a time of fun and excitement; it is also a time of danger.

5. Many elements have gone into the creation of the modern "light shows" which are common at rock palaces, large clubs and many college dances. They apparently started with the effort to simulate an acid trip; hence the names "The Acid Test," "Freak Out," and "Trips Festival." These early shows used mainly overhead projections, from which came the name "wet shows." "Wet shows" are various special dyes in water placed in shallow dishes or clock lenses, on top of an overhead projector. About the same time came another element, the color organ. This organ emitted certain colors that corresponded to the keyboard notes, giving a special light effect. This soon gave way to "Vortex Concerts" in San Francisco's Morrison Planetarium (1957–1959) where a filmmaker named Jordan Belson used seventy projectors, slides, and film clips in a fifty-minute program with composer Henry Jacobs' electronic music. Although the color wheel (a large wheel with multicolored windows), the strobascope (a high-intensity light flashing rapidly on and off), and Op Art patterns thrown by light projectors have been added, the modern "light show" is an up-dated Belson's "Vortex" concert. The modern "light show" is a complex affair, using numerous liquid projectors, Op patterns, color wheels, strobascopes, slides and motion picture clips from underground films, cartoons and TV commercials.

Principle 4: An Effective Paragraph Is Unified

Paragraph unity is the product of several forces working together in harmony. A clear, precise, and limited topic sentence helps produce unity. So does disciplined reasoning and care that you get that reasoning into your paragraph. But, most importantly of all, paragraph unity is produced by your having a firm grasp of just what your duty in a particular paragraph is.

A. The principle cause of a lack of paragraph unity is writing on the *subject* of the topic sentence rather than supporting the *assertion* about the subject.

Never, in composition, think of yourself as writing *on a subject.* You should *never* write *on* a subject. Instead, in an individual paragraph you support and develop and amplify and illustrate one particular and definite *assertion* about a subject. That assertion is made in the topic sentence. As we saw in our discussion of analysis, most subjects are extremely complex and can be examined at length from many different points of view. Inevitably, the result of writing *on* a subject is an unfocused hodgepodge of ideas and hence a paragraph with no clear direction.

The paragraph that follows illustrates what happens when one writes on a subject rather than supporting a particular assertion about a subject:

Four out of five American couples use some kind of birth control to improve the quality of family life. Unfortunately, sometimes tragically, many women and their husbands are using old-fashioned, rather ineffective methods of contraception, when they could be using the new and more effective pill. This is an oral method of birth control and may be prescribed for women only by a physician. There are a number of pills on the market today, and they all work about the same way. Twenty to twenty-one consecutive pills are taken, one a day beginning on the fifth day of the menstrual cycle. When taking the pill not a single day must be omitted, for it is not effective if the cycle is interrupted. By dissolving and entering the blood stream the pill stops the activity of certain glands and prevents ovulation. A two- to four-year time limit has been placed on taking of some of the pills because of aftereffects. The pills are very effective if used properly under the care of a physician.

☞ NOTE: Presumedly, the second sentence is the topic sentence. It leads the reader to expect a contrast between the *ineffectiveness* of several specific "old-fashioned" contraceptive methods and the *effectiveness* of the "pill." Instead of making this contrast, however, the writer puts down everything she can think of concerning the *subject,* the "pill."

B. A second major cause of a lack of paragraph unity is the writer's ignoring his topic sentence assertion.

This second basic cause of a lack of paragraph unity is closely related to the first, since one is ignoring his topic sentence assertion when he writes on the subject in general. However, in paragraphs like the one we've just examined, there is generally a gradual drift away from supporting the assertion to writing about the subject. In paragraphs that lack unity because the writer ignores his topic sentence assertion, the writer generally makes a strong assertion in his first sentence, and then simply ignores it and his responsibility to develop and support it. It's as if he told the reader he was going to bring him a pepperoni pizza, and then delivered one with mushrooms. For example:

There are many problems to be faced when entering a college. It is easier to face up to them if a student likes the atmosphere of the school he attends. If he likes the campus he has some incentive to study hard so he will stay there. If he does not like the campus he does not want to stay there; consequently, he does not apply himself. If a student likes the school he attends, he is more likely to graduate.

☞ NOTE: The first sentence leads the reader to expect a discussion of various "problems" that face the entering college freshman. But the student ignores the topic sentence assertion and makes overgeneral, unsupported assertions about the importance of liking the college one attends.

UNITY TEST

The model argumentative paragraph lends itself to a simple "unity test." In the topic sentence of such a paragraph you make an assertion that must be supported and developed in one of the two fashions we've already examined. You can easily test all sentences in support of the topic sentence assertion for relevance by using one of two terms, whichever fits—*because* or *for instance*.

A. When you develop a topic sentence assertion with reasons, you should be able to place each reason immediately after the topic sentence *assertion* with "because" in between. To illustrate:

Limited Subject: Depression and the Freshman

Topic Sentence 1:	A freshman *is vulnerable to a feeling of depression.*
Reason 1 (because):	He is away from home for a long period, perhaps for the first time.
Reason 2 (because):	He is responsible for his own success or failure.
Reason 3 (because):	He may find himself without a feeling of purpose and direction.
Topic Sentence 2:	Such a feeling of depression *is self-perpetuating.*
Reason 1 (because):	It is difficult to study when one is depressed.
Reason 2 (because):	When one doesn't study, his grades suffer.
Reason 3 (because):	Falling grades generate more depression.
Topic Sentence 3:	Depression *can be conquered.*
Reason 1 (because):	Making new friends to replace those left at home helps.
Reason 2 (because):	Joining campus organizations helps.
Reason 3 (because):	Forcing oneself to study, instead of brooding, helps.

When you support your reasons, you should be able to put each supporting statement immediately after the reason it supports with *because* or *for instance* in between. Hence:

Topic Sentence:	A feeling of depression is self-perpetuating.
Reason 1:	It *is difficult to study when one is depressed.*
Support (because):	When one is depressed he is overcome by lassitude and indifference.
Support (because):	Any effort seems to require more energy than one can muster.
Reason 2:	When one doesn't study, his grades *suffer.*
Reason 3:	Falling grades *generate more depression.*
Support (because):	Grades are a primary index of achievement in college.
Support (because):	As his grades fall the freshman feels he is failing to live up to his own and his parents' expectations.
Support (because):	This feeling of failure intensifies the freshman's feeling of despair and hopelessness.

B. When you develop a topic sentence assertion with examples or details, you should be able to place each example or detail immediately after the topic sentence assertion with *for instance* in between:

Topic Sentence:	The principal's office *was a shambles.*
For instance:	All the windows were shattered.
For instance:	Water stood in puddles on the floor and stained the once handsome drapes.
For instance:	The large desk which had stood in the center of the office was upended in one corner, its drawers open, and their contents scattered about the floor.
For instance:	Obscene scrawls from colored crayons disfigured the walls.

If you mentally insert these two unity words as you develop your paragraph, you can quickly catch yourself if you start to drift off into the uncharted sea of irrelevancy. Notice this student paragraph:

Cassius Clay, in my opinion, is one of the greatest boxers there ever has been. I have seen all of his fights that were televised. And I can honestly say that it was really enjoyable to watch him fight. Why then is he forbidden to fight in the United States?

Topic Sentence:	Cassius Clay, in my opinion, *is one of the greatest boxers there ever has been.*
Because?:	I have seen all of his fights that were televised.
Because?:	It was really enjoyable to watch him fight.
Because?:	Why then is he forbidden to fight in the United States?

Obviously, none of the three sentences which the student uses to "support" his topic sentence assertion will follow that assertion with "because" mentally inserted between. The student is writing in a free associational manner on his *subject,* Cassius Clay, rather than supporting his *assertion* about the subject. All three sentences are irrelevant to the topic sentence assertion and must be kicked out.

☞NOTE: The unity test is designed to alert you to sentences in your paragraph which, though intended to support the topic sentence assertion, do not do so. Often, a sentence in a paragraph will have some function other than support of the topic sentence assertion. It may be a transition, or a qualification, or a definition, or a clarification, or a restatement, or a conclusion. But if a sentence that is intended to support the main point of your paragraph fails the unity test, it must be omitted or revised until it does meet the test for unity.

Exercises: Paragraph Unity

1. Turn back to the sentence outlines on pp. 43–45. Assume that each sentence designated by a roman numeral is a topic sentence. Underline the assertion in each of these sentences and then put the appropriate unity term (*because* or *for instance*) to the left of each element under a particular topic sentence.
2. Analyze the following "paragraphs" and indicate with a check (√) those sentences which *do not* support the topic sentence assertion and which are, therefore, irrelevant. In each case, indicate whether the lack of unity is caused by "writing on the subject" or "ignoring the topic sentence assertion."

1. Since primitive times man has been aware of laughter and humor and has been looking for anything that might make him smile. If life didn't have humor, it would become depressing and hostile. To the average person a sense of humor means the ability to laugh and see life in a happier way. The majority of people would like to say that they possess a sense of humor, but what they want to say is not always true. To say that one has humor is just the same as saying that some people get mad or excited when they really don't. Laughter and humor are natural instincts, and because of this people have to be reminded not to laugh at certain things. That many foreigners think that the American people all have a humorous nature is because America's billboards are pasted with advertisements showing smiling faces. Humor can be defined in many ways because it means different things to different people.

2. On my first day at work I was taught how to fill out an admission summary sheet, an out-patient form, and a set of insurance papers. All of these reports must be completed upon a patient's admission to the hospital. I often had to open the mail before the morning coffee break. It was not unusual to see papers all over the receptionist's desk before the morning was through. There is never a dull moment in a hospital. If you aren't busy at your assigned job, you are busy improving your skills.

3. Not all of the workers displaced by automation can find other work. Though other jobs are created, many of these displaced workers are not skilled or trained enough to be hired. For many workers,

assembly-line work causes problems within themselves because they are not satisfied with doing only a small part of the product. These people must be able to look at a finished product with pride knowing that they did all of the work. They have no ability or training for another job. Since they must have money to live, they go to work everyday as a part of a machine.

4. Alone a man is meek and shy and would do no harm to his fellowman. This same man, though, would react completely differently when faced by a similar situation when he is no longer alone. He doesn't have to be frightened of someone he would ordinarily fear for his friends are there to support him verbally and physically. Ten such men together feel big and fearless and think they can lick anybody.

5. The fears of an atomic bomb are pushing people to seize the present moment. An atomic bomb can destroy an entire city. A powerful blast is created only a few moments after the bomb explodes due to the release of a great quantity of explosive power. The blast waves move through the air at a speed greater than that of sound and create high amounts of pressure which knock down buildings and incur great destruction. Destruction is also brought about by the atomic bomb because it produces a glowing ball of fire that may reach millions of degrees. Radiant energy is involved in the fireball, which travels out from "point zero" (the point directly below or above the point of detonation) at the speed of light. A heat effect such as this can kill people, scorch paper, wood, and foliage up to one-and-a-half miles from point zero. Closer into point zero the intense heat ignites fires which in turn create other fires. The ultimate effect is a blazing fire storm that can wipe out an entire city. A realization of these facts cause people to try to seize the present moment, especially teen-agers.

Principle 5: An Effective Paragraph Is Coherent

To "cohere" means to "stick together," and coherence devices are used to make a series of sentences all relevant to the same point stick so closely together that the reader passes effortlessly from one to another. The best coherence devices are progressive development and unity. If your paragraph has a clear, precise, and limited topic sentence, if the topic sentence assertion is fully and progressively developed, and if the paragraph contains no irrelevant material, it will inevitably have a logical coherence even if you don't use a single one of the coherence techniques we are going to discuss. It will have the coherence of the great public buildings of ancient Greece. No mortar was used in the construction of these buildings, yet each stone was so closely fitted to its neighbor that none was needed.

Coherence devices, in other words, are no substitute for close reasoning, a lesson Snoopy has yet to learn:

© 1969 United Feature Syndicate, Inc.

But coherence devices do have a valid function as fine mortar to bridge the fissure from one block to another, to allow the reader to pass smoothly from sentence to sentence within the paragraph.

Some coherence devices, such as *pronouns* and *repetition* murmur to the reader, "Relax, take it easy; I'm still talking about the same point." Others, such as certain *relation words* are like road signs that warn the driver of a curve, an intersection, a detour. They alert the reader that he is coming to a qualification, to a contrast, to an example, to a clarification, to a conclusion.

PRONOUNS

A pronoun is a one-word summary. By using a pronoun you remind the reader of what you've just said even as you move forward; you keep the subject of your remarks constantly before him. Notice how "they," "them," and "these" are used (perhaps in excess) to tie together the sentences of this paragraph:

Approximately 30,000,000 Americans change their address each year. And millions of *these* movers strive in their home-hopping to upgrade themselves socially with each hop. *These* highly mobile citizens are also the nation's prize consumers. *They* not only try to upgrade their home with each move, but, market studies show, *they* have a tremendous "upgrading urge" when it comes to the extras. If *they* move into an area where the neighbors have clothes driers or air conditioners, *they* feel *they* must have them, too, and quickly. Experts on consumer motives find *they* are ripe for any goods sold to *them* as "keys to social acceptance." (Vance Packard)

☞ NOTE: A word of caution here. Every pronoun you use must have a clear and unambiguous referent. Two pronouns that often lack a clear and unambiguous referent are *this* and *which:*

This: When you use "this," it is often wise to follow it with a word or phrase that indicates exactly what your "this" refers to. This practice will eliminate the vagueness that often accompanies the use of "this."

Hence: "this concept is . . ." rather than "this is . . ." or "this belief that most people are materialistic was . . ." rather than "this was . . ."

Which: Whenever you use *which,* be sure there is one, and *only one,* possible antecedent for the pronoun. Don't use *which* to refer to the general "idea" of a statement: *Unclear:* "Man is a sad animal, and a happy animal, and a cruel animal, *which* is really too bad." (What is "too bad"?—That man is a kind animal? That man is made up of opposites? That man is an animal?—Who knows?) *Unclear:* "Within the last ten years America has become a fascist, anarchistic, ungodly, communist, materialistic, flipnik-ridden mess, *which* is a pretty poor way to run a country." (*"Mess* is a pretty poor way to run a country"? No. That doesn't make sense. Here again, there is no specific antecedent for *which.*)

REPETITION

Repetition of the same word or phrase in two or more successive sentences creates coherence in much the same way that the use of pronouns creates coherence. Notice Steinbeck's repetition of an introductory *the* and his repetition of *red country* and *grey country* in this, the opening paragraph of *The Grapes of Wrath:*

To the *red country* and part of the *grey country* of Oklahoma, the last rains came gently, and they did not cut the scarred earth. *The* plows crossed and recrossed the rivulet marks. *The* last rains lifted the corn quickly and scattered weed colonies and grass along the sides of the roads so that the *grey country* and the dark *red country* began to disappear under a green cover. In *the* last part of May the sky grew pale and the clouds that had hung in high puffs for so long in the spring were dissipated. *The* sun flared down on the growing corn day after day until a line of brown spread along the edge of each green bayonet. *The* clouds appeared, and went away, and in a while they did not try any more. *The* weeds grew darker to protect themselves, and they did not spread any more. *The* surface of the earth crusted, a thin hard crust, and as the sky became pale, so the earth became pale, pink in the *red country* and white in the *grey country.*
(John Steinbeck)

Repetition of the same *syntactical pattern* (parallelism) in two or more successive sentences is an extremely effective means of achieving coherence. It shows that you care how you say what you have to say:

In the process of creating these new values, Black Power *will*, its advocates hope, *build* a new sense of community among black people. It *will try* to forge a bond in the black community between those who have "made it" and those "on the bottom." It *will bring* an end to the internal back-biting and suspicious bickering, the squabbling over tactics and personalities so characteristic of the black community. If Black Power can produce this unity, that in itself *will be* revolutionary, for the black community and for the country.

(Charles V. Hamilton)

RELATION WORDS

Relation words and phrases point out a *relation* or *connection* between two ideas. Be sure the relation word or phrase you choose indicates the *kind* of relation you mean. Here are a few types:

1. *Plus* relation words:
   and — in addition
   moreover — furthermore
2. *Qualification* relation words:
   however — although
   of course — needless to say
3. *Contrast* relation words:
   on the other hand — yet
   but — nevertheless
4. *Comparison* relation words:
   similarly — comparably
   like — in the same way
5. *Clarification* relation words:
   for instance — to illustrate
   for example — specifically
6. *Sequence* relation words:
   first — then
   secondly — finally

7. *Conclusion* relation words:

therefore	hence
thus	so

Notice how appropriate relation words allow us to follow with ease this writer's argument:

Nevertheless, the difference in social acceptability between *I ain't* and *I am not,* between *hern* and *hers,* and so forth, is a real fact. If my child is likely to run into trouble later on for saying *I done it* or *hisn,* I will try to keep him from getting into the habit of using those forms which are actually not acceptable socially and which may cause others to react unfavorably towards him. But, if I am sensible about it, I will realize that the reason I want him to avoid these "incorrect" forms is not any inherent badness or evil character that they may have, but a purely practical consideration, that of their social acceptability. . . . Of course, as soon as people in any given group stop treating, say, *he don't* as socially unacceptable, it automatically becomes "correct."

Principle 6: An Effective Paragraph Begins with a Transition

That hypothetical construct perched on your shoulder is not only an incurable skeptic but something of a dullard, to boot. Give him half a chance and he will throw up his hands in despair and cry, "I'm lost! I don't follow you!" So when you move from one paragraph to another, use a transition to help him along.

A. You can use a *relation word* or *phrase.*

At the level of sheer logic, one of the most curious features of the "theological era" of the past is that most people feared and sought to avoid death at any and every cost, except sometimes for honor's sake. Even though they professed to have faith in personal survival after death, it was their Worst Enemy. Nowadays, when faith is waning not only in the prospect of hell but even of heaven, there is a trend toward accepting death as a part of reality, just as "natural" as life. Churchmen, even clergymen, are dropping the traditional faith in personal survival after death, just as many unbelievers do. Curiously, it is the skeptics about immortality who appear to face death more calmly. They seem somehow less inclined to hang on desperately to life at the cost of indescribably and uncreative suffering for themselves and others.

But a painful conflict persists.   (Joseph Fletcher)

B. You can use a *pronoun* that has its antecedent in the preceding paragraph.

Forced to a reason for his hostility, the white Chicagoan—or Ciceroan—returns again and again to his property, and, less often but often enough, to his safety. In *Cicero* at night, on the residential streets, you can still hear crickets; on a humid night in August, you can still meet two or three solitary strollers in as many blocks, some of them women, who don't cross the street or even seem agitated as you, a stranger, approach.

It is, in fact, not a part of a modern urban complex at all, but an American small town out of the 1930's. . . .   (Gene Marine)

C. You can *incorporate* in the first sentence of your paragraph a key word or phrase from the preceding paragraph.

Windows were opened again, and lights went on in many apartments. The *assailant* got into his car and drove away. Miss Genovese staggered to her feet. A city bus, 0-10, the Lefferts Boulevard line to Kennedy International Airport, passed. It was 3:35 A.M.

The *assailant* returned.   (Martin Gansberg)

D. You can *restate* the main point of the preceding paragraph.

This is all of one piece with the fact that *teachers are so badly underpaid.* The people of the commercial society are no fools. They understand perfectly well that there are a few people who, because of their careers, have no frontiers in the social structure. These are the teachers, of course, and the creative people . . .

It is not only that teachers are underpaid, but also that they are interfered with by the "outside," that forces them to become quasi-politicians. . . .   (Harry Golden)

E. You can use a *combination* of these techniques.

To undertake a discussion of the modern woman and yet speak sympathetically of her awareness of power is obviously a risky business. Not only in our personal relations but even in our public affairs we Americans dislike the idea of power; we prefer the ideas of helpfulness and cooperation. Progressive education favors the helpful cooperative child over the forceful child. So-called enlightened politics prefers to co-exist with communism rather than throw our whole moral weight against it. *Power* is a dirty word in our society.

Yet the impulse to *power* is entirely human. . . . (relation word, incorporation)   (Diana Trilling)

American marriage is dangerously weakened at its inception because of our preference for moonlight and poison ivy—the lies elders tell the young about marriage, and the hourly elaboration of these lies, cunningly persuasive, by many magazines, the radio, the movies, national advertisers. It is rarely portrayed for what it is: a difficult and demanding exercise in human relationships; a partnership, not without austerity, in which losses as well as profits are shared; an undertaking dynastic as well as individual. More commonly—vulgarly and infantilely—marriage is portrayed as a gumdrop *heaven:* soft, gooey, chewy, and oh, so sweet.

It is, of course, a *heaven* of huge dimensions. . . . (pronoun, incorporation)   (David L. Cohn)

Romantics, who want love's desiring to be conclusive, though endless, often linked it to death: if nothing further can happen and rival its significance, if one dies before it does, love indeed is the end. But this is ending the game as much as winning it—certainly an ambiguous move. The religious too perpetuate longing by placing the beloved altogether out of physical reach. The "bride of Christ" who retires to a convent longs for her Redeemer—and she will continue to yearn, as long as she lives, for union with a God at once human and divine, incarnating life and love everlasting. In its highest sense, love is a reaching for divine perfection, an act of creation. And always, *it is a longing.*

Since love is longing, experts in the Middle Ages held that one could not love someone who could not be longed for—for instance, one's wife. . . . (relation word, restatement, incorporation)
(Ernest Van Den Haag)

Exercises: Coherence and Transitions

1. In the following paragraphs indicate the use of pronouns, repetition and relation words for *inter-sentence coherence by* single underlining.
2. Circle *transitions* between paragraphs in those instances where the first part of the succeeding paragraph is given. Indicate the type of transition used: relation word or phrase, pronoun, incorporation, restatement, combination.

1. The roles of male and female are increasingly merged in the American household. The American man is found as never before as a substitute for wife and mother—changing diapers, washing dishes, cooking meals, and performing a whole series of what once were considered female duties. The American woman meanwhile takes over more and more of the big decisions, controlling them indirectly when she cannot do so directly. Outside the home, one sees a similar blurring of function. While men design dresses and brew up cosmetics, women become doctors, lawyers, bank cashiers, and executives. "Women now fill many 'masculine' roles," writes the psychologist Dr. Bruno Bettelheim, "and expect their husbands to assume many of the tasks once reserved for their own sex." They seem an expanding, aggressive force, seizing new domains like a conquering army, while men, more and more on the defensive, are hardly able to hold their own and gratefully accept assignments from their new rulers. A recent book bears the stark and melancholy title *The Decline of the American Male.*

Some of this evidence, it should be quickly said, has been pushed too far.   (Arthur Schlesinger, Jr.)

2. Each wad has its discipline. The fish prepare to mate. Each male capelin seeks a female, darting from one fish to another. When he finds one, he presses against her side. Another male, perhaps two males, press against her other side. The males urge the female on toward the beach. Some are struck down by diving seabirds but others take their places. Cod dash among them and smash their sexual formations; they re-form immediately. Cunner rise and rip at them; flounder dart beneath them toward the beach.

The first wad runs into beach wavelets, and a hundred nets hit the water together. . . .   (Franklin Russell)

3. No woman—no reasonably normal woman—wants to assert superiority over men, let alone dominate them. On the contrary, women want to be cherished and protected by men and dependent on men's superior strength. It is by this that they are made to feel most feminine.

But the modern man seems incapable of the traditional assertions of masculinity. He cannot give a woman the emotional support she desires because he has come to believe that it is he who needs the supporting, from a woman. Instead of exercising the authority which was once thought to define a mature man, he tries to impose himself by demands for deference and attention which are essentially childish. He often retreats into passivity, forcing women into attitudes alien to their sexual disposition—and then he resents them for being more active and positive than he.   (Diana Trilling)

4. The median age of girls when they marry is now about twenty, and the preoccupation with marriage becomes fairly persistent when this age is past. One can observe this frequently among graduate students. Today a young lady of twenty-one who is still single is apt to think of herself as an old maid. She prefers, however, to see herself as well settled with the man of her choice, or of her dreams, who loves and cherishes her and by whom she will eventually have about four children. Once she has met him, she often appears to care little about how much money they will have, what side of the tracks he was born on, his social or ethnic background, or his religion. Love is what counts, or at least what seems to be love. And she thinks she wants a man whom she can look up to, who has been exposed to at least an equivalent formal education and is perhaps a little better in his studies than she is. This makes her feel more secure.

One hears a great deal about security. It has become the golden calf of today. When one stops to analyze what is meant by it, one soon learns that it has little to do with jobs, with income, or with social status, but is a subjective feeling derived usually from a certain sense of approbation and depending more on self-approbation than on anything else.   (Carl Binger, M.D.)

5. It is possible that the bad reputation of marihuana and other forms of this drug reflects in part the bias of upper classes against and indulgence of the lower strata. Since hemp grows luxuriantly without cultivation in many parts of the world, it is available to many of its devotees at extremely low cost—in India, for example, at about one-twentieth the price of good quality whiskey in 1894, when the

English carried out an extensive inquiry into the subject. Denunciations of the weed come characteristically from persons of those classes which prefer whiskey, rum, gin, and other alcoholic beverages and who do not themselves use marihuana. Such persons, overlooking the well-known effects of alcohol, commonly deplore the effects of hemp upon the lower classes and often believe that it produces murder, rape, violence, and insanity.

Despite the prevalence of these beliefs among the drinkers of rum and whiskey and the upper classes generally, impartial investigations invariably have shown no such results.

(Alfred R. Lindesmith)

6. The idea that marriage must be coextensive with love or even affection nullifies it altogether. (That affection should coincide with marriage is, of course, desirable, though it does not always happen.) We would have to reword the marriage vow. Instead of saying, "till death do us part," we might say, "till we get bored with each other"; and, instead of "forsaking all others," "till someone better comes along." Clearly, if the couple intend to stay "married" only as long as they want to, they only pretend to be married: they are having an affair with legal trimmings. To marry is to vow fidelity regardless of any future feeling, to vow the most earnest attempt to avoid contrary feelings altogether, but, at any rate, not to give in to them.

Perhaps this sounds grim. But it needn't be if one marries for affection more than for love.　　　　(Ernest Van Den Haag)

7. The present American family system is cutting directly into this age-old style of preparing young men for leadership and responsibility. By the time they reach high school they are expected to have settled career objectives, to work hard to attain them, and to begin to spend enough time with girls so that an early marriage will be assured. They are expected to drive carefully, to abstain from pranks of all kinds, to study hard enough—but not too hard—to make the educational grade. They are expected to marry very young, to have children at once, and to support their wives and children while going to school. Enormous numbers of our future doctors and lawyers, engineers and statesmen, are holding down eight-hour-a-day jobs, trying to do at least passing work in school and college, and giving their wives a hand all night and all weekend in the care of two or three or four small children.

In this steady rush towards domestic responsibility, many valuable things have been sacrificed.　　　　(Margaret Mead)

8. When adults first become conscious of something new, they usually either attack or try to escape from it. This is called the "attack-escape" reaction. Attack includes such mild forms as ridicule, and escape includes merely putting out of mind. The attack on the first man to carry an umbrella in London was an exhibition of the same reaction as has so often been displayed toward startling new discoveries in science. These attacks are often accompanied by rationalizations—the attacker giving the "reasons" why he attacks or rejects the idea. Scepticism is often an automatic reaction to protect ourselves against a new idea. How often do we catch ourselves automatically resisting a new idea someone presents to us? As Walshe says, the itch to suffocate the infant idea burns in all of us.

(W. I. B. Beveridge)

9. He led me down a winding staircase into a narrow passage, deep underground, and so low that I had to stoop in places. It was stiflingly hot and very dark, with only dim, yellow bulbs several yards apart. There seemed to be miles of dark labyrinthine passages—actually, I suppose, a few hundred yards in all—that reminded one queerly of the lower decks of a liner; there were the same heat and cramped space and warm reek of food, and a humming, whirring noise (it came from the kitchen furnaces) just like the whir of engines. We passed doorways which let out sometimes a shouting of oaths, sometimes the red glare of a fire, once a shuddering draught from an ice chamber. As we went along, something struck me violently in the back. It was a hundred-pound block of ice, carried by a blue-aproned porter. After him came a boy with a great slab of veal on his shoulder, his cheek pressed into the damp, spongy flesh. They shoved me aside with a cry of "*Sauve-toi, idiot!*" and rushed on. On the wall, under one of the lights, someone had written in a very neat hand: "Sooner will you find a cloudless sky in winter, than a woman at the Hotel X, who has her maidenhead." It seemed a queer sort of place.   (George Orwell)

10. *Playboy* really feeds on the existence of a repressed fear of involvement with women, which for various reasons is still present in many otherwise adult Americans. So *Playboy*'s version of sexuality grows increasingly irrelevant as authentic sexual maturity is achieved.

The male identity crisis to which *Playboy* speaks has at its roots a deep-set fear of sex, a fear that is uncomfortably combined with fascination.   (Harvey Cox)

Review Exercise: Body Paragraphs

For the exercise at the end of Section One you practiced the three preliminaries to composition on two subjects. Later, you wrote an introductory paragraph for a theme on each of these subjects. Review your outlines, theses, and introductory paragraphs. Now develop each thesis in the appropriate number of body paragraphs, following the principles we have discussed. (Be sure to begin each paper with the introductory paragraph that you have already written.)

When this exercise is returned to you, you should retain it for further development.

3

Conclusion
Paragraphs

Your essay should convey an impression of *organic unity*. Such an impression is conveyed when the essay has a clear beginning, a well and progressively developed middle, and an end which follows naturally and logically. Avoid the expressions "in summary," "to summarize," "in conclusion," "in concluding," and "to conclude." They alert the reader to go to sleep.

SUMMARY

Summary tells the reader *where* he's been, but it doesn't tell him *why* you took him there or the *significance* of the sights he has seen. Hence, summary *alone* is inadequate as the conclusion of an argumentative essay because summary does not conclude. Furthermore, you should not summarize at length in a short essay because the reader can be expected to remember the three or four main points that you have made. If you present a detailed summary in such a situation, you will simply annoy him and insult his intelligence. The reassertion of your thesis (which we will look at in a moment) is usually sufficient summary in a standard length theme. More detailed summary prior to conclusion is only necessary in longer papers.

CONCLUSION

In your conclusion paragraph you should:

1. Reassert your thesis. The thesis is a conclusion which the body paragraphs justify. When you stated it at the end of your introduction paragraph, the reader said to himself, "Oh yeah? Prove it." When you reassert it at the beginning of your conclusion paragraph, the reader says to himself, "OK. But so what?" Answering this question is your job in your conclusion paragraph.

2. Further develop the relationship (established in your introduction paragraph) between subject and context. In developing this relation further, build your discussion around one or two key expressions in the introduction paragraph. This technique ties your ending to your beginning and creates an impression of unity and wholeness. It makes the reader believe that you had your conclusion in mind when you began your essay.

3. Make a conclusion about this relationship between subject and context. This conclusion may take numerous forms. It may take the form of a warning, of an admonition, of a lament, of a judgment, of a forecast, of a directive.

To illustrate:

Limited Subject: Parental Discipline of Children by Spanking

Introduction Paragraph: Most agree that a child must be subject to discipline. But about the proper administrator of discipline and the form it should take there is less unanimity. Some say it should be left to school authorities; others claim it is solely the responsibility of the family. To some discipline is a mild verbal reproof; to others it is a beating. Parental discipline of children by spanking, however, arouses little controversy. It lies in a neutral zone between a permissive and an authoritarian approach to discipline. But spanking as a means of disciplining children is not as innocent as it may appear. The reasons parents give for such discipline are partially discredited by unacknowledged motives. Similarly, though such discipline may bring about desired changes in the behavior of the child, it may produce undesirable emotional reactions.

Developing the Conclusion Paragraph

1. Reasserting your thesis

As we have seen, spanking is not quite as innocent a form of discipline as it appears. The unacknowledged motives of the parents belie their stated reasons for spanking. And, though such discipline may lead the child to reform and conform, the emotional reactions it tends to arouse are far from desirable.

☞ NOTE: Though the thesis is *reasserted* at the beginning of the conclusion paragraph, it is not mechanically *repeated*. Notice, too, the use of a key word, "innocent," from the introduction paragraph.

2. Developing further the relation between context and subject

Since even such a mild form of discipline as spanking springs, at least in part, from unworthy motives and creates undesirable emotional reactions in the child, the authoritarian position which advocates liberal use of the "rod" is particularly suspect.

☞ NOTE: The limited subject is "spanking," the larger context "discipline." The sentence above makes an assertion about those who advocate harsh discipline, an assertion that follows from what has been discovered about one form of discipline, spanking.

3. Making a conclusion about the relation of context and subject

---

If a parent wishes to use stronger methods of discipline than spanking, he should ask himself whether it is the child's welfare, or the release of his own pent-up aggressive needs, that he is trying to achieve.

☞ NOTE: The final sentence is a judgment about the relation of context and subject and a thinly veiled admonition.

The completed conclusion paragraph

As we have seen, spanking is not quite as innocent a form of discipline as it appears. The unacknowledged motives of the parents belie their stated reasons for spanking. And, though such discipline may lead the child to reform and conform, the emotional reactions it tends to arouse are far from desirable. Since even such a mild form of discipline as spanking springs, at least in part, from unworthy motives and creates undesirable emotional reactions in the child, the authoritarian position which advocates liberal use of the "rod" is particularly suspect. If a parent wishes to use stronger methods of discipline than spanking, he should ask himself whether it is the child's welfare, or the release of his own pent-up aggressive needs, that he is trying to achieve.

Limited Subject: Racial Intermarriage Between Negroes and Whites in America

Introduction Paragraph: Prejudice dies slowly. Anti-Semitism lingers on in Germany and flourishes in the Arab world. Britain acted to halt the influx of Asians. And Australia has not yet repealed her discriminatory immigration laws. In America prejudice manifests itself most blatantly in the attitudes of many whites toward the Negro.

Even those who claim to be free of prejudice towards the Negro often "draw the line" at interracial marriage. The racially intermarried couple will find it easier to combat the prejudice many will feel toward them if both are college graduates and if they have an income that puts them in the upper middle class.

Conclusion Paragraph

1. Reasserting your thesis

Since a college degree and a relatively high level of income command respect in American society, and since the racially intermarried couple who possess both violate the common stereotype, they are better able to combat prejudice.

☞ NOTE: Here the major reasons why a college degree and a substantial income help the racially intermarried couple combat prejudice are summarized in the first portion of the sentence. Notice the recasting of a key phrase, "combat the prejudice," from the introduction paragraph.

2. Developing further the relation between context and subject

---

Though prejudice dies slowly, it is harder to maintain when the stereotypes it produces are dramatically violated. The racially intermarried couple that is both highly educated and economically successful denies the prejudiced person his smug rationalizations.

☞ NOTE: Another key statement from the introduction paragraph, "prejudice dies slowly," is repeated. The relation between *prejudice* and a racially intermarried couple who are educated and successful is developed.

3. Making a conclusion about the relation of context and subject

---

But, most importantly of all, each couple that braves the condemnation of society through racial intermarriage, whatever their educational background or financial level, brings America a little closer to the day when intermarriage between black and white will no longer shock. Man is often outraged by the exception. The rule he seems always to accept.

☞ NOTE: The conclusion is in the form of a forecast, with reasons for its validity.

The completed conclusion paragraph

Since a college degree and a relatively high level of income command respect in American society, and since the racially intermarried couple who possess both violate the common stereotype, they are better able to combat prejudice. Though prejudice dies slowly, it is harder to maintain when the stereotypes it produces are dramatically violated. The racially intermarried couple that is both highly educated and economically successful denies the prejudiced person his smug rationalizations. But, most importantly of all, each couple that braves the condemnation of society through racial intermarriage, whatever their educational background or financial level, brings America a little closer to the day when intermarriage between black and white will no longer shock. Man is often outraged by the exception. The rule he seems always to accept.

Exercise: Conclusion Paragraphs

A. Return to the sentence outlines on pages 43–45 for which you have already written introduction paragraphs. Write a conclusion paragraph for each outline in which you successively:

1. Reassert your thesis.
2. Further develop the relationship between subject and context.
3. Make a conclusion about the relationship of subject and context.

Underline the key words or phrases taken from the relevant introduction paragraph.

B. For the exercise at the end of Section One you analyzed two subjects, constructed topic outlines of your analyses, and wrote appropriate thesis statements. For subsequent exercises, you wrote introduction and body paragraphs for these two essays. Complete these two essays by writing a conclusion paragraph for each, following the pattern discussed in this chapter.

Review: Essays for Analysis

Following are five freshman essays. Each essay adheres to the various principles for introduction paragraphs, body paragraphs, and conclusion paragraphs that have been discussed. Analyze each essay carefully.

1. Indicate the three parts of an introduction paragraph in each essay.
2. Label the topic sentence in each body paragraph.
3. Note the manner in which each topic sentence assertion is developed.
4. Indicate coherence devices by single underlining.
5. Circle transitions from paragraph to paragraph.
6. Indicate the three parts of a conclusion paragraph in each essay.

HIPPIE VOCABULARY

Timothy Leary, sometimes styled the father
of the hippie movement, has charged us all to "Tune in,
turn on, drop out." However, before we progress to
"turning on," much less to "dropping out," we
should know the nature of the world that Leary
would have us drop into. The vocabulary of the hippie
culture provides us with a clue to the nature of this
world. Though one group of words associated with
hippie life reveals a theme of simplicity and
communion, another group shows a world characterized
by irresponsibility and tinged with fear and madness.

Many of the words associated with hippie life
communicate a closeness to nature and a natural
simplicity. Such terms as "grass," "flower people,"
"flower children," and "incense," call to mind the aromas
of nature. Other terms, such as "maryjane" and
"beautiful people" are child-like expressions. "Love,"
"love-in" and "peace," other terms often used by
the hippies have soft, peaceful connotations. All of
these expressions create a picture of a tranquil, gentle,
simple society that wants only to live in harmony
with nature.

However, quite a different aspect of the hippie
world is revealed by a second group of terms
associated with the subculture. These expressions
reveal a world characterized by irresponsibility and
tinged with fear. "Speed," "high," "trip," and "turn-on"
connote a desire for kicks, for movement, a dissatisfaction with what "is" that contrasts markedly
with the gentleness of the terms of the first group.
And in such terms as "bad-trip," "bummer," "fit,"
"freak-out," and "crash," there is an element of
fear, and even a hint of insanity.

Though the image of their life that the hippies
would have the "straight" world accept is indeed

projected by the first group of words which we've examined, the second group at least partially discredits this image. The hippie world may be sweetness and light, but it is not all sweetness and light. There is a dark side to this world, as the second group of words reveals. A person contemplating the giant step from "tuning in" to "turning on" would do well to consider the possible price.

INDIVIDUALITY

Virtually all agree that a man must be free if he is to have self-respect and dignity. And inseparable from freedom is individuality. If a man lacks individuality, he can scarcely be said to be free. But the essence of individuality does not lie in being "different." It does not necessarily manifest itself in action or appearance. Rather, individuality is an attitude of mind.

Certainly individuality is not a quality that is determined by externals, by either actions or appearance. If it were, one could achieve "instant individuality" by moon-bathing from two to five every morning or by purchasing bizarre "one of a kind" articles of clothing. No, individuality is internal; it resides in attitudes and outlooks.

A man who passively adopts the values and attitudes of his culture is not an individual. Such a man resembles W. H. Auden's "unknown citizen"; he is a culturally conditioned automaton. Instead, a man is an individual when he holds no truths self-evident and no values so sacred that they are not open to question, examination, and discussion. Such a man is an individual because he exercises freedom of choice, because he actively determines for himself his values and his attitudes. Like the slave to Mencken's "bitch goddess," success, he may decide to leave a job that is emotionally satisfying for one less gratifying but more lucrative. However, the man who is an individual will not make the switch out of blind loyalty to the equation of success and level of income. He will make his decision after weighing the satisfactions he gets from his present job against those he believes a higher income will open for him. He might just as well change from a lucrative to a relatively poor-paying job. The yardstick is his, not society's.

A man who holds no truths to be self-evident is also an individual because he is able to determine for himself his reaction to those various institutions and forms of behavior which tend to elicit automatic "either-or" responses among the mass of men. A person who responds with a shout of approval to "marriage" and "steady work" and who responds with a cry of indignation to "Communist party" and "free love" cannot be styled an individual because he is bound by societal values and attitudes.

Individuality, then, is indeed an attitude of mind. A man who is an individual is necessarily a free man, because he demands and exercises the freedom to determine for himself those values and attitudes which he holds. Such a man, needless to say, is a boon in a democracy, a bane in a totalitarian state.

TWAIN'S ATTITUDE TOWARD THE SOCIALLY CONDITIONED CONSCIENCE IN *Huck Finn*

Mark Twain uses *Huckleberry Finn* as a format for airing some of his attitudes toward life and people in general. By using Huck as his instrument, Twain is able to communicate his views without putting his opinion as an author directly into the book. One of Twain's major themes, the nature of "morality," is shown to us through the inner conflict apparent in Huck—a conflict between his natural sense and his socially conditioned conscience.

In *Huckleberry Finn* Twain sets up a Southern society in which we find inverted values. Thus, when Huck's conscience (Twain speaks of conscience as a socially conditioned instrument) tells him to do what is "right" according to society, it is actually telling him to do what Twain regards as "wrong."

Twain's preference for natural sense is evident throughout the book, and comes into focus especially in Huck's relationship with Jim. Huck was brought up to regard a Negro as an inferior person, to feel that by virtue of his color alone, a white was better than his black neighbor. This idea was drilled into Huck by his social environment, so when Huck lied to Jim, it was very difficult for him to apologize. In Huck's words: "It was fifteen minutes before I could work myself up to go and humble myself to a nigger; but I done it, and I warn't ever sorry for it afterward neither." In this case, Huck's natural sense, which told him that Jim was a human being and should be treated as such, won out over his socially conditioned conscience.

Another dilemma that Huck must resolve is whether or not to turn in Jim to the authorities. Again, his conscience tells him that the "right" thing to do is to tell on Jim, but in his heart Huck knows better. However, Huck does come close to following his conscience, and in one scene we find him saying: "My conscience got to stirring me up hotter than ever, until at last I says to it, 'Let up on me—it ain't too late yet—I'll paddle ashore at the first light and tell.'" At the end of the scene, though, when it comes to the actual accomplishment of the deed, Huck decides to follow his natural sense, instead.

The climax and most ironic part of the book comes when Huck utters the words, "All right, then, I'll go to hell," after he decides not to let Miss Watson know where Jim is. Huck has finally let his natural conscience triumph over the socially conditioned one. The irony lies in the fact that Twain, as the author, feels that what Huck has done is right, whereas Huck (still under the influence of his social upbringing), feels that he will go to hell for the terrible wrong he has committed.

Thus, Twain has shown us through Huck what he believes to be true—that people should be guided by their natural sense of what is "right," not by what other people tell them is "right." Although this view of morality may seem hopelessly subjective, it implies a common core of humanity in all men. And it is not a view held by Twain alone. Ernest Hemingway, one of the greatest American writers of this century, adopts an identical position when he states that one has acted morally when he feels "good afterwards." The best ethics, both Twain and Hemingway feel, are empirical ethics.

CAPITAL PUNISHMENT: A SENSELESS,
OUTMODED PRACTICE

Society is presently going through a period of self-examination. Techniques used in the past to clear up medical, mental, and social problems are being questioned, and discarded or revised. One area under investigation is that of the treatment of criminals. They are being given rights that, heretofore, persons convicted of crime were denied, and the motives behind their actions are being considered far more than ever before. As this concern for the criminal increases, it becomes more and more obvious that a decision must be made: is capital punishment a fair and sensible practice or not? And soon the answer will be clear: capital punishment must be abolished.

Execution as a form of punishment—and we may infer from the term "capital punishment" itself that execution is meant, at least in part, as punishment—is not sensible. In the first place, if punishment is meant to make a person suffer, imprisonment would be more effective than execution. After all, death takes place in a matter of seconds, after which there is no feeling of pain and no sense of being punished. But the agony of imprisonment, of being cut off from society and from one's family and friends, of living a sexless, rigidly circumscribed existence, lasts much longer.

Capital punishment also fails as a means of protecting society. Since it is the convicted criminal—one who has already committed the crime—and not the potential criminal who is executed, society has already suffered. Neither does capital punishment protect society by acting as a deterrent to potential criminals. It has not been demonstrated that punishment, of whatever sort or severity, deters, since a person, when he commits a crime, does not expect to be caught.

A way of protecting both society and the criminal can easily be devised and, without extreme difficulty, be carried out. That way would include rehabilitation of the criminal and reduction of societal factors conducive to crime. To aid the criminal (and, ultimately, society), prisons might be converted into institutions similar to modern mental hospitals, with facilities and personnel conducive to helping the criminal. In such an institution the criminal could make restitution for his deeds—not as punishment but as one might pay a debt. To aid society (and, ultimately, therefore, the criminal), a more intense examination of the conditions which seem to produce crime and a more fervent attempt to erase these conditions should be undertaken. And aid, psychiatric, vocational, and economic, should be made even more available to the public.

Obviously, capital punishment is an outmoded

practice which fails to punish, fails to protect, and fails to deter. In an age of reassessment, capital punishment demands reassessing. Abolition of this outmoded vestige of the past would be one hopeful signal, at least, that man is able to act rationally and change outdated behavior to meet the demands of a changing world.

PRIVACY AND THE FRESHMAN

Many have noted and criticized the increasingly blatant "invasion of privacy" in America today. The typical college freshman does not suffer from this invasion, however, for his privacy has already been conquered. He lives in a world virtually devoid of opportunity for privacy. He has no privacy for meditation and reflection, no privacy for his personal life.

The facilities of colleges are set up in such a way that the freshman has no chance to be alone when he wishes to be alone, no place that he can call his own and infuse with his particular personality. Typically, the freshman lives in a college dormitory where he shares a room with one or more other students; he eats his meals at the dorm cafeteria among a crowd of fellow students; he studies in the library surrounded by others, attends classes surrounded by others, spends his leisure time at union or theater or game surrounded by others. Almost never is he alone.

This lack of privacy makes meditation and reflection difficult, for both require solitude and silence. Thus, the freshman has little opportunity, even if he has the inclination, to integrate the many "facts" he is learning or to reflect upon the significance of his newly acquired knowledge. Often, his "in class" experiences remain isolated from and irrelevant to his "out of class" life, for the atmosphere in which the relation of the two might be perceived is absent.

The freshman also lacks privacy in which to conduct his personal relationships. Unless he has a car or can borrow a friend's apartment, the freshman must date, love, and even quarrel in public. On Friday and Saturday nights, especially, couples returning from dates form long queues in the entrance halls of the women's dorms. Almost shoulder to shoulder with couples on either side, they passionately embrace, or whisper endearments, or, in undertones, fight. Instead of being able to conduct his private life in private, the freshman has no choice but to conduct it in public.

The freshman, in short, has no privacy to defend against invasion. Yet the very outcry that invasions of privacy such as wiretapping, electronic snooping devices, and accessible personal data files evoke is evidence that privacy and freedom, privacy and human dignity, are closely allied. Surely the freshman has as valid a claim to these democratic rights as the rest of the American population.

Section Three

POLISHING
COMPOSITION

The greatest barrier to careful polishing of composition is psychological. When you have written the last word of the last sentence of your conclusion paragraph the impulse to head for the nearest bed or bar is almost overpowering. Theodore Dreiser, the author of Sister Carrie, *refused to revise and edit his manuscripts. When he was through, by God, he was through. But for whatever Dreiser is now remembered and studied, it is not the lucidity of his style.*

Resist the impulse to pass over imprecise expression and awkward syntax in your writing. Polish.

Principles of Precise Expression

Most students will go along with their instructor's comments on reasoning errors and matters of paragraph development. After all, a false analogy or a causation fallacy is there for all to see, and for all to agree upon. Similarly, a paragraph either has a transition or it doesn't, a general assertion is either supported or it isn't. A meeting of minds is generally possible.

But in matters of syntax and diction, in matters of sentence structure and word choice, such a meeting of minds comes much less readily. Often a student reacts to such markings as "wordy," or "imprecise," or "word choice," or "awkward" with a vague, "He doesn't like the way I said this." The implication is that someone else might like the way it was said. And quite possibly someone else might.

Cleopatra's "infinite variety" pales before the variety of sentence patterns and words, and the ways in which the two can be effectively combined. Of course, flat rules are possible, as long as the terms in them are left unconcretized (and thus meaningless). "Precision is preferable to imprecision"; surely. "Clarity is preferable to obscurity"; who would disagree? "Gracefulness of expression is preferable to awkwardness"; by all means. No, we have no time for word games of this sort, for one man's delicate turn of phrase is another's precious pomposity.

The chapter that follows sets forth seven specific principles of precise expression. They are not rules; there are times when exaggeration is effective; there are times when the passive provides welcome variety. But as guidelines, as principles to be violated only for deliberate and consciously conceived effects, they are helpful. Perhaps their greatest value lies in their compelling you to become self-conscious about the words you use and the sentence structures you employ. For, as mentioned before, the cardinal rule of composition is "know *what* you are doing and *why* you are doing it." Learn these principles, follow them in the normal course of your writing, but feel free to ignore them *when you have reason.*

Principle 1: Use the Sound Test

Your ear is your best friend. Never *write* a sentence that you would feel foolish speaking. If you're writing an out-of-class theme, read aloud each sentence you write and see if it "sounds right." If you're writing in class, read each sentence silently and test it against your ear.

You should be especially careful to avoid *inflated diction, jargon,* and *wordiness.*

Inflated diction: Man, analytically viewed, connotes a relatively concrete image possessed of a fairly definite designation.
Jargon: The family man motivates his own life pattern and thus assumes total responsibility for his self-actualization.

☞ NOTE: Inflated diction and jargon have a way of suffocating thought. Both of the above statements are totally opaque. They communicate nothing.

Wordiness: There was no way Twain could hide the fact that inhumanity to man was present in human life when he wrote *Huck Finn.*

☞ NOTE: The idea in this statement is that "In *Huck Finn* Twain shows man's inhumanity to man." If you can make your point in nine words instead of twenty-three, do so.

Many sentences that fail the sound test do not exhibit inflated diction or jargon, nor is their failure to pass the test due to simple wordiness. Note, for example, these two statements:

Her father is drunk very often, therefore not always going to work or collecting his pay check causing much concern.

One rainy Saturday afternoon in the year 1956, as I was dancing on a limb of my favorite tree in all the yard to be an airplane or hang from, thereby becoming a superman, I leapt from it, breaking my arm.

By applying the sound test, you can *recognize* sentences of your own which, like these, demand revision. However, if you adhere to the various principles of precise expression that follow, you should find very few of your sentences failing the sound test. For to write well is also to write euphoniously.

Principle 2: Be Literal

Don't be one of those who must always complain, "But you *know* what I mean." *Say* what you mean. Remember the reader doesn't possess the omniscience of God. He can only go by what you *say*.

Nonliteral: One example *can be found* in the United States Post Office.

☞ NOTE: This statement can be taken to mean that the example is *hidden* somewhere in the United States Post Office.

Literal: One example *is* the United States Post Office.

Nonliteral: Alcoholism is a *habit* that has ruined the lives of many people.

☞ NOTE: Alcoholism is not a *habit*.

Literal: Alcoholism is a *disease* that has ruined the lives of many people.

Nonliteral: One childhood misery *would be* a nightmare about a big black crawling spider.

☞ NOTE: Do not use *would* when you can substitute *is*.

Literal: One childhood misery *is* a nightmare about a big black crawling spider.

Nonliteral: The draft is a *very necessary* part of modern society.

☞ NOTE: This is like the girl who's "almost a virgin." You can't have it both ways.

Literal: The draft is a *very* important part of modern society.

or

The draft is a *necessary* part of modern society.

Nonliteral: In the 1800s and early 1900s the old flour mill was used by the whole community. But today no one uses it. It just *sits* by the creek and *watches* the water flow by.

☞ NOTE: How sad.

Nonliteral: A stark naked man appeared at their window and started pounding fiercefully and making every conceivable sound. He would not depart with the girls and the tree house until after one continuous hour of pounding and peeping. The man was mentally deranged, so the damage he could have done (if the girls had not had such good lungs and muscles) was unlimited.

Notice the various absurdities in these three sentences:

1. "started pounding *fiercefully*"—a combination of *fearfully* and *fiercely*.
2. "making every conceivable sound"—*caw, click, ugh, grunt, shh, skk, rurr, plop, buzz*—it would take far more than an hour to make every conceivable sound.

3. "He would not depart with the girls and the tree house"—
   if the man is strong enough to depart carrying girls, tree
   house, and all, it is unlikely that the girl's strong lungs and
   muscles will be much help.
4. "one continuous hour of pounding and peeping"—apparently
   the man peeps and then pounds. Or does he pound and then
   peep? Perhaps, he peeps while he pounds. Most men, if they
   had to pound for an hour, would lose interest in peeping.
5. "the damage he could have done . . . was unlimited"—how
   many times have you read of people sustaining "unlimited
   damage"?

The conventions of written English are different from those
of spoken English. Although you should be able to speak
naturally and unaffectedly every sentence you write, you should
not write every sentence you can comfortably speak.

Speech tends to be less precise than writing should be. When
you speak, your audience can ask you to clarify, amplify, explain.
When you speak you employ a repertoire of aids to communication denied you when you write: gestures, intonation, emphasis,
inflection, facial expressions.

Composition is a one-shot affair. If your meaning is unclear,
the reader can't say, "What do you mean?" If your syntax is
awkward, the reader can't exclaim, "Run through that again!"
So, in composition, you must be a literalist.

Principle 3: Choose the Exact Word

A person who uses a screwdriver as a crowbar or a wrench
as a hammer rather than search for the correct tool for the job
is lazy at best and probably incompetent. Words are properly
instruments of precision. Many, like old tools, have become dull
and ineffective from overuse. Though they may lie conveniently
close at hand, they are not the best for the job. As you write and
as you revise, take time to search for the exact word which
conveys your exact meaning.

USE SPECIFIC NOUNS

The more specific your noun, the more precise your meaning. Always use the least general noun possible.

Vague: He hit the man with a *thing.*
Vague: He hit the man with an *object.*
Vague: I'm in a *predicament.*
Vague: I'm in a bad *situation.*
Vague: I got a lousy *deal* on the car I bought.

Use the process of analysis and classification, which we have discussed, to find the most specific noun:

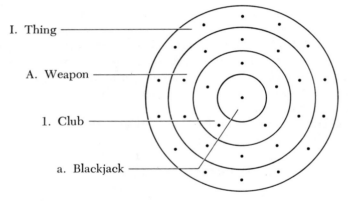

I. Thing

   A. Weapon

      1. Club

         a. Blackjack

You should always search for the classification that encompasses the least number of alternatives. Whenever you use a vague noun, you must concretize it to satisfy the reader's legitimate curiosity. If you state that "Crime in the streets is a *problem,*" the reader wants to know *why.* If you state that "He was beaten with a blunt *object,*" the reader wants to know *what.* If you state that "Yvonne is in a bad *situation,*" the reader wants to know *how.* Therefore, whenever possible, you should forget the vague label and concentrate instead on the concretization. The reader will supply the label himself and you will avoid unnecessary verbiage:

Wordy: Crime in the streets is a *problem.* Many urban dwellers are afraid to walk in the city at night.
Improved: Many urban dwellers are afraid to walk in the city at night.

Wordy: He was beaten with a blunt *object.* The weapon turned out to be a baseball bat.
Improved: He was beaten with a baseball bat.

Wordy: Yvonne is in a bad *situation.* She has a date with Pete, but she wants to go out with C. S.
Improved: Yvonne has a date with Pete, but she wants to go out with C. S.

AVOID BLAND MODIFIERS

Many adjectives and adverbs, like many nouns, cover a multitude of sins. They are so general and imprecise that they convey no exact meaning to the reader. *Interesting, kind, great, really,* and *truly* are examples of bland modifiers. Showing is always preferable to telling. Simply asserting that a fact is *interesting* will not convince your reader. *Make* the fact interesting, don't *tell* the reader that it is.

Unconvincing: An *interesting* fact is that blind people often feel that they are ugly.
Improved: Blind people often feel that they are ugly.

Some additional examples of bland modifiers are *exciting, beautiful, lovely, sweet, nice, pretty.* Making love is a *nice* feeling; so is scratching a mosquito bite. "She's a *pretty* girl and that's *pretty* important these days" tells the reader less than nothing.

When you use modifiers of this sort you are feeding your reader oatmeal without salt, sugar, or milk. They are words without flavor, without color. They communicate virtually nothing.

Modifiers of this sort are unconcretized abstractions to boot.

The reader can validly demand, "What do you mean by *exciting, beautiful, lovely, sweet?*" So if you feel you *must* use a modifier of the sort we've mentioned, *always* give the concretization too.

Oatmeal: The party was *really exciting*. The host did *lots* of *funny* things (bland modifiers italicized).
Palatable: The party was exciting. The host, in drunken exuberance, declared that there should be another door into the kitchen, so people could come in one and go out the other. He took an ax from the garage and created the second door. Later, just before he passed out, he tried to play George of the Jungle from the living-room light fixture. It pulled from the ceiling and blue flame shot from the bare wires. Then all the lights in the house went out.

MAKE YOUR VERBS WORK

Don't use colorless verbs. Like nouns and modifiers, verbs vary in their precision. A precise verb communicates a precise meaning.

One sign that you are using a vague, imprecise verb is the use of bland adverbs. Often a bland verb and a bland adverb can be replaced by a single vivid verb:

Poor: The man *walked quickly* into the room.
Improved: The man *strode* into the room.

Poor: I *looked carefully* at the bracelet.
Improved: I *scrutinized* the bracelet.

Principle 4: Do Not Convert Verbs into Nouns or Verbals

Many English verbs have noun counterparts. For example:

VERB	NOUN
determine	determination
confuse	confusion
evaluate	evaluation

Verbs can also be converted into nouns and adjectives by adding -*ing*:

VERB	VERBAL
run	running
see	seeing
call	calling

Do not use the noun or verbal form if you can express your meaning through the verb itself. Such usages cause wordiness, redundancy, and awkward, involuted, even incomprehensible, constructions.

VERB INTO NOUN

Awkward: The chaos came to an *end.*
Improved: The chaos *ended.*

Awkward: Each float received much *evaluation* on it.
Improved: Each float *was* extensively *evaluated.*

VERB INTO VERBAL

Awkward: My friend, *being* on the freshman football squad, made college football a frequently *discussed* topic.
Improved: Since my friend *was* on the freshman football squad, he and I frequently *discussed* football.

Awkward: Because of its *being* a complex subject, we will examine only one aspect of it.
Improved: Since the subject *is* complex, we will examine only one aspect of it.

Principle 5: Avoid Exaggeration

In speech, we commonly overstate:

My head feels as big as a *watermelon.*

That was a *fabulous* party.

All hell broke loose!

He's the *world's greatest liar.*

In argumentative writing, exaggeration should be avoided. An exaggerated statement is imprecise; you should be literal and exact. An exaggerated statement is ineffective; it annoys the reader because it's obviously a lie. For example, to validly assert that a particular person is "the world's greatest liar" would require personal acquaintance with the lying ability of every person on earth, an obvious impossibility.

USE STRONG MODIFIERS WITH CARE

Remember the boy who cried "Wolf!" Don't say that it was a *terrible* party if you mean "unpleasant" or "dull." Don't call a movie *great,* or an incident *tragic,* or a girl *beautiful* unless the adjectives are warranted. Show some discrimination, some sense of proportion. That you find a film exciting does not make it *great;* that six members of a family are killed in an auto accident is saddening, but it is certainly not *tragic;* that the girl you hope to date has a fresh complexion and a shapely figure does not mean she's *beautiful.* Strong adjectives like "great," "tragic," and "beautiful" are unconcretized abstractions. Give the concretization and forget the adjective.

Similarly, be sure the modifier you *use* says what you *mean.* If you call a matter *urgent,* you haven't supported your assertion if you only show it to be *pressing.* If you call a matter *crucial* you haven't supported your assertion if you only show it to be *significant.* *Several, a few, some, many, most* indicate quite different degrees. Choose your modifiers with care.

☞ NOTE: Learn to distinguish between ineffective overstatement and *hyperbole.* When you overstate you are making a *literal* assertion that you cannot support. Hyperbole, on the other hand, is a figure of speech. It is deliberate, conscious, and *extreme* exaggeration without the purpose of literal persuasion. It is used to heighten effect or to create comic effect. Like analogy, it can be used in addition to, but not as a substitute for, reasoned argument. For example:

Board of Education members are typically mindless automatons programed by a reactionary computer to run wild slapping down all new ideas and attempts at reform.

Principle 6: Shun the Passive Voice

The passive voice is a curse. Think of it as an insidious disease, a deadly menace, a peril, a thief bent on robbing your writing of freshness, directness, clarity. It stalks you. It slips in when your attention wanders. Beware!

Using the passive voice is like writing a "who-done-it" without ever telling the reader "who done it."

"A young coed was savagely attacked last night!" Who done it?

"This aspect of the subject was chosen." Who done it?

"An evasive response was made." Who done it?

We have an instinctive desire to know the perpetrator of an act. The passive voice frustrates this desire. The passive voice hides the actor deep in the sentence or leaves him out altogether.

You are using the passive voice whenever you write a form of the *to be* verb followed by a past participle:

is attacked
is *being attacked*
was attacked
was *being attacked*
has *been attacked*
had *been attacked*
may have *been attacked*
etc.

In English we normally progress from *subject* through *verb* to *object*. The passive voice inverts normal word order and puts the *object* of the verb before the verb.

Awkward: The pressures on college students should be attempted to be relieved.
Improved: Administrators and instructors should attempt to relieve the pressures on college students.

Awkward: The younger generation is considered to be disrespectful and immoral by many older people.
Improved: Many older people consider the younger generation disrespectful and immoral.

Using the passive is like turning off the freeway onto country by-roads. Unless you know exactly what you are doing and where you are going, you will soon be hopelessly lost in a maze of jumbled syntax. The result is often a sentence that must be entirely recast.

Awkward: Whenever a good talk is present, an abrupt joke *is entered* by him.
Improved: He frequently interrupts serious conversation with a joke.

Awkward: Bachelors *should be able to be distinguished* from married men by looking at their left hand.
Improved: A bachelor doesn't wear a wedding ring.

Awkward: Because of these two incidents, this girl's life *has been altered* to the extent that she can't ride a bus for fear of a closed-in space.
Improved: These two incidents caused the girl's claustrophobia.
or
Her fear of closed places is so severe that she is even unable to ride in a bus.

Awkward: Within the last two years it *has been brought* to my attention that a considerable amount of questioning *has been conversed* over the question, should eighteen-year-olds have the right to vote. *Improved:* I have only recently learned of the controversy over allowing eighteen-year-olds to vote.

☞ NOTE: Like errors in reasoning, errors in writing hang together. Observe the various types of errors in the awkward sentence above:

1. Unjustified use of the *passive* voice
2. Misuse of *amount* and *conversed* (diction errors)
3. Use of potential verbs as nouns: "attention," "questioning," "question"
4. Wordiness
5. Awkward sentence structure
6. Fails sound test

THE CASE AGAINST THE PASSIVE VOICE

1. The passive is *wordy.* When you change a passive construction to an active one, you save words.
2. The passive is *awkward.* It leads to involuted constructions that fail the sound test.
3. The passive is *impersonal.* It eliminates the individual, the "doer."
4. The passive is *dull.* Wordy, awkward, impersonal writing stupifies the reader.

ACCEPTABLE USE OF THE PASSIVE VOICE: EMPHASIS

Of the various acceptable uses of the passive voice, its use for *emphasis* is the most common. In English sentences, the subject position is typically the position of emphasis. Therefore, if you wish to emphasize the *recipient* of an action, you may use the passive.

Use the passive with *by* when the actor, though worthy of mention, is less important than the recipient of the action.

The student was bitten by a rabid squirrel.
The new novel was praised by the critics.

Use the passive without *by* when the actor is unknown, unimportant, or self-evident.

Actor unknown: The bank was robbed of $50,000 in cash.
The man was murdered.

Actor unimportant: The matter was brought up at the meeting.
The flight scheduled to leave at 5:10 P.M. has been canceled.

Actor self-evident: The senator was not re-elected.
John was busted last night.

Exercises: Precise Expression

A. Indicate the principles of precise expression that each of the following sentences most obviously violates. So far we have examined six principles:

1. Use the sound test.
2. Be literal.
3. Choose the exact word.
4. Do not convert verbs into nouns or verbals.
5. Avoid exaggeration.
6. Shun the passive voice.

B. Rewrite each sentence in conformity to the principles the original violates. For example:

My mother, being president of the local chapter of the DAR, is always busy.

Principle violated: Do not convert verbs into verbals.
Revision: My mother's duties as president of the local chapter of the DAR keep her busy.

1. One of the problems with joining campus organizations is finding the time for all the things you have to do.
2. Lots of interesting situations make the book fun to read.
3. It has been seen that these attitudes were often communicated to the child by his parents.
4. John began to fight like a mad dog and soon annihilated his opponent.
5. Because of being both a narrator and a chief character in the novel, Nelly is able to give a good account of the story.
6. I sat thinking of how much suffering my aunt and uncle were going through.
7. My stomach left its original place and got caught in my throat; my skin seemed to want to get up and run away, leaving me there; it was the day of my first speech to the class.
8. The two girls, being as they enjoyed each other's company so much, decided to travel together.
9. I knew there was someone in heaven, but I was never fully aware of the whole situation.
10. While one is away at school, the attraction for another person may be taken.
11. When having read this book, I invariably thought back to how the people on Noah's Ark had gotten along.
12. The protagonist did not care much for the important things in life.
13. Being a military funeral, rifles were shot and bugles were played.
14. When reaching the age of eighteen, a large number of these females were either divorced or widowed.
15. The reasons for many happenings in life will create disturbances in the mind.
16. The Catholic religion never ate meat on Fridays because it was immoral.
17. When he announced that he was quitting explosions started right and left.
18. As time passed man developed into a complex society.
19. An animal is characteristic to the fleshy part of man and its attributes as opposed to the spiritual.

20. An exception is taken in this paper to the standard interpretation of the poem.

Principle 7: The *Idea Subject* of a Statement Should Be the *Grammatical Subject* of the Statement, and the *Assertion* About the Idea Subject Should Be the *Verb*

Grammatically, a statement is a sentence which exhibits a subject and a predicate. Semantically, a statement is an assertion about something or someone.

Before you write the final version of any statement, you should have clearly in mind your *idea subject—the something or someone you wish to make an assertion about.* Then, as you write the sentence, you should make the *grammatical subject* correspond to the *idea subject* and the *verb* correspond to the *assertion* about the idea subject. Awkward sentence structure results when the grammatical subject of a statement does not correspond to the idea subject and when the verb does not embody the central assertion about the idea subject.

As you read over a statement you've written, or as you write a statement, mentally label the grammatical subject. Then ask yourself: "Is this grammatical subject the *idea subject* of my sentence?" If it isn't, you should revise the sentence to make idea subject and grammatical subject correspond. To illustrate:

s v
Awkward: It is here that Holden faces his biggest disappointment when he sees Phoebe.

Note: In this sentence, *it* is the grammatical subject. But the idea subject, the subject about which the student is writing, is *Holden, not it.* Therefore *Holden* should be made the grammatical subject of the sentence and the central assertion about him the verb.

s v
Revised: Holden faces his biggest disappointment when he sees Phoebe.

Awkward: Of all the ridiculous laws we have, the *one*^{s} I disagree with most *is*^{v} the age of drinking.

Note: In this sentence *one* is the grammatical subject. But the idea subject is *law*, not one. In other words, that which the student wishes to express his opinion about is a particular *law*, not a *one*.

Revised: Of all the ridiculous laws we have, the *law*^{s} which prohibits the purchase of alcoholic beverages by minors *is*^{v} the one I disagree with the most.

Awkward: Medea's *mind*^{s} *is pulled*^{v} into a state of vengeance and confusion when she finds that her husband is leaving her.

☞ NOTE: The student is writing about *Medea*. *Medea* should, then, be the subject.

Revised: *Medea*^{s} *becomes*^{v} vengeful and confused when she finds that her husband is leaving her.

On the other hand, notice how idea subject and grammatical subject, verb and assertion about idea subject, *do* correspond in this passage:

We shall not flag or fail. We shall fight in France, we shall fight on the seas and the oceans, we shall fight with growing confidence and growing strength in the air, we shall defend our island, whatever the cost may be, we shall fight on the beaches, we shall fight on the landing grounds, we shall fight in the hills; we shall never surrender.
(Winston Churchill)

☞ NOTE: The idea subject is *we*, the British people. The assertions about them are what they *shall* and *shall not* do. And Churchill makes the two correspond to grammatical subject and verb in *every* clause.

Careful adherence to Principle 7 not only eliminates many kinds of awkward constructions but also greatly reduces overuse of and overreliance on the *to be* verb. Adherence to the principle thus sharpens your writing by forcing you to use verbs that *work*.

Furthermore, careful adherence to Principle 7 enforces proper subordination. Since the principle requires you to make your idea subject and your assertion about it subject and verb of an independent clause, there is no danger of your burying the main idea in a dependent clause. And once you have established the grammatical dominance of your main idea, the lesser ideas will tend naturally to a properly subordinate position.

Finally, adherence to Principle 7 tends to eliminate verbosity because many wordy constructions depend on phrases or clauses that subordinate the idea subject. Making the idea subject the grammatical subject entails cutting out such unnecessary verbiage.

$\qquad\qquad\qquad\quad$ s $\qquad\quad$ v
Wordy: John's most personal *characteristic* *is* the fact that he's all messed up.

☞ NOTE: The student is making an assertion about *John*. *John* should therefore be the subject, the assertion about him the verb.

$\qquad\quad$ s $\;$ v
Improved: John *is* all messed up.

$\quad$ s $\;$ v
Wordy: *It seems* that as hemlines go up, girls' morals go down.

☞ NOTE: The student is making an assertion about girls' morals. The sentence should be recast to make *morals* the subject.

$\qquad\qquad\qquad\qquad\qquad\quad$ s $\qquad$ v
Improved: As hemlines go up, girls' *morals go down.*

            s   v
Wordy: One *item* that we must consider *is* the effect of mini-skirts on the sexual fantasies of male midgets.

☞ NOTE: The idea subject is *mini-skirts.* Here the writer has substituted verbiage for his assertion about mini-skirts, and the reader is left completely frustrated.

                s   v
Improved: Mini-skirts have enriched the sexual fantasies of male midgets. (lucky devils)

Exercise: Grammatical Subject versus Idea Subject

    In the sentences that follow, underline the *grammatical* subject and verb of each *independent* clause. Then state the *idea* subject of each sentence. Finally, rewrite each sentence, making the idea subject the grammatical subject, and the assertion about it the verb. To illustrate:

                       s   v
Awkward and wordy: Maybe *why* the hotel caught fire *is* because someone forgot a burning cigarette.

☞ NOTE: The idea subject is *hotel.* The key assertion is that it *caught fire.*

                s   v
Improved: The *hotel may have caught fire* because someone forgot a burning cigarette.

or

                    s   v
Maybe the *hotel caught fire* because someone forgot a burning cigarette.

1. The reason why I like blind dates is because you never know what the guy will be like.
2. One of the causes of marital conflict is when the couple have financial difficulties.

3. So it might be wise to think that a limitation of tenure is an effective safeguard against that type of problem.

4. Another reason that television has hurt comedy is that there are many similar programs that carry the same type of comedy.

5. It seems to me that everyone has his own idea of what liberty is.

6. It seems as though grandmother has some sort of "sixth sense."

7. I must confess that I had drunk the potent stuff before, but never in such quantities.

8. The picture one forms when looking at an inner-city ghetto is that of very poor living conditions.

9. There are many different forms of love which are included in life, four of these being: love of country, love of God, love of self, and love of one's fellow man.

10. The only way college is essential is for those who pursue a career which requires a higher education.

11. Throughout the work of W. B. Yeats there appear to be three major influences.

12. Due to the fact that I have never been personally involved in a conflict between blacks and whites, it seems that my feelings are not as strong as fear and hatred.

13. The main reason why I think universal military training is essential is because if our country should be attacked by an enemy we would have a standing army.

14. Dependent upon the ideas and ideals of the past is the amount of freedom we enjoy today.

15. It seems that a person who puts on a big front is trying to make an impression with his personality or possessions.

16. One reason that alcoholism is such a problem is that more automobile accidents are caused by drunken drivers than by any other group.

17. One reason for high-school pregnancies is when the girls lack sex education.

18. When listening to politicians discussing foreign aid, all I hear is them raving on and on about the United States acting as an "angel of mercy" to poor defenseless countries.

19. I think the play *Desire Under the Elms* proves that a tragedy can be successful even if the characters do not possess great social stature.

20. It seems as though man has an acute feeling of insecurity because he wanders through life thinking that someone is watching over him and protecting him from harm.

2
Two Diversions

You master sentence structure by learning to manipulate it, by playing with it until it loses its mystery. And, in the process, you gain a feeling for written language.

In both of the "diversions" that follow you will be required to write relatively long sentences. Longer sentences are the ones in which difficulties in modification and parallelism tend to arise. So in the process of manipulating structure you will gain a greater feeling for and competency at these matters too.

GENERATING SENTENCES

We have seen that when the idea-subject of a sentence does not correspond to the grammatical subject, the sentence is often awkward and wordy. Therefore, before you set about writing the final version of a sentence, you should first formulate in your mind the idea-subject of that sentence.

But, *you don't have to have the rest of the sentence in mind.*

To write an effective sentence, once you have the idea-subject firmly in mind simply:

1. Write toward your subject until you come to your subject.
2. Then write away from your subject until you come to your verb (or verb modifiers).

3. Then write away from your verb until you have finished the sentence.

In other words, you should have the idea-subject of your sentence in mind before you begin the sentence, and you should make it correspond to the grammatical subject. After writing this subject, you should keep it in mind until you come to your verb. Then, you should keep both subject and verb in mind until you have finished the sentence.

For example, take the subject "man":

1. Write toward your subject until you come to your subject:

$$s$$
This hot, rumpled and furious *man* / . . .

2. Write away from your subject until you come to your verb:

$$s$$
This hot, rumpled and furious *man* / who spit at me yesterday and who kicked my poor dog and who took my sister's candy from
$$v$$
her hot, sticky little hands *walks* / . . .

3. Write away from your verb until you have finished your sentence (but don't forget your subject):

$$s$$
This hot, rumpled and furious *man* / who spit at me yesterday and who kicked my poor dog and who took my sister's candy from
$$v$$
her hot, sticky little hands *walks* / indifferently down the street with the self-satisfied smirk of a person content with himself on his ugly, stupid face.

Let's take another example, using the subject "students":

1. Write toward your subject until you come to your subject:

$$s$$
Some women *students,* / . . .

2. Write away from your subject until you come to your verb:

Some women *students*, / having nothing better to do with their
time or their parents' money, *enroll* / . . .

3. Write away from your verb until you have finished your sentence:

Some women *students*, / having nothing better to do with their
time or their parents' money, *enroll* / in college in order to search
for a pot of gold, disguised as a man.

Of course, either your idea-subject or your verb, or both, may
be compound. But as long as you start out with a clearly conceived idea-subject, make it the grammatical subject, and work
from there, mentally labeling additional subjects as you go, and
then mentally labeling each verb as you come to it, you will have
no difficulty. The key to the whole business is beginning with your
idea-subject in mind, mentally labeling it "grammatical subject"
when you write it, and then mentally labeling all additional subjects and all verbs, and checking them against each other for
agreement, as you write the sentence.

The author of the following sentence may well have had
in mind only his subject, *Princeton Pond,* when he began his
description:

"Princeton Pond ripples prettily when there is a breeze, reflects
the shapes of the taller buildings around it and the airplanes that fly
above it, shimmers handsomely when the sun is at its zenith, and
darkens under passing clouds." (St. Clair McKelway)

Notice how the sentence develops:

"*Princeton Pond* / *ripples* prettily when there is a breeze . . ."

(At this point we can almost sense the author pausing, repeating *Prince-*
ton *Pond* / *ripples* to himself, and then continuing)

/ *"reflects* the shapes of the taller buildings around it and the airplanes that fly above it . . ."

(Again the pause, and a mental repetition of *Princeton Pond* / *ripples,*
reflects)

/ *"shimmers* handsomely when the sun is at its zenith . . ."

(Another pause, and a silent repetition of *Princeton Pond* / *ripples,*
reflects, shimmers)

/ "and *darkens* under passing clouds."

Exercise: Generating Sentences

Make each of the nouns listed below both idea subject and grammatical subject of a sentence at least thirty words in length.

1. Write toward your subject until you come to your subject.
2. Write away from your subject until you come to your verb (or verb modifiers).
3. Write away from your verb until you have finished your sentence.

To illustrate:

Unit: $\overset{\text{s}}{People}$ $\overset{\text{v}}{vent}$

Expansion: Many $\overset{\text{s}}{people}$ of the "over-thirty" generation / $\overset{\text{v}}{vent}$ . . .

Many $\overset{\text{s}}{people}$ of the "over-thirty" generation who are seething with repressed anger at their own empty, unhappy lives / $\overset{\text{v}}{vent}$ . . .

Many $\overset{\text{s}}{people}$ of the "over-thirty" generation who are seething with repressed anger at their own empty, unhappy lives / $\overset{\text{v}}{vent}$ that anger on those student protestors who threaten them . . .

Many $\overset{\text{s}}{people}$ of the "over-thirty" generation who are seething with repressed anger at their own empty, unhappy lives / $\overset{\text{v}}{vent}$ that anger on those student protestors who threaten them by daring to oppose the Establishment.

1. Idea
2. Car
3. College
4. Blacks
5. Hippies

6. Convict
7. Dorms
8. Morals
9. Love
10. President Nixon

PERIODIC AND LOOSE SENTENCES

Periodic Sentences

A *periodic sentence* is one in which the normal progression from subject to verb or, when a linking or transitive verb is used, from verb to complement, is deliberately interrupted. There are three ways to interrupt this normal progression:

1. Keep the subject in reserve.
2. Keep the verb in reserve.
3. Keep the complement in reserve.

The effect of such a delay is to throw extra emphasis on the element, be it subject, verb, or complement, which has been kept in reserve. This emphasis results from the sudden end to the suspense that has been created.

1. Keeping the subject in reserve:

Despite their protestations to the contrary, despite their insistence on the purity of their motives, despite their innumerable rationalizations, despite, in other words, all their attempts at self-justification, most *flipniks are* neurotic failures.

2. Keeping the verb in reserve:

The *establishment* of a volunteer army, though appealing to those who dislike the thought of military service, though desired by those who advocate a more professional military, though defended by those who feel it would reduce the military budget, *is* fraught with danger to democracy.

3. Keeping the complement in reserve:

$$\overset{s}{S}he\ \overset{v}{became},$$ after four racking years of study during which she learned—and promptly forgot—forty-seven different ways to clean a coffee pot, eighty-two ways to beat whipping cream, and one hundred eight ways to remove doggy stains from carpets, a genuine, bona fide, certified $\overset{c}{Home\ Economist!}$

If you really want to put your reader on edge, you can keep your subject in reserve, and then, after grudgingly giving it to him, keep your verb in reserve, as in this sentence that describes Ishmael's emotions at a climactic moment in *Moby-Dick:*

As the watch narrated to each other their unholy adventures, their tales of terror told in words of mirth; as their uncivilized laughter forked upwards out of them, like the flames from the furnace; as to and fro, in their front, the harpooners wildly gesticulated with their huge pronged forks and dippers; as the wind howled on, and the sea leaped, and the ship groaned and dived, and yet steadfastly shot her red hell further and further into the blackness of the sea and the night, and scornfully champed the white bone in her mouth, and viciously spat round her on all sides; then the rushing $\overset{s}{Pequod},$ freighted with savages and laden with fire, and burning a corpse, and plunging into that blackness of darkness, $\overset{v}{seemed}$ the material counterpart of her monomaniac commander's soul.

Obviously, a reader can't take too much of this sort of tension at a time, so you should save your grand efforts at periodicity for grand moments in your writing.

Loose Sentences

Most of your sentences will be of the "loose" variety, with just a hint of periodicity created by standard modification:

     s   v
A *man* who harbors attitudes of this sort *is* unlikely to feel at ease in the company of political liberals.

                                 s   v
Though understandably widespread, this *view* is no longer tenable.

A *loose* sentence, like the one I'm writing here, is one in which you just go along, adding phrases and clauses in a natural order without attempting to create suspense by holding certain elements in reserve.

The difference between a periodic sentence and a loose sentence is, perhaps, best understood in terms of the three steps of sentence construction that we discussed in the chapter, "Generating Sentences."

To write a *periodic* sentence, you spend considerable time writing *toward* your subject, or *away from* your subject, or both. This creates suspense by withholding from the reader the subject, or the verb, or both. In the sentence from *Moby-Dick,* Melville writes at length *toward* his subject, *Pequod,* and then writes at length *away* from it before he finally gives us his verb, *seemed.*

To write a *loose* sentence, providing your verb needs no complement, you go ahead and give your reader the subject and verb, and then write *away from* the verb. For example:

    s   v
The *group left* in an old Ford that bucked and backfired and rocked and pitched like a miscegenous union of wild bronco and storm tossed rowboat.

To write a loose sentence when you use a verb that requires a complement, you go ahead and give your reader the subject, verb, and complement, and then write *away from* the complement. For example:

 s   v   c
He reached the *ticket office* after waiting five hours in a downpour that started the moment he got in line and ended the moment he left.

$$\overset{s}{What} \; \overset{}{might} \; \overset{v}{have \; been} \; \overset{}{is} \; \overset{c}{an \; abstraction} \; remaining \; a \; perpetual \; possi-$$

What might have been is an abstraction remaining a perpetual possibility only in the realm of speculation.   (T. S. Eliot)

Exercises: Periodic and Loose Sentences

1. Construct five periodic sentences of at least thirty words each by writing at length *toward* the subject. (Keep the subject in reserve.)
2. Construct five periodic sentences of at least thirty words each by writing at length *away from* the subject. (Keep the verb in reserve.)
3. Write a "loose" version of each of these ten sentences by putting additions after the main clause.

Review Exercise: Polishing Composition

Revise the two essays which you have written as part of the continuing exercise begun at the end of Section One. Adhere to the seven "principles of precise expression" that we have discussed unless you have a reason for violating one of them. In this case, put a check ($\sqrt{}$) in the left margin to indicate that you are aware of what you are doing and are prepared to justify it. Be able to identify those of your sentences which are periodic, and those which are loose.

Section Four

SPRINGBOARDS
TO
COMPOSITION

ℰach of the five writing as-
signments in the following section
is preceded by a short story that
suggests certain topics for composi-
tion. Read the short story and the
brief note that follows. Then choose
that particular theme topic which
most interests you. In writing your
essay, try to follow all of the prin-
ciples of composition that have been
discussed.

Ken W. Purdy

Big Daddy Says Yes, Big Daddy Says No[*]

"Myself, I would not have believed all this," Tazio said. "Before, I would not have thought it possible."

"I, too, was a nonbeliever," Juan said. "Although Spanish and a Catholic, I was a nonbeliever."

"Is it a question of belief?" Peter said. "I think I'm dreaming. I don't believe it's *happening*."

"Certainly it is happening," Tazio said. "*I* am here. I speak. I know I speak, I hear myself speaking, it is happening to *me*."

"In my dream, it is happening to you," Peter said.

"You are dead," Juan said. "Dead men don't dream."

"I tell you something," Karl said. "We all dream, is not possible? Each dreams, and all the others are in his dream, yes?"

"Where are we?" This one was a little way off, by himself.

"You are . . . ?" Tazio said.

"Jerry."

"*I* don't know where we are," Karl said. "This place I have never before seen."

"Place?" Juan said. "How can you call it a *place*? There's nothing here, aside from ourselves."

"Hell with it," Jerry said. "Place or no place, I am goddamn well not dreaming. I'm dead, and I know I'm dead, because I can remember dying. I was pushing a helicopter from J.F.K. to

Newark and the thing threw a blade over the East River. I had twenty-four people and a baby in that mother. It went straight in, chung! Son of a bitch. It was my day off, too. I was just filling in for a guy. I said no when he asked me the first time, then I got greedy and said yes."

"I have heard," Tazio said, "that there is a thing called a Jesus wheel in a helicopter?"

"Jesus nut," Jerry said. "When the Jesus nut goes, everything goes."

"Did your Jesus nut go?"

"Dunno," Jerry said. "I saw a blade come off and I knew we were through."

"I think with Karl," Juan said. "You dream, and I dream in your dream."

"Don't give me that," Jerry said.

"I think it strange that we are all men here," Tazio said.

"No," someone said. "Not all."

"Where are you?" Peter said.

She stood up, a small woman, almost pretty. "Marie," she said. "And I am not dreaming, either. I remember dying. I was a photographer for *Agence Montafe*. I was in Vietnam, just outside a village in the Nouc valley. I was with some American Marines. They had called in an air strike. I got up, just a little way, barely my head off the ground, I thought, to make a quick shot. I was using a Hasselblad and I remember thinking I should have used the Nikon, to keep my head down, when I was hit. Boom. In the middle of my chest. I felt it clearly and I died immediately."

"I, while the young lady talked, have been counting," Karl said. "We are thirty-two people. Now, of the thirty-two people, is there anyone who died in bed?"

"I," said a man, tall, thin, black. "Michael. I was walking on North Halsted. It was raining. I decided I'd have me a beer until it stopped. There was a bar across, so I started over there. This brother was up on a scaffolding. He must have slipped. I heard somebody yell. I looked up; there he was, right on top of me, coming from five floors. They got me to the hospital, only just about. I dunno about him."

"I died in bed," someone said. "Larkin." He was fat and old. "My wife was after me to exercise, walk to work every day. One day I walked three blocks, then a bus came along, so I took it. I had just sat down, a woman next to me sneezed right in my face. I could never prove it, but nobody can tell me that didn't do it. I had pneumonia three days later."

"This is extraordinary," Peter said. "Karl, how did you die?"

Karl said, "I was on a walking trip in England. I was in a place called Eastbourne, on the Channel, a high cliff. We were going away—I was with a party of friends—when I decided I must have a last look. I could go right or left; I went right, no reason. I went too close to the edge. A piece of grass, turf you would say, broke under me, and I fell. You, Peter? How was it by you?"

"I don't know," Peter said. "I don't. . . ." The others had formed a semicircle around him. They were staring. The mass of them, as a unit, scimitar-shaped, began to move toward him. He woke. Ruth was sitting up in bed beside him, holding his hands. The white light of morning filled the room.

"*That* must have been a beauty," Ruth was saying. "You were screaming 'No! No! No!' at the top of your voice. What in hell was going on?"

"I was in this crowd, everybody was dead," Peter said. "They were each telling how it happened: this one because he said yes instead of no, this one because he went right instead of left, all little, insignificant things got them killed. . . . They asked me how *I* died, I said I didn't know, then they moved in on me, and that was when I woke up. Not too soon, either. Jesus, I've had some dreams, but——"

"Poor lamb!" Ruth said. "Stay put and I'll bring up your breakfast." She propped his pillows behind him, and hers. He picked up a Simenon he'd been reading the night before. He'd got through a couple of pages when the buzzer went.

"Bacon or sausage?" Ruth said.

"I don't know," he said. "Whichever you want."

"I'm dieting, idiot. You're not. Sausage or bacon?"

He tried, he tried hard, but he couldn't say it, not bacon, not sausage, not the one word or the other. ■

☞ NOTE: "Big Daddy" is Purdy's irreverent term for whoever or whatever determines whether we shall live or die. And whether Big Daddy says "yes" or "no" seems to be strictly a function of our random, unimportant "nonchoices." Each of the five characters who tells of the circumstances of his death died as a result of an apparently insignificant decision. At the end of the story Peter is paralyzed. For who knows? Big Daddy may be waiting to say "yes" or "no" depending on whether Peter chooses to eat sausage or bacon.

Theme Topics Suggested by the Story

1. Discuss the role that *chance* plays in a person's life. (Consider, for example, the role of chance in meeting your "one and only," the role of chance in automobile accidents, in contracting a disease, in choosing a school, in securing a job, and so forth.)

2. Discuss the contrasting views of man's position implied by the two designations of God as "Our Lord in Heaven" and "Big Daddy."

John Collier

The Chaser[*]

Alan Austen, as nervous as a kitten, went up certain dark and creaky stairs in the neighborhood of Pell Street, and peered about for a long time on the dim landing before he found the name he wanted written obscurely on one of the doors.

He pushed open this door, as he had been told to do, and found himself in a tiny room, which contained no furniture but a plain kitchen table, a rocking-chair, and an ordinary chair. On one of the dirty buff-colored walls were a couple of shelves, containing in all perhaps a dozen bottles and jars.

An old man sat in the rocking-chair, reading a newspaper. Alan, without a word, handed him the card he had been given. "Sit down, Mr. Austen," said the old man very politely. "I am glad to make your acquaintance."

"Is it true," asked Alan, "that you have a certain mixture that has—er—quite extraordinary effects?"

"My dear sir," replied the old man, "my stock in trade is not very large—I don't deal in laxatives and teething mixtures—but such as it is, it is varied. I think nothing I sell has effects which could be precisely described as ordinary."

"Well, the fact is—" began Alan.

"Here, for example," interrupted the old man, reaching for a bottle from the shelf. "Here is a liquid as colorless as water, almost tasteless, quite imperceptible in coffee, milk, wine, or any other beverage. It is also quite imperceptible to any known method of autopsy."

"Do you mean it is a poison?" cried Alan, very much horrified.

"Call it a glove-cleaner if you like," said the old man in-differently. "Maybe it will clean gloves. I have never tried. One might call it a life-cleaner. Lives need cleaning sometimes."

"I want nothing of that sort," said Alan.

"Probably it is just as well," said the old man. "Do you know the price of this? For one teaspoonful, which is sufficient, I ask five thousand dollars. Never less. Not a penny less."

"I hope all your mixtures are not as expensive," said Alan apprehensively.

"Oh dear, no," said the old man. "It would be no good charging that sort of price for a love potion, for example. Young people who need a love potion very seldom have five thousand dollars. Otherwise they would not need a love potion."

"I am glad to hear that," said Alan.

"I look at it like this," said the old man. "Please a customer with one article, and he will come back when he needs another. Even if it *is* more costly. He will save up for it, if necessary."

"So," said Alan, "you really do sell love potions?"

"If I did not sell love potions," said the old man, reaching for another bottle, "I should not have mentioned the other matter to you. It is only when one is in a position to oblige that one can afford to be so confidential."

"And these potions," said Alan. "They are not just—just—er—"

"Oh, no," said the old man. "Their effects are permanent, and extend far beyond casual impulse. But they include it. Bountifully, insistently. Everlastingly."

"Dear me!" said Alan, attempting a look of scientific de-tachment. "How very interesting!"

"But consider the spiritual side," said the old man.

"I do, indeed," said Alan.

"For indifference," said the old man, "they substitute de-votion. For scorn, adoration. Give one tiny measure of this to the young lady—its flavor is imperceptible in orange juice, soup, or cocktails—and however gay and giddy she is, she will change altogether. She will want nothing but solitude, and you."

"I can hardly believe it," said Alan. "She is so fond of parties."

"She will not like them any more," said the old man. "She will be afraid of the pretty girls you may meet."

"She will actually be jealous?" cried Alan in a rapture. "Of me?"

"Yes, she will want to be everything to you."

"She is, already. Only she doesn't care about it."

"She will, when she has taken this. She will care intensely. You will be her sole interest in life."

"Wonderful!" cried Alan.

"She will want to know all you do," said the old man. "All that has happened to you during the day. Every word of it. She will want to know what you are thinking about, why you smile suddenly, why you are looking sad."

"That is love!" cried Alan.

"Yes," said the old man. "How carefully she will look after you! She will never allow you to be tired, to sit in a draught, to neglect your food. If you are an hour late, she will be terrified. She will think you are killed, or that some siren has caught you."

"I can hardly imagine Diana like that!" cried Alan, overwhelmed with joy.

"You will not have to use your imagination," said the old man. "And, by the way, since there are always sirens, if by any chance you *should*, later on, slip a little, you need not worry. She will forgive you, in the end. She will be terribly hurt, of course, but she will forgive you—in the end."

"That will not happen," said Alan fervently.

"Of course not," said the old man. "But, if it did, you need not worry. She would never divorce you. Oh, no! And, of course, she herself will never give you the least, the very least, grounds for—uneasiness."

"And how much," said Alan, "is this wonderful mixture?"

"It is not as dear," said the old man, "as the glove-cleaner, or life-cleaner, as I sometimes call it. No. That is five thousand dollars, never a penny less. One has to be older than you are, to indulge in that sort of thing. One has to save up for it."

"But the love potion?" said Alan.

"Oh, that," said the old man, opening the drawer in the kitchen table, and taking out a tiny, rather dirty-looking phial. "That is just a dollar."

"I can't tell you how grateful I am," said Alan, watching him fill it.

"I like to oblige," said the old man. "Then customers come back, later in life, when they are rather better off, and want more expensive things. Here you are. You will find it very effective."

"Thank you again," said Alan. "Good-by."

"*Au revoir*," said the old man. ▬

☞ NOTE: Some psychologists have asserted that the "need to be loved" is man's greatest need. Certainly, "love" is one term that almost never evokes an unfavorable response. We all want it, we all need it, we feel it to be an unmitigated blessing.

Alan Austen, the young man in the story, loves, but his love is not returned. The apothecary sells him a love potion for the token price of one dollar, a potion that will make the girl he loves devoted and adoring; that will make her cling jealously to him, her sole interest in life; that will make her want to know his every thought and make her solicitous of his every need; that will make her totally faithful. The young man is overjoyed at the prospect.

But the apothecary knows Alan will return. He will return with 5,000 carefully hoarded dollars to purchase the potion that will kill Diana. For this sort of love, which youth so desires, is in the long term suffocating. It is not a blessing but a curse; it brings not happiness but rage. It robs the one so loved of freedom and joy. It becomes an unbearable blight.

Theme Topics Suggested by the Story

1. Many child-rearing manuals stress that, above all else, the parent should "love the child." Describe the characteristics of "smother love," the sort of love that harms the child.

2. Discuss: "Romantic love is not a valid basis for marriage."

3. Many young people feel disgusted at the sight of people in their late forties or fifties kissing and cuddling and cooing in public (or even in private). Write a theme in which you analyze the reasons for this common reaction.

4. Discuss: "Marriage cures the jealousy by curing the love."

Dashiell Hammett

Nightshade*

A sedan with no lights burning was standing beside the road just above Piney Falls bridge and as I drove past it a girl put her head out and said, "Please." Her voice was urgent but there was not enough excitement in it to make it either harsh or shrill.

I put on my brakes, then backed up. By that time a man had got out of the sedan. There was enough light to let me see he was young and fairly big. He moved a hand in the direction I had been going and said, "On your way, buddy."

The girl said again, "Will you drive me into town, please?" She seemed to be trying to open the sedan door. Her hat had been pushed forward over one eye.

I said, "Sure."

---

* From *Half-a-hundred,* ed. Charles Grayson, pp. 114–117. Reprinted from Colliers, 1934, by permission.

The man in the road took a step toward me, moved his hand as before, and growled, "Scram, you."

I got out of my car. The man in the road had started toward me when another man's voice came from the sedan, a harsh warning voice. "Go easy, Tony. It's Jack Bye." The sedan door swung open and the girl jumped out.

Tony said, "Oh!" and his feet shuffled uncertainly on the road; but when he saw the girl making for my car he cried indignantly at her, "Listen, you can't ride to town with——"

She was in my roadster by then. "Good night," she said.

He faced me, shook his head stubbornly, began, "I'll be damned if I'll let——"

I hit him. The knockdown was fair enough, because I hit him hard, but I think he could have got up again if he had wanted to. I gave him a little time, then asked the fellow in the sedan, "All right with you?" I still could not see him.

"He'll be all right," he replied quickly. "I'll take care of him all right."

"Thanks." I climbed into my car beside the girl. The rain I had been trying to get to town ahead of was beginning to fall. A coupé with a man and a woman in it passed us going toward town. We followed the coupé across the bridge.

The girl said, "This is awfully kind of you. I wasn't in any danger back there, but it was—nasty."

"They wouldn't be dangerous," I said, "but they would be—nasty."

"You know them?"

"No."

"But they knew you. Tony Forrest and Fred Barnes." When I did not say anything she added, "They were afraid of you."

"I'm a desperate character."

She laughed. "And pretty nice of you, too, tonight. I wouldn't've gone with either of them alone, but I thought with two of them . . ." She turned up the collar of her coat. "It's raining in on me."

I stopped the roadster again and hunted for the curtain that belonged on her side of the car. "So your name's Jack Bye," she said while I was snapping it on.

"And yours is Helen Warner."

"How'd you know?" she had straightened her hat.

"I've seen you around." I finished attaching the curtain and got back in.

"Did you know who I was when I called to you?" she asked when we were moving again.

"Yes."

"It was silly of me to go out with them like that."

"You're shivering."

"It's chilly."

I said I was sorry my flask was empty.

We had turned into the western end of Hellman Avenue. It was four minutes past ten by the clock in front of the jewelry store on the corner of Laurel Street. A policeman in a black rubber coat was leaning against the clock. I did not know enough about perfumes to know the name of hers.

She said, "I'm chilly. Can't we stop somewhere and get a drink?"

"Do you really want to?" My voice must have puzzled her; she turned her head quickly to peer at me in the dim light.

"I'd like to," she said, "unless you're in a hurry."

"No. We could go to Mack's. It's only three or four blocks from here, but—it's a nigger joint."

She laughed. "All I ask is that I don't get poisoned."

"You won't, but you're sure you want to go?"

"Certainly." She exaggerated her shivering. "I'm cold. It's early."

Toots Mack opened his door for us. I could tell by the politeness with which he bowed his round bald black head and said, "Good evening, sir; good evening, madam," that he wished we had gone someplace else, but I was not especially interested in how he felt about it. I said, "Hello, Toots; how are you this evening?" too cheerfully.

There were only a few customers in the place. We went to

the table in the corner farthest from the piano. Suddenly she was staring at me, her eyes, already very blue, becoming very round.

"I thought you could see in the car," I began.

"How'd you get that scar?" she asked, interrupting me. She sat down.

"That." I put a hand to my cheek. "Fight—couple of years ago. You ought to see the one on my chest."

"We'll have to go swimming sometime," she said gaily. "Please sit down and don't keep me waiting for my drink."

"Are you sure you——"

She began to chant, keeping time with her fingers on the table, "I want a drink, I want a drink, I want a drink." Her mouth was small with full lips and it curved up without growing wider when she smiled.

We ordered drinks. We talked too fast. We made jokes and laughed too readily at them. We asked questions—about the name of the perfume she used was one—and paid too much or no attention to the answers. And Toots looked glumly at us from behind the bar when he thought we were not looking at him. It was all pretty bad.

We had another drink and I said, "Well, let's slide along."

She was nice about seeming neither too anxious to go nor to stay. The ends of her pale blond hair curled up over the edge of her hat in back.

At the door I said, "Listen, there's a taxi stand around the corner. You won't mind if I don't take you home?"

She put a hand on my arm. "I do mind. Please——" The street was badly lighted. Her face was like a child's. She took her hand off my arm. "But if you'd rather . . ."

"I think I'd rather."

She said slowly, "I like you, Jack Bye, and I'm awfully grateful for——"

I said, "Aw, that's all right," and we shook hands and I went back into the speakeasy.

Toots was still behind the bar. He came up to where I stood.

"You oughtn't to do that to me," he said, shaking his head mournfully.

"I know. I'm sorry."

"You oughtn't to do it to yourself," he went on just as sadly. "This ain't Harlem, boy, and if old Judge Warner finds out his daughter's running around with you and coming in here he can make it plenty tough for both of us. I like you, boy, but you got to remember it don't make no difference how light your skin is or how many colleges you went to, you're still nigger."

I said, "Well, what do you suppose I want to be? A Chinaman?" ▬

☞ NOTE: The action of this story takes place in the Prohibition period (1920 –1933), yet the story still has the ring of truth about it. Does this suggest that "white racism" has really not declined significantly in the last 40 –50 years?

The girl doesn't realize that the narrator is a black until after they have entered the speakeasy. Then her ease vanishes. As the narrator says, their attempt to pretend that his color didn't matter "was all pretty bad."

It is precisely the sort of behavior that we see in the story, behavior that would be considered admirable and praiseworthy in a white, that has caused Jack Bye to be regarded as a "desperate character." For he doesn't "know his place."

Theme Topics Suggested by the Story

1. Discuss contemporary signs of white racism.
2. Discuss difficulties that face a white girl who dates a black.
3. Discuss the statement "black is beautiful" in terms of the symbolism of the color "black" in Western culture.
4. Discuss reasons for racial prejudice against blacks.

Alberto Moravia

A Middling Type[*]

I at once found myself at ease in my new home. It was a three-room flat, on the first floor of a modern block, in a quiet, respectable suburban quarter. My satisfaction was due, above all, to the conviction that the flat was not just any sort of a flat but was really mine, made in my own image and likeness, and consequently, it must be believed—since no one is exactly like anyone else—unique. I had spent a couple of months fitting it up, selecting every piece of furniture, every trifle, with extreme care. For a further two months, I had been contemplating these furnishings with the same untiring, rapt complacency with which I sometimes chanced to contemplate my face—it, too, being unique just because it was mine—in a looking glass.

Furthermore, as well as the flat, I also liked the house, which was neither too old nor too new, middle class, in a not too clearly defined style; and also the street, with its flowering oleanders and its shops on the ground floor, modern shops, with conspicuous signs and large windows: the tobacconist's, the hairdresser's, the perfumery, the delicatessen shop, the baker's, the stationer's. Right opposite my windows there was a flower shop. Through its window one could catch a glimpse of plants, of tall, slender vases full of flowers, of the jet of a small, decorative fountain. The florist was a pretty, dark girl, tall and shapely, with slow gestures and quiet movements, who did not look more than 25.

---

[*] Reprinted with the permission of Farrar, Straus & Giroux from *Command and I Will Obey You* by Alberto Moravia. Copyright © 1968 by Farrar, Straus & Giroux, Inc., originally appeared in *Playboy* magazine.

She was alone; she would arrive in the morning, pull up the roller blind, would move about for a little as she arranged the flowers and would then wait for customers. For the most part, she stayed inside the shop, sitting behind the counter, reading comic-strip papers. But often she would appear in the doorway and hang about, looking at the street, in which, however, there was nothing to look at and nothing ever happened.

I immediately noticed the pretty florist, and since it was the beginning of September and all my friends were still on holiday and I spent most of my time at home, I ended by devoting a great deal of my time to her.

I was working at my desk, for I had to draw up an industrial report; but every ten minutes, I would get up and go and look at the flower shop. Down there was the girl, behind the counter at the back of the shop, her dark head bent over the comic strips. Or again she might be in the doorway, leaning against the doorpost. I would look at her for a little and then go back to work.

Finally, I had an idea: In order to attract the girl's attention, I would reflect a ray of sunlight onto her by means of a mirror. It seemed to me that this was an original, a truly new, idea. So, using a little pocket mirror, I started directing the sunlight at the flower shop. First the ray of light moved across the glass of the window, then onto the shop sign and, finally—like a piece of thread that after many efforts penetrates through the eye of a needle—it went through the narrow doorway and settled, like a caressing hand, upon the girl's bowed head. It paused for a little on her hair, then slithered down her bare arm, then reached the page of the comic paper and remained there, moving slightly from time to time. The girl went on reading for a short time, then raised her head and looked toward the door. Almost frightened by my own boldness, I retreated hastily back into my room.

But after a moment, I again rose and went to the window. The girl was standing in the doorway, her eyes fixed on the street. I focused a ray of sunlight and directed it onto her, raising it gradually from her feet and up over her body as far as her breast. Then, with sudden decision, I planted the spot of light on her face. This time she raised her eyes, saw me and smiled at me. I smiled, too, and made a gesture, as much as to say: "Come up, come up to my flat and pay me a visit." The girl hesitated and then made a sign with her hand, as if to say: "Yes, but later on." Filled with joy at so rapid a success, I pointed to the watch on my wrist and asked her: "When?" Again by means of gestures, she replied: "At half past twelve." It was now 11 o'clock. I waved to the girl, went back into the room, made a pirouette, rubbing my hands together, then went over to a looking glass, gazed at myself and gave myself a kiss.

I found it difficult to work and was looking at my watch every five minutes. From time to time, I got up and went over to the window: The girl was there, behind the counter, her head bent over her comic strips. At one moment, I watched her as she was choosing some roses for a woman customer: I observed her fine figure as she leaned forward, her strong, bare arm as it slipped cautiously among the flowers, took a rose, withdrew, was again stretched forward. I reflected then that she was truly a most attractive girl and that there was something very disturbing about the way in which she had so easily and so mysteriously accepted my invitation.

When it was 25 minutes past 12, I went for the last time to the window sill: The girl, in a slow, calm, stately manner, was coming and going about the shop, rearranging flowers. Then she came out and composedly, with three movements, lowered the roller blind. I saw her cross the street and then disappear as she entered the main door.

Feeling excited, I took up my position in the entrance hall, behind the door. I noticed with satisfaction that a large plant of the Ficus family, which I had bought the day before, made a very fine effect in the corner between the two doors. Moreover, I had had the same thought a little earlier as I cast an eye round the sitting room, which was all in the modern, Swedish style. The flat was elegant and original, and I was sure it would make a good impression upon the girl.

At last I heard the lift as it stopped with a jerk at the landing, and then there was the sound of the lift doors being opened and closed and, finally, that of heels on the floor outside. A brief silence and then the ring of the bell. In order not to give the impression that I was waiting behind the door, I went on tiptoe into the sitting room and then came back, making as much noise as possible, and opened the door.

I was a little disappointed. From a distance, she had seemed to me beautiful; close to, one could see that she was merely young and pleasing. She was dark, with a face that was slightly plump in the lower part, a big mouth, an aquiline nose and eyes that were large and black and bovine in expression. As she came in, she said, in a good-natured voice with a regional accent: "I ought not to have come. I've come just to welcome you, you see. We're neighbors; it was just to make your acquaintance."

"You must excuse me," I said, "but if I hadn't had the idea of the mirror, I don't really know how I could have got to know you."

I noticed that she shrugged her shoulders slightly. "At first," she said, "I thought it was the engineer. Then I realized it was you."

"What engineer?"

"The engineer who lived here before you came. He began in that way, too, by dazzling me with a mirror. But perhaps it was he who suggested to you that you might play this trick on me to attract my attention?"

"No, really, I don't know him."

"Sorry, but very often, you know, things do happen like that."

She walked in front of me, familiar and talkative; but in the doorway, she stopped. "Why, everything here is just as it was. You took the flat furnished, did you?"

This time, I thought for a moment before answering. It seemed to me that something had suddenly come between me and the girl, something extraneous, embarrassing and humiliating that I couldn't yet define. In the end, I said: "No, the place was empty; it was I who furnished it."

"Well, what a coincidence: Here in the entrance hall there always used to be a plant like this one. A little smaller, perhaps. It's a Ficus, isn't it?"

"Yes. It's a Ficus."

"The engineer thought the world of it. He explained to me that it had to be watered twice a week."

I wondered at this point whether, since the girl had noticed the beauty of the plant, I myself should not also provide her with information of the same sort, and I hesitated: I could not entirely exclude the idea of doing so. The girl went on: "I say, how curious! The engineer had this same little picture."

Annoyed, I remarked: "Abstract art looks all the same, but it isn't, really."

We went on into the sitting room. The girl clapped her hands with delight. "Why, the sitting room is exactly the same! The same furniture. Perhaps the arrangement is just a little different."

This time, I said nothing. The girl went and sat down on the sofa, crossing her legs and unbuttoning her coat over her ample bosom: She seemed very pleased, and it was clear that she expected me to start making love to her. I made a move to put a record on the record player, but then changed my mind and went over, instead, to the sideboard, where I had placed a bottle of aperitif and some glasses ready on a tray. But, again, I thought better of it and went and sat down opposite the girl. Then I said: "May I ask you some questions?"

"Yes, of course."

"Did the engineer, the first time you came here, put a record on the record player?"

"Yes, I think he did."

"And did he then offer you something, a liqueur, an aperitif?"

"Yes, he offered me a vermouth."

"And then, immediately afterward, he sat down beside you, didn't he?"

"Yes, he sat down, but why . . . ?"

"Wait. And did he start making love to you?"

The girl was evidently somewhat disconcerted by this question. "But excuse me," she asked, "why d'you want to know these things?"

"Don't worry," I said, "I won't ask any indiscreet questions.

Only about details of what might be called a peripheral kind.
So he started making love to you, that's understood. And tell
me"—I reflected a moment—"did he, in order to get things going
and to be on confidential terms, did he not, at a certain moment,
suggest that he might read the lines in your hand?"

The girl started laughing. "Yes, that's exactly what he did.
But how did you come to guess it? You must be a bit of a
wizard!"

I should have liked to reply: "That's what I was going to
do myself," but I hadn't the courage. I looked at the girl and
it seemed to me now that she was enveloped in a dangerous,
impassable aura, like the aura that surrounds the poles that carry
high-tension cables. I was, in fact, unable either to do or to say
anything to her that had not already been done and said by
the engineer. And I seemed to see that the engineer, in turn,
was merely the first of an unending line of shaving mirrors in
which, as far as the eye could see, I should behold only myself.
At last I asked her: "Now tell me: Did the engineer resemble
me?"

"In what sense?"

"Physically."

She gazed at me for quite a long time and then said: "Well,
yes, in a way, yes. You're both of you middling types."

"Middling?"

"Well, yes, neither ugly nor good-looking, neither tall nor
short, neither young nor old: middling."

I said nothing, but I looked at her, saying to myself with
helpless, angry annoyance that the adventure, at this point, might
be said to have evaporated: The flower seller was now, for me,
taboo, and the only thing to do was to find a decent excuse to
send her away. The girl became conscious of my change of
mood and inquired in some alarm: "What's the matter with you?
Is there something wrong?"

With an effort, I asked her: "In your opinion, are there a
great many men like myself and the engineer?"

"Well, yes. You're part—how shall I say?—of the mass." I
squirmed, and all of a sudden, the girl exclaimed: "Now I under-

stand. You're offended because I told you you were a middling, ordinary type. Isn't that so?"

"Not so much offended," I replied. "Let's say—paralyzed."

"Paralyzed; why?"

"It's like this: It seems to me that I do what everyone does, and so I prefer to do nothing."

The girl sought to console me. "But you shouldn't feel paralyzed with me. Besides, I swear to you that I prefer men like you, who are not too original, who don't stand out from the crowd and about whom one knows in advance what they'll do and say."

"Well, I have work to do," I announced, rising to my feet. "Forgive me, but I have an urgent job that has to be finished in a hurry."

We went through into the hall. The girl did not appear too pained; she was smiling. "Don't be so angry," she said. "Otherwise, you'll really be behaving like the engineer."

"What did the engineer do?"

"When I told him, one day, that he was a man just like so many other men, ordinary, in fact, he got into a rage, just like you, and turned me out." ■

☞ NOTE: Every person, no matter how common or dull he may appear to others, is secretly convinced of his own uniqueness. In his heart of hearts, everyone feels "I'm different; I'm special." It is this universal vanity that Moravia is exposing and mocking. Tell someone that he's the most hateful, cruel, and calloused person in the world, and he will privately preen himself—"I'm different." But tell him what is most probably the truth—that he's just average, one of the mass, a "middling type," and watch out!

The narrator cannot bear the thought that he is just like the departed engineer—in his tastes, in the way he seduces a girl, in his appearance. His vanity is insulted. So he determines to show that he is indeed "different" by turning the girl out. But even in this action he is conforming—for the engineer reacted in exactly the same way when the girl, one day, told *him* that he was "just like so many other men, ordinary, in fact."

Theme Topics Suggested by the Story

1. Discuss: "The way to a man's (or woman's) heart is through his vanity."
2. Discuss the ways in which love can be seen as a "mutual admiration society."
3. Teen-agers often dread more than almost anything else being labeled "different." Yet all people, Moravia suggests, feel that they are "different" and derive great satisfaction from this conviction. Contrast those ways man *does not* want to be thought "different" with those ways he *does* want to be thought "different."
4. Discuss: "The strongest love is self-love."

Brendan Gill

Truth and
Consequences[*]

She had straight blond hair and a red mouth, and she was lame. Every day she played golf and went swimming in the center of a crowd of boys. Charles, sitting with his mother on the hotel porch, watched her and nodded while his mother repeated, "Isn't it extraordinary, a girl like that? I wonder what in the world they see in her." Charles took to walking past the pool during the morning as the girl and boys lay there side by side, laughing. He listened carefully to her voice. It was low, unhurried, forceful. So, he thought, was her language. Every other word seemed to him to be "damn," "hell," and worse. She spoke of God, to whom Charles was preparing to dedicate his life, as if He were a friend in the next block. "I swear to God," the girl said. "I must have told you this one, for God's sake." Charles walked out of range of the jokes that followed. He was eighteen and he was spending this last vacation with his mother before entering a seminary. In eight more summers he would be a priest. The girl's language sent sharp lightnings through him. He had never seen or heard anyone like her before in his life.

One night after dinner, while his mother was upstairs swallowing a pill, the girl sat down beside him on the hotel porch. Her lips were smiling, her eyes the color of her blue, open blouse. "We ought to know each other," she said. "You ought to join the rest of us at the pool."

"I'm with Mother."

The girl covered his hand with hers. "Well, for God's sake, you're old enough to swim by yourself, aren't you?"

Charles felt that he ought to explain before it was too late, before she had said something he could never forget. "I'm going to be a priest," he said.

The girl kept smiling. "A priest? With a turn-around collar and everything?"

He nodded.

"So you can't come swimming with the gang?"

"That hasn't anything to do with it. I just thought I ought to tell you. I always do tell people."

"You can still come dancing with us if you want to?"

"Certainly."

"Could you take me to a movie if you wanted to?"

"Yes."

"I never met a boy who was going to be a priest. Could you take me out for a ride tonight if you wanted to?"

He said in relief, "We didn't bring our car."

"Oh, hell, I mean in my car. I mean just for example. I didn't say I'd go with you." She stared at him slowly from head to foot. "It would be funny, with a boy who was going to be a priest."

Fortunately, Charles thought, his mother would be coming downstairs at any moment now. She would make short shrift of the girl. "You oughtn't to keep swearing like that," he said.

He expected her to laugh, but she didn't. She ran her hand up and down the bare brown leg that was shorter than the other. "Like what?" she said.

"Like 'for God's sake.' That's taking the name of the Lord in vain. That's one of the Ten Commandments."

"I'm an awful damn fool," the girl said. "I talk like that to keep people from thinking about my leg. But I didn't know you were going to be a priest."

Charles wanted to get rid of her, but he didn't know how. He stood up and said, "I don't think you ought to worry about things like that. I hadn't even noticed."

She stood up beside him. Her eyes shone in the mountain light. "Oh, damn you, please don't lie to me," she said. "Of course you've noticed. But does it bother you? Does it make you want to stay away from me?"

"No," he said. "Oh, no."

She slipped her hand under his arm. "Thanks for saying that so nice and hard. I haven't asked anybody that in a long time."

Without having willed it, stupidly, Charles found himself walking the length of the porch beside the girl. Her blond hair touched the shoulder of his coat. It was difficult to tell, looking down at her, that she was lame. He bent his head to smell her perfume. "Tell me what you do," he said.

"You mean, bang, just like that, what do I do?"

"Not that you have to tell me."

"But I do. It's just that there aren't any surprises in me. I'm not beautiful or tormented—or not much tormented. I don't do anything. I got out of Walker's and I had a party and now I guess I'll be on the loose like this for a couple of years. Finally somebody may ask me to marry him, and quick like a fish I will. I hope I'll have sense enough for that. And I'll be terribly glad when I've done it. I'll try to let him win most of the arguments we'll have. I'll try to be good about satisfying him, the way all those awful books say, and about having good kids for him, and all that."

Charles felt himself stumbling. She had told him everything about herself. She had told him the truth, which he hadn't wanted. They reached the end of the porch and stood facing the valley between the mountains. Two old men were playing croquet in the gathering darkness, the wooden mallets and balls knocking softly together, the white trousers moving like disembodied spirits across the lawn. Charles and the girl could hear, below them in the kitchen, the clatter of dishes being washed and stacked and the high, tired voices of the waitresses.

"Now talk about you," the girl said. "You think you want to be a priest?"

"Why—yes."

"It isn't just a vow your mother made while she was carrying you?"

Charles laughed, and was surprised at how easily he laughed. "Well," he said, "I guess Mother's always wanted me to be a priest, especially after Dad died. We went abroad then, Mother and I. We spent the summer in Rome. We had an audience with the Pope—the old one, a little man with thick glasses and a big ring. We got so we were going to Mass and even to Communion every day. When we came back to this country I started in at a Catholic school. I liked it. I graduated this year. I'm going down to the seminary in the fall. I guess I'll like that, too."

"But isn't there more to it than that?" the girl said. "I'm not a Catholic—I'm not anything—but don't you have to have some kind of a call, bells ringing, something like that?"

"You mean a vocation. Yes. Well, I guess I have a vocation all right."

"But what is it? How can you be sure?"

Charles gripped the railing of the porch. He had never been able to answer that question. He remembered kneeling beside his mother's bed, month after month, year after year. "Don't you feel it, darling?" his mother had whispered. "Don't you feel how wonderful it will be? Don't you feel how God wants you?" Charles had told himself finally that he was able to answer that question. The next day his mother, dabbing her eyes, had said, "Here's my boy, Father Duffy. I'm giving him to you." And Father Duffy had said, "Ah, you're an example to Irish mothers everywhere. Are you sure you want to come with us, boy?" "Yes, Father, I do," Charles had said, watching his mother. He had spoken an answer, written an answer, lived an answer, but he had never believed it. He had been waiting to believe it. Now he heard himself saying, for the first time, "No, I can't be sure."

The girl said, "Then you're not going to be a priest. You mustn't be. Why are you so damned afraid to face the truth?"

Charles saw his mother walking heavily along the porch. He studied her as if she were a stranger. What an enormous old woman she was, and how strong she was, and how she had driven him! He took the girl's hand. It was cool and unmoving. He felt the porch floor trembling under his mother's approach.

☞ NOTE: Charles, like the girl, is lame. His lameness is psychic—his inability to "stand up" against his mother's dominance. He lies to the girl about not noticing her lameness, as he lies to himself. But the girl demands truth, and practices truth, and her honesty has made her strong. Toward the end of the story, after Charles has admitted his private doubts about being called to the priesthood, the girl demands: "Why are you so damned afraid to face the truth?" The answer, of course, lies in the description of the mother's approach that immediately follows. She bears down on her son with heavy, implacable force. When the boy seizes the girl's hand, we can almost hear his silent cry for the strength to face the "consequences" of truth.

Theme Topics Suggested by the Story

1. Discuss the implications of the statement: "Above all else, to thine own self be true." (Be sure to support your assertions with specific situations and cases.)
2. Discuss the difficulties that a son or daughter faces in breaking free of parental dominance.
3. Discuss reasons for parents' reluctance to relinquish control of their children's lives.
4. Discuss reasons why people hide the truth from themselves. (For example the truth of ceasing to love another, the truth of dissatisfaction with school or job, the truth of unfulfilled sexual desires.)

Section Five

Clear
Thinking
for
Composition

In "Yvonne and the Dirty-Minded Instructor" and "Yvonne and the Tender Trap" we glanced at several of the most blatant blocks to logical thinking. In this section we will examine the matter of logical thinking in more detail and depth. We will analyze those forces—cultural, psychological, and linguistic —that interfere with clear thinking and observe how uninformed opinions and specific reasoning errors block logical thought. For expository writing is a vehicle for communicating thought. No matter how well-developed an essay is, no matter how cogent the expression, that adept development and that cogent expression are no more than empty technique if richness of thought is lacking.

In other words, effective composition is not an end in itself; it is a means to an end. Up to this point the emphasis has been more on "form" than on "content," more on "how" than on "what." But form and content are, ultimately, inseparable. High-quality writing does not exist in a vacuum. "How well you say" cannot be divorced from "what you have to say."

◢
Cultural
Conditioning

The chances are that you will agree with most, or even all, of the following statements:

1. Drinking in college dormitories should not be allowed because intoxicated students would disturb others.
2. Oral contraceptives should not be given to undergraduate girls at their request because to do so would lead to increased sexual activity.
3. We should not allow Communist teachers in our schools because they could influence the minds of their students.
4. If parents would remember the effects of a broken home on the children, they might think twice before getting a divorce.
5. A child should be encouraged to say his prayers because saying prayers will strengthen his religious faith.
6. Capitalism is desirable because it encourages free enterprise.

Apparently, each of these statements contains *two* assertions which we can call *judgment* and *reason*. For example:

Judgment: Capitalism is *desirable*.
Reason: Capitalism *encourages free enterprise*.

Judgment: A child *should be encouraged to say his prayers*.
Reason: Saying his prayers *will strengthen his religious faith*.

So, if you are writing a paragraph and one of these statements is your topic sentence, your job would appear to be to show

how and why capitalism encourages free enterprise or how and why saying prayers strengthens religious faith. And if you do show how and why your *reason* is true, the *judgment* would seem to follow. But the *judgment does not follow.*

IMPLIED ASSERTION

The judgment does not follow because each of these statements actually contains not two, but *three* assertions. This third assertion we shall call an *implied assertion* because it is an assertion *suggested* by the other two. The point to remember about this implied assertion is that it is *hidden.* It is not spelled out like the other two; it is merely suggested. Nevertheless, it is still there.

For example, take the statement that "Capitalism is desirable because it encourages free enterprise." The assertion that "Capitalism is desirable" (judgment) does not follow from the assertion that "Capitalism encourages free enterprise" (reason) unless it is true that "Free enterprise is desirable" (implied assertion).

"But," you may say, "*everybody* knows that free enterprise is desirable."

No!

Communists obviously don't believe that free enterprise is desirable. Socialists such as those in England who have supported nationalization of key industries obviously don't believe that free enterprise is desirable, Americans who tried to set up Utopian communities in which everybody shared equally obviously didn't believe that free enterprise was desirable.

What you mean when you say that "Everybody knows free enterprise is desirable" is that most Americans today believe that free enterprise is desirable.

But so what? Since when has the fact that a large number of people believe something to be desirable been, in itself, evidence of its desirability? After all, people used to believe that draining blood out of a sick man was desirable. Was it?

Furthermore, those very people who say that free enterprise is desirable don't really mean it. After all, a thief who picks your pocket is exercising free enterprise. So is the murderer who poisons his wife to collect the insurance. So is the doctor who refuses to treat a dying person until he is assured of payment. Is such free enterprise desirable?

Once you have written out the *implied assertion,* you can *concretize* it to test its accuracy. But the danger is that you will never even realize that a given statement contains a hidden assertion. The reason you may completely overlook the existence of an implied assertion can be traced to *cultural conditioning.*

CULTURALLY CONDITIONED ASSUMPTIONS

We are, to a large degree, creatures of our particular age. We grow up in a certain "climate of opinion." And this climate of opinion determines the form of many of our *attitudes* and *values.* Unfortunately, these attitudes and values tend to change rather slowly. There is a tendency for them to lag behind changes in social structure, economic realities, scientific discoveries, and so forth. Thus many people have values and attitudes that don't reflect the reality of the world they live in. The result, needless to say, is an inability to think rationally and objectively about many subjects.

Let's look at some examples.

1. *Individuality*—Most people in America "believe in" individuality. In other words, it is a value toward which they have a favorable attitude. Yet these same people are often quite critical of people who assert their individuality, who refuse to conform. They may

criticize "peaceniks," people who oppose the war in Vietnam; they may criticize hippies or "flower people"; they may criticize people who are aggressive in pursuit of their own ambitions. Furthermore, people who "believe in" individuality are often looking for a job with security; they often fear Communists, socialists, and atheists; they may well despise black power and resist the attempts of blacks to move into their neighborhood.

2. *The American Dream*—Many people in America today believe that if you work hard and save your money, you can become wealthy. They believe that it is possible, through hard work and education, for an average fellow to advance "from rags to riches." Of course, once upon a time we had a wide-open, laissez-faire economic system, taxes were low, population was light, the resources of the country were largely undeveloped. A belief in the American dream made some sense then, though not much. But today American society has changed. It is highly structured; the population, compared to the past, is dense; taxes are high; opportunities to "make a killing" are few; upward mobility is limited. Today the American dream, the belief that hard work and integrity will alone lead to the highest levels of wealth and power, is absurd, yet it is still widely believed in.

3. *War*—Americans, prior to the second half of the twentieth century (and with the possible exception of their own Revolutionary War), had had experience with only one kind of war—war in which armies faced armies along a "front." When the armies of one nation were no longer capable of resisting the advance of the armies of another nation, they were "defeated"—they surrendered and peace followed. There is no widespread recognition of the *essential difference* between this type of "front" war and modern guerrilla war. However, analysts who are aware of the difference have amassed much evidence that, given certain conditions, a guerrilla war can never be "won" in the sense that a front war can be won. The enemy can never be defeated, he will never surrender, peace will never be achieved.

The point of citing these three examples of culturally conditioned values and attitudes is simply this: Because you live in a particular country, in a particular part of the world, in a particular age; because you were raised in a particular class and educated in a particular educational system by teachers who were also in many ways the product of their culture, *you possess a large collection of attitudes and values whose accuracy, truth, or merit you have never questioned.*

These attitudes and values can be called *assumptions,* because you *assume* them to be accurate; you don't question them; you probably don't even see them as open to question.

However, these *assumptions* are really *assertions.* And, in composition, any assertion must be both *stated* and *supported by evidence.*

One of the things that a liberal education is all about is learning to question your assumptions. But you obviously can't question them until you train yourself to recognize them.

When you realize that you are making an assumption, write it out in the form of an assertion. Then test the accuracy of the assertion by *concretizing* it. Almost all culturally conditioned assumptions involve unconcretized abstractions. In other words, they tend to be quite general. Thus, it is especially important that you bring them down to concrete instances.

Let's take a couple of examples:

Judgment and Reason: The unregulated dispensing of oral contraceptives to unmarried coeds should be prohibited because it would lead to greater sexual activity.
Assumption (stated as assertion): Premarital sex is wrong.
Concretization: Recall the analysis of this assertion in "Yvonne and the Dirty-Minded Instructor."

Judgment and Reason: Drinking should not be allowed in college dormitories because intoxicated students would disturb others.
Assumption (stated as assertion): If a person drinks, he will become intoxicated.
Concretization: Do I become intoxicated every time I drink? Do all the people I know who are allowed to drink become intoxicated every time they drink? Does to allow drinking in dorms mean to allow drunkenness?

When you state and concretize your various assumptions in this way, you will undoubtedly retain some as accurate, reject some as inaccurate, and modify others to conform more closely with reality. In examining your assumptions, you will be converting them into rationally held opinions. Instead of your mind being a passive, uncritical receptacle for every half-baked notion floating around in the general culture, it will become an active, questioning intelligence.

The unexamined life is not worth living, Socrates has observed. It is equally true that the unquestioned assumption is not worth having.

Before we leave the subject of cultural conditioning we should take a brief look at two related matters which are also blocks to logical thinking: moral judgment and compartmentalization.

MORAL JUDGMENT

The tendency to make a hasty *moral judgment* about a subject is probably *the* most ingrained block to logical thinking and *the* greatest barrier to meaningful communication and understanding. A hasty emotion-laden moral judgment bears the same relation to a reasoned value that a prejudice bears to an informed opinion. Both prejudices and hasty moral judgments are essentially non-rational; both are signs of righteousness and intolerance; both substitute preconception for perception. The first and foremost aim of logical thinking is insight and understanding, not moral judgment.

You are making a moral judgment whenever you use words like "right," "wrong," "good," "bad," "sinful," "evil," "shameful" *and* whenever you adopt an attitude that implies judgmental words of this sort—an attitude of shock, disgust, hate, revulsion; an attitude of righteousness or righteous indignation. The fantastically successful catch phrase "Does she . . . or doesn't she?" gets part of its effectiveness from our desire to jump in with a decisive moral judgment if she "does."

We have a strong tendency in our society to label actions and ideas according to whether they lie in the Devil's camp or God's. Perhaps this tendency can be traced to our Puritan heritage—who knows?

What is important is to fight against it. We should fight this tendency to make hasty moral judgments because the tendency blocks logical thinking. Analysis attempts to understand what something *is,* and hasty moral judgment prevents such understanding.

Think for a moment of what would happen to medicine (and to your willingness to see a doctor) if doctors responded to their patients with *moral judgment* rather than attempting to *understand:*

☛ THE MORALISTIC MEDICS

SCENE: *Clinic in a middle-sized town. Various rooms accommodate specialists in different fields.* JOHN ACNE, *a young man of nineteen whose face is covered with pimples, is entering the dermatologist's office.*

JOHN ACNE (*hesitantly*): Uh . . . doctor . . .

DERMATOLOGIST (*interrupting him*): My God! Just look at you! What a mess! You look like a freak!

JOHN ACNE (*hiding his face behind his hands*): I'm sorry.

DERMATOLOGIST (*pulling his hands away*): Didn't I tell you to stop eating sweets? Didn't I?

JOHN ACNE (*in a weak voice*): Yes.

DERMATOLOGIST (*shaking his fist*): Well, why didn't you? What kind of slob are you anyway?

JOHN ACNE (*unconsciously raising his hand and fingering a particularly ripe pimple*): I tried . . .

DERMATOLOGIST: And just look at you, picking away. You make me sick!

We now move to the obstetrician's office.

MARY PREGNANT (*a young girl of seventeen in her third month of pregnancy. She wears no wedding ring.*): Hello, doctor. I want to get a checkup to see how my baby's doing.

OBSTETRICIAN (*looking at the third finger of Mary's left hand*): Where's your wedding band?

MARY PREGNANT (*blushing and covering her hand*): Well, you see, I'm . . . I'm not married.

OBSTETRICIAN (*jumping up from his desk and glaring down at Mary*): What! Not married? Pregnant, and not married?

MARY PREGNANT (*mildly*): Yes, doctor.

OBSTETRICIAN (*ignoring her comment*): And you expect me to examine you? You expect me to dirty my hands by touching a fallen woman? (*He raises his arm and points dramatically.*) Away, wanton creature! Don't darken my door again!

Obviously, neither one of these physicians is fit to practice medicine. Similarly, no person who indulges in hasty moral judgment is fit to practice logical thinking.

You should approach any subject in the same way that a competent physician approaches a patient. Indeed, a given subject of investigation is to your intelligence as a patient is to a doctor. The doctor's goal is to gain insight into and to understand the nature of his patient's physical state. Your goal is to gain insight into and to understand the various aspects of your subject. In both cases, hasty moral judgment makes achieving the goal of understanding and insight impossible, and, in both cases, hasty moral judgment is a sign of incompetence.

COMPARTMENTALIZATION

Compartmentalization is what allows us to *say* we believe one thing while *acting* as though we believed something else, without perceiving any contradiction. It is what allows us to make a general statement which contradicts a more specific statement, without perceiving any contradiction.

For example, a student wrote a theme on mercy killing in which he took the position that mercy killing should not be allowed because only God has the right to take a human life. A week or so later he wrote a theme on the war in Vietnam in which he said that we should send more troops and step up the bombing of the North. He saw no contradiction.

Another student wrote that censorship of pornography is necessary to prevent the minds of our nation's youth from becoming corrupted. Later, the following dialogue took place:

INSTRUCTOR: Do you consider high-school students part of the "nation's youth"?

STUDENT: Yes.

INSTRUCTOR: Did any of your friends in high school ever read "pornography" like *Fanny Hill, Candy, My Life and Loves, Justine, Story of O, The Pearl?*

STUDENT: Sure.

INSTRUCTOR: Have you read these books or others like them?

STUDENT: Yes.

INSTRUCTOR: How many of your high-school friends have become sex perverts, sex fiends, or morally corrupt degenerates?

STUDENT: What kind of friends do you think I have?

INSTRUCTOR: Do you consider your mind to have been morally corrupted by what you've read?

STUDENT: No, of course not.

Perhaps man could not live if he did not indulge in some degree of compartmentalization, but the smaller that degree, the better. There's something a bit ridiculous about the man who heads the local chapter of the Society for the Prevention of Cruelty to Animals and yet puts into practice at home the axiom "To spare the rod is to spoil the child."

There are two principal ways to reduce compartmentalization:

1. Trace out the basic principle that is implied by a given belief that you hold.

Take the man who heads the local chapter of the SPCA. Implicit in support for this organization is the basic principle that *inflicting unnecessary pain is wrong*. If inflicting unnecessary pain is wrong, it is at least as wrong to inflict excessive pain on children as it is to inflict such pain on animals. If this man is to avoid compartmentalization, he must either start sparing the rod or resign from the SPCA.

2. Concretize your belief to determine if there are exceptions to it on the level of specific instances.

Compartmentalization thrives on absolutes. When a man maintains the truth of numerous absolutes, he *has* to compartmentalize to prevent reality—concrete instances, everyday experiences—from showing the falseness of his beliefs. Such a man may tell his daughter, "Never marry a man that drinks," and yet admire and respect numerous people, all of whom drink. He may maintain that "A girl who becomes pregnant out of wedlock is nothing but a tramp," and yet have several middleclass friends whose daughters became pregnant before they married. He may maintain that "A man who won't look you straight in the eye can't be trusted," and yet trust implicitly several people who have never looked him straight in the eye. He may maintain that "Motherhood is sacred," and yet give evidence in court to show why a certain mother is unfit to retain custody of her children.

A man such as this has safely insulated his culturally conditioned values and attitudes from danger of being modified by reality. However, he scarcely strikes us as a person to admire for his clarity of thought.

Exercises: Cultural Conditioning

1. State the culturally conditioned moral judgment that each of the following subjects evokes. Then, from your own experience, show how these culturally conditioned attitudes are frequently compartmentalized. For example, the culturally conditioned moral judgment evoked by "honesty" is "good," "desirable." But what do many people do when they discover that they've received too much change after making a purchase?

a. Monogamy	f. Judging by appearances
b. Chastity	g. Romantic love
c. Adultery	h. Miscegenation
d. Bribery	i. Women's rights
e. Success	j. Cheating on exams

2. The truth of each of the statements printed below is considered self-evident by many, perhaps even most, Americans. Identify the implied assertion (the culturally conditioned assumption) inherent in each statement and explain how cultural conditioning is responsible for the widespread acceptance of these assumptions.

a. I believe we shall continue to build the strongest, finest, freest way of life the world will know.
b. It is time we placed the responsibility of the individual *with* the individual.
c. Man is part angel, part animal.
d. Many books today contain so many obscene words that you can't let your children read them.
e. He's no Christian; I've never seen him in church.

f. If at first you don't succeed, try, try again.
g. Don't marry until you find the right man.
h. A good wife is faithful to her husband.
i. Neither a lender nor a borrower be.
j. A bird in the hand is worth two in the bush.

2

Unconscious
Needs and Fears

Did you ever, as a young child, wake up in the middle of the night, in the dark, terrified and crying, just in time to save yourself from falling from a high ledge to rocks a hundred feet below? Did you ever lie rigid in your bed, awakened by some strange ominous sound, and dare not get up to turn on the light for fear the lurking beast would get you? Did you ever, when you went to bed at night, after turning off the light, jump into the bed from several feet away to escape the grasping paw of some sinister creature crouched beneath your bed, waiting to grab your leg when you approached? Did you ever, when you had gone out after dark, run for your life, trying in terror to reach the door of your home before the shadowy monster chasing you caught up and jumped you from behind, not daring to look back over your shoulder for fear of what you would see and managing to reach your home and slam the door behind you just as the unseen pursuing fiend, its panting breath on the back of your neck, was reaching forward to grab you?

Oh, you've outgrown these terrors, you say. You're not so irrational anymore. These strange fears have been put behind you. You are a rational person now.

Don't count on it!

Most adults are no more rational than the poor terror-ridden children whose secret fears they pretend to find amusing and absurd. They have simply learned ways of disguising these fears and emotions, both from others and, more significantly, from themselves. But these irrational, scary feelings are still there, deep in the unconscious. Most adults, it is true, don't reveal these feelings by screaming in the night and fleeing unseen monsters; but they reveal them in other ways, as the scene below from John O'Hara's *Appointment in Samarra* illustrates:

JULIAN: "Did you hear [mother] telling the old gent not to say masticate? You know she hasn't the remotest idea why she doesn't like the word."

CAROLINE: "I'll bet she has. Women aren't that dumb."

JULIAN: "I say she hasn't the remotest idea why she doesn't like the word. . . . Did you ever masticate?"

CAROLINE: "None of your business."

Man is not naturally a rational creature, as most men want so badly to believe. At best a small part of him is rational, like the one-ninth of an iceberg that projects above the surface. The rest, like the great bulk of the iceberg, is hidden, and a shift or break somewhere in that deep submerged part may dip the rational portion completely beneath the surface into the realm of the irrational.

William Butler Yeats, the great Irish poet, has expressed the essentially nonrational nature of man in this way: "Our thoughts and emotions are often but spray flung up from hidden tides that follow a moon no eye can see." Yeats is comparing the way the moon controls the tides of the ocean and the way our unconscious, a hidden moon deep in ourselves, controls the thoughts and emotions that we *think* we control ourselves in a rational manner.

So, if you are to learn to think rationally—something most adults never do learn to do—you must take away some of the power of that moon deep inside you to control the way you think. The way to do this is to understand something about the unconscious, the hidden, irrational part of your mind, and how it affects the way you think about many subjects.

Of course, acquiring this understanding about yourself is no guarantee that you will be able to think creatively and logically. But if you do not acquire it, you will never be able to do so. The situation here might be compared to walking. Having legs is no guarantee that you will be able to walk—perhaps polio or a broken spine makes your legs useless. But without legs at all, it is a sure thing that you will never be able to walk. The best you may be able to manage is a poor imitation of natural walking through the use of artificial limbs or devices. Similarly, most people never do learn to think in even a largely rational way. The best they can manage is a poor imitation of creative, uninhibited thinking, just as the person with artificial limbs can manage only an unsatisfactory imitation of the walking ability of a person with the full use of his legs. But the difference is that while the person with artificial legs knows that his walking ability is impaired, the average person whose thinking processes are similarly stunted denies with great indignation any suggestion that he lacks the ability to think logically and rationally about any subject. Hopefully, you do not want to join the ranks of these self-deceived people.

SOME DIFFICULT TRUTHS

Let us, then, take a brief look at some of the truths about yourself that you would discover if you were to spend a couple of years on an analyst's couch probing this hidden realm:

You have homosexual desires.

You hate your parents.

You have incestuous desires toward your sister or sisters (if you are male), toward your brother or brothers (if you are female).

You desire to be loved and to be made love to by your father (if you are a woman), by your mother (if you are a man).

You have sadistic impulses that cause you to take pleasure in inflicting pain on others.

You feel secretly ashamed of masturbating.

You would like to kill or mutilate anyone who dares insult you or criticize you.

You would like to kill, castrate, or otherwise destroy your sexual rivals.

You feel secretly inferior to others.

"But," you claim, and let's take a man's point of view here, "I have a girl friend" (and, in your mind, you think smugly of other conquests). "I love both my parents; I think my sister's an ugly, sexless pig and pity the guy she's trying to catch; my mother lost her sex appeal before I was old enough to know the difference; and I am considered a very kind fellow—I stopped pulling the wings off flies before any other kid in my block."

I believe you.

"Then you're crazy. I tell you I love my parents, I tell you I don't want to sleep with my sister, and you say you believe me. But you still say that I don't love them and that I do want to. What kind of logic is that?"

The logic of reality rather than the logic of Aristotle!

THE LOGIC OF REALITY

In the everyday world of external, physical reality it is true that two different objects cannot occupy the same space at the same time or be two different objects simultaneously. For example, if there is a solid block of wood 3 inches square sitting on your table, there cannot be a block of plastic 3 inches square sitting in the same place at the same time; and if the block of wood is there, it cannot be a block of plastic at the same time —they are *mutually exclusive*. But when this type of logic is applied to *concepts* such as democracy or marriage or to states of the mind such as love or desire, it is *absolutely false*.

The logic of mutual exclusiveness is valid *only* in dealing with physical, external *objects*. It is *not* valid when applied to products of the human mind, such as abstractions, feelings, wishes, impulses. Apparently mutually exclusive opposites, such as love-hate, kindness-cruelty, exist in the same space at the same time—in your mind and right now.

But, and this is what is so important, the average person applies a false logic to his thoughts and emotions, a logic applicable only to external, physical objects. He feels that if he hates his parents, he cannot love them; that if he has homosexual impulses, he is a homosexual and a dirty pervert, not a heterosexual who can love a person of the opposite sex.

REPRESSION AND DENIAL

Now, in our society, to be a homosexual, or to hate one's parents, or to want to sleep with one's sister is very threatening. It is scary. It makes a person feel "bad," "dirty," "evil." Therefore, at a very early age we *repress* these "evil" emotions in ourselves—that is, we shove them out of our conscious mind, out of our awareness. The result is that we honestly and sincerely feel that we *do not* have the wishes, longings, and impulses that we really do have. In other words, as a result of this repression we are able, with a clear conscience, to *deny* the existence of such horrible, threatening feelings in ourselves.

But these feelings *are* there, buried deep inside us, out of sight, and they manifest themselves in strange and devious ways, ways that *seriously* impair our ability to think logically, rationally, and objectively about many, many subjects.

Let's take a look at a fairly obvious example of this process before turning to some more complex ones. This example of the way a repressed feeling can cause illogical behavior is suggested by a book called *Games People Play* by Eric Berne. This game, which is not played for fun, culminates in "Slamming Doors":

The husband comes home from the office about six o'clock after a hard day at work and a fatiguing ride on the commuter train. He is tired. He knows he will have to be up by six o'clock the next morning. All he wants to do is to have a beer, eat dinner, watch TV for an hour, and go to sleep. After dinner, as he is relaxing on the couch in front of the TV set, his wife, who has done nothing all day except watch soap operas on television and do a bit of shopping, comes and sits close to him. After a few moments she unfastens a couple of buttons on his shirt and strokes his chest. Soon the husband begins to criticize her. Perhaps Sally's dress had a tear in it, perhaps the dog has made a small spot on the carpet. It doesn't matter. He finds something and harps on it until he has created a major argument. Then he jumps up, stalks to the guest bedroom, yells "Goodnight," and slams the door.

Why this argument? Apparently because of the tear in Sally's dress, the spot, or whatever. *Actually,* however, the husband knows that if he goes to bed with his wife, she will want him to make love to her, and he doesn't want to. It will fatigue him further and keep him up later. He will be tired in the morning. But in our culture a man is not a man unless he is ready to make love to any willing woman anytime, anyplace. So the husband is scared. If he goes to bed with his wife and she wants to make love, he will have to realize he isn't up to it, and this he would find threatening. So he manages to *deny* his lack of sexual desire by creating an argument that allows him to get out of making love with his wife without admitting to her *or to himself* that he has no desire.

Now, if he had been able to recognize that he felt no desire that evening and that feeling no desire when exhausted did not mean that he was not a "man," he would have been able to speak to his wife openly and avoid the whole pattern of irrational behavior.

Repression and denial of certain feelings and impulses can cause irrational thinking, as well as illogical behavior, and it is with such that we are primarily concerned here. Let's take, as our first illustration, one of the most sensitive of the subjects we have mentioned, homosexuality, and see how denial of the homosexual desires that we all have can block logical thinking.

First, due to the false logic of mutual exclusiveness which we have noted, most people feel that to admit to homosexual feelings is to be a "queer," which in this society is generally regarded as very bad. Therefore, these feelings are repressed and then denied. So far, so good. The average person feels, "I have no homosexual feelings." But let us not forget that he does.

PROJECTION AND REACTION FORMATION

When a person represses or denies an emotion or impulse, it can manifest itself indirectly in a number of ways, among which are "projection" and "reaction formation." You may already have come across these terms in a psychology course. *Projection* is ascribing to others feelings, impulses, or characteristics which you yourself possess but which you have repressed and deny that you possess. *Reaction formation* is excessive sensitivity to and reaction against feelings, impulses, or characteristics which you yourself have but which you have repressed and deny that you have.

CASE I: *Homosexual Colleague*

A friend and colleague of mine, who is now married, told me a few years ago of an incident that befell him at a party. He is a very outgoing, spontaneous, and uninhibited fellow and, unfortunately, some of his mannerisms are those that certain people consider "feminine." His voice is rather high, he sometimes holds his hand limply at the wrist, and his lips are full and fleshy. At this party, after an hour or two, he found himself talking to a stranger. Excited by the subject and forgetting himself, he laid his hands on the stranger's shoulders and arms a number of times. Suddenly, after he had again placed his hand on the other's arm to make a point, his new acquaintance yelled, "Get your damned hands off me!" causing people all over the room to look around, and then stalked indignantly away. For the rest of the evening he studiously avoided my friend and went about whispering to others and pointing at him.

We can understand the stranger's irrational and cruel behavior by tracing the irrational thinking that led to it. Having
repressed and denied his own homosexual impulses, this man
was highly sensitive to any behavior in others that might appear
evidence of homosexuality. This oversensitivity caused him to
misperceive reality and interpret simple individual mannerisms
as signs of homosexuality. He then *projected* his own homosexual impulses which the behavior of my friend aroused in
him onto my friend. This projection led him to the erroneous
conclusion that "This man talking to me is a homosexual."
Finally, through the workings of *reaction formation,* he *reacted*
with violent, cruel, and irrational disgust and horror to my
friend's touching him, an indication of his violent hatred of his
own *unperceived* (because repressed and denied) homosexual
longings.

What would have been the thoughts of a person who
acknowledged that he himself, while not a homosexual in any
sense, had homosexual impulses? First, he wouldn't be oversensitive to any mannerisms that might be construed as signs
of homosexuality. Therefore, he probably wouldn't have even
noticed my friend's touching except as evidence of his friendly,
outgoing nature. If, on the other hand, he did notice the full
lips, limp wrist, and touching, he would have made one of two
observations to himself, *neither of which would have led him
to irrational behavior or erroneous conclusions:*

1. Here is a friendly, outgoing fellow with some effeminate
   gestures.
2. Here is a friendly, outgoing fellow with some effeminate
   gestures that may, though it is not likely, indicate that he is a
   homosexual. I'll find out more about him and decide.

These are the rational, logical thoughts of a man in control of
that moon that controls most men.

THE DANGER SIGNALS OF IRRATIONAL THOUGHT

From this illustration we can draw two very important conclusions. There are certain *danger signals* of irrational thought that you can learn to recognize. Whenever you perceive one of these two reactions in yourself, BEWARE! It is certain that unconscious forces are at work.

1. An immediate, strong, emotional reaction against something (this "something" may be an individual person, a proposition, a concept, an abstraction, and so forth);
2. A feeling of "primary certitude" about something (that is, an immediate, strong, emotional feeling: "I know the truth about that!").

Either of these responses indicates that unconscious fears or unconscious needs are at work. In other words, you are reacting, at least in part, nonrationally.

Let's take some examples:

Danger Signal 1—an immediate, strong, emotional reaction against something.

SUBJECT	RESPONSE
Physical violence	Bad
Incest	Bad
Torture	Bad

Danger Signal 2—primary certitude about something.

SUBJECT	RESPONSE
Courage	Good
Mother	Good
Love	Good

From these two sets of examples we can perceive that people tend to react to many subjects in an "either-or" manner and with hasty moral judgment. Both of these reactions are blocks to logical thinking.

EITHER—OR THINKING

Either–or thinking is thinking which *ignores the complexity* of a subject. We are all familiar with the statement "The more I learn, the less I know." What this means, of course, is that the more a person learns, the less sure he is that he "knows the truth" about various matters. Or, put more precisely, he comes to realize that there is no "Truth," but rather many "truths" about most matters, depending on how one looks at them.

There are many reasons for the prevalence of either–or thinking. One reason is the desire all men have for certainty, and it is much easier to be certain about a matter if you ignore the complexities, the subtleties, the exceptions. Another reason is cultural conditioning. A third is the tendency to apply the logic of mutual exclusiveness to other than object relationships. And a fourth, not to be underestimated, is the essentially antithetical nature of our language, which encourages us to think in terms of "opposites": noisy-quiet, hard-soft, love-hate, good-bad, black-white.

Either–or thinking causes us to deny the complexity of ourselves and others, as well as causing us to ignore the complexity of subjects and issues:

If you loved me, you wouldn't say nasty things like that to me. (Nonsense.)

Boys who love their mommy don't get mad at them and make them unhappy, Johnny. (And after awhile, Johnny learns not to feel anger, consciously, toward his "mommy," but at the cost of knowing himself.)

It is the kind of thinking that leads a girl to wish to be loved for "herself alone" rather than for her "body," a wish that can never be granted, as Yeats points out to one such girl: *

> 'Never shall a young man
> Thrown into despair
> By those great honey-coloured
> Ramparts at your ear,
> Love you for yourself alone
> And not your yellow hair.'
>
> 'But I can get a hair-dye
> And set such colour there,
> Brown, or black, or carrot,
> That young men in despair
> May love me for myself alone
> And not my yellow hair.'
>
> 'I heard an old religious man
> But yesternight declare
> That he had found a text to prove
> That only God, my dear,
> Could love you for yourself alone
> And not your yellow hair.'

---

* "For Anne Gregory" by William Butler Yeats is reprinted from The Collected Poems of W. B. Yeats. Copyright 1933 by The Macmillan Company, renewed 1961 by Bertha Georgie Yeats. By permission of W. B. Yeats and The Macmillan Companies of New York, London, and Canada.

MORAL JUDGMENT

"But surely," you may claim, "despite your condemnation of impulsive moral judgment in the preceding chapter, no logical and rational defense of some actions can be made. Take torture, I *know* it is wrong, evil, bad. This is a case where both either–or thinking *and* moral judgment are justified."

You must train yourself, however, to realize that no such "thing" as "torture," in the abstract, an entity in itself, exists any more than "truth" exists as an entity in itself. You must ask yourself: "Torture *when?*" "Torture *where?*" "Torture *of whom?*" "Torture *how?*" "Torture *for what purpose?*"

You must always *concretize*. There is no such "thing" as torture, there is only the deliberate infliction of pain on a particular individual, at a particular time, in a particular place, by a particular person, by a particular means, for a particular purpose.

AMBIGUITY

Can you not conceive of a situation in which torture might be necessary, even, from a particular point of view, desirable? There are no absolutes. Trite as it may sound, life is complex and ambiguous. Discipline yourself to be always aware of this complexity and ambiguity. Learn to be content in uncertainty. This does not mean that you may have no values, no beliefs, no convictions. Rather, it means that your thoughts will reflect what *is,* rather than what you feel *should be.*

Perhaps the deliberate infliction of pain on another *should be* always wrong and bad. Perhaps love *should* always bring . happiness. But such is not what *is.*

Take for example, the case of a man who has planted a high-explosive bomb in some crowded office building in a large city. When it explodes, it will kill and mutilate scores of people. If every method short of torture has been tried and he has not confessed to the location of the bomb, is not the infliction of pain on one person justified to prevent its infliction on fifty or a hundred?

"So!" you may assert, "The end justifies the means! Therefore, police brutality is justified, since the end, law and order, is desirable. Destroying civilian centers in nuclear war is justified, since the end, defeat of the enemy, is desirable."

No! Absolutely not! No such generalization follows from our hypothetical example. In our "torture" illustration we asserted that *all* alternatives short of the infliction of pain had been tried. And the infliction of pain on one person was weighed against its *inevitable* infliction on scores of people. Furthermore, beware of the *false dilemma*. Have *all* alternatives *really* been tried? For example, the entire downtown district could be evacuated until the bomb either exploded or was located.

The point is that many subjects cannot validly be responded to in terms of simple right or wrong. They are too complex and ambiguous. You must *recognize and respect* this complexity, *concretize*, and *avoid hasty moral judgment*.

REACTION FORMATION AND FAILURE TO CONCRETIZE

Let us now return for a moment to the subject of homosexuality and, using an actual contemporary political event, show how the unconscious process of *reaction formation*, combined with *a failure to concretize*, led to a type of absurdity this world can do without:

CASE II: *Security Risk*

If you happen to be a homosexual, you should think twice before choosing government employment. The Army, the State Department, in fact, any government branch, doesn't want you. Why? Because you're a "security risk."

The idea is that a homosexual is especially vulnerable to blackmail. If someone who wants to get government secrets that this person has access to finds that he is a homosexual, he can force this person to reveal the secrets by threatening to expose the fact of his homosexuality if he doesn't cooperate. The homosexual is thus seen as more of a threat to government security than the "healthy hetero." So if you have access or potential access to sensitive information and the government discovers that you are homosexual, you will, as a matter of policy, be fired as a security risk. At first glance this policy seems a rational one, not a rationalization. But let's look at how it works in the specific instance:

At the height of the Johnson-Goldwater presidential campaign, a top aide and close friend of President Johnson went down to the men's room of the local YMCA and entered a toilet stall with another man. What he didn't know was that Big Brother was watching. The police had equipped an old storage cubicle with peepholes and spent their time peering down over the tops of the toilet stalls for any hanky-panky.

The aide was discovered and arrested, and it wasn't long before the story broke. Johnson's key advisor was exposed as a homosexual (though of a rather funny sort, since he had a wife and children). As a result of this "discovery" he was forced to resign his post and *his security clearance was revoked.*

Now, let's examine the absurdity of the "reasoning" that led to the destruction of this man's public and private life.

The "official" argument for the dismissal of known homosexuals is that they are subject to blackmail and are hence security risks. However, the main weapon in the hands of the hypothetical blackmailer is his threat to expose the homosexual as such. In other words, the homosexual is subject to blackmail *only* as long as he is not generally known to be homosexual. As soon as he is "exposed" as a homosexual, he is no longer subject to blackmail and hence no longer a potential security risk.

But, and here the absurdity reaches a climax, it is only *after* a homosexual is exposed as such, it is only *after,* in other words, he is *no longer* subject to blackmail and hence *no longer* a potential security risk that he is dismissed as being subject to blackmail and as being a security risk!

It is quite obvious, then, that the "official argument" justifying the dismissal of homosexuals is simply a smoke screen disguising the *real* reasons, which probably lie in the reaction-formation-based fear and loathing that many people have toward homosexuals.

Moral: There are two-legged as well as four-legged asses. The more the two-legged sort bray with passionate intensity, the more skeptical and dispassionate the reasoning man becomes.

In *The Wall Street Journal* is published a weekly "odd-lot index" which shows whether John Q. Public thinks the market is going to go up or down. Some professionals have guided their investment policies by this index, buying when the public is pessimistic and selling when it is optimistic.

A good rule of thumb is that the *popular* view on a subject should be presumed stupid until proved wise.

PRIMARY CERTITUDE

In Case I and Case II we have seen the working of reaction formation, which sets Danger Signal 1 flashing. Let's now turn, in our third illustration of the way in which unconscious needs and fears block logical thinking, to a subject which often starts Danger Signal 2 blinking by evoking a feeling of "primary certitude."

CASE III: *Get Tough!*

A major problem in America's large cities today is what is known as "crime in the streets"—sudden, savage, and apparently senseless beatings, rapes, and murders of average people going about their business. What is the solution?

CRACK DOWN ON CRIME!
GET TOUGH WITH CRIMINALS!
INCREASE THE PENALTIES FOR CRIME!
UNLEASH THE POLICE!

Danger Signal 2 is flashing. A strong, immediate, emotional conviction that you "know the truth" about this problem. A feeling of "primary certitude."

Why "get tough"? Why increase the penalties?

The standard argument is that getting tough will deter potential criminals from breaking the law. If a man knows that he will receive much "pain" for a little "pleasure," he will not commit criminal acts.

But this argument contains an all-important implied assertion —that man is a rational creature who always weighs potential pleasure against potential pain before he acts. As we have seen, such an assumption is unjustified and false.

The briefest investigation into the field of criminality will show that no causal relation has ever been established between the severity of physical punishment (such as imprisonment) and the rate or seriousness of criminal acts.

But most people never make this investigation, never try to understand the actual causes and cures of criminal behavior. They, instead of becoming suspicious of their opinion when Danger Signal 2 flashes, perceive this feeling of "primary certitude" as evidence that they know the truth, that any fool knows that the way to stamp out crime is to get tough with the criminals. And so they march proudly and blindly on, following the pull of that hidden moon deep in themselves as pathetically and as inevitably as the children of Hamelin Town followed the Pied Piper to the hole in the mountain; as proudly and blindly, we might add, as most of the citizens of Nazi Germany followed that master manipulator of unconscious needs, Adolph Hitler, to their own and their nation's doom.

Don't join the ranks of these benighted people. Learn to *recognize* and *respect* the two danger signals of irrational thought when they occur in your thinking. If you do learn to recognize and respect them, you will be able to stop short, analyze the motivations for your irrational reaction, force yourself to suspend moral judgment, avoid either-or thinking, and achieve objectivity. And having done so, you will be in a position to think logically and rationally about the subject at hand. You will be able to analyze it as an intelligent, thoughtful person rather than merely *reacting* to it with about as much intelligence as the rat in the experimental psychologist's cage displays when it runs mindlessly to the feed trough at the flashing of a light.

IRONY

It has been said that one of the surest tests of intelligence and sophistication is the ability to recognize irony. The perception of irony always necessitates suspension of moral judgment, intellectual detachment (objectivity), and recognition of the various points of view from which a subject may be regarded. Thus you should cultivate your ability to recognize irony as a means of cultivating your ability to think logically. Irony always involves incongruity or contrast. This contrast may take many forms: contrast between what appears to be and what is, contrast between what is intended and what is achieved, contrast between what is said and what is meant, contrast between what is and what should be.

All three cases which we have examined in this chapter reveal numerous ironies. In Case I there is irony of appearance-reality; my colleague "appeared to be" homosexual while in reality it was the man reacting against him that had strong homosexual impulses. In Case II there is irony of intention-achievement; governmental practices designed to weed out people subject to blackmail cause people to be fired only after they are no longer subject to blackmail. And in Case III there is irony of appearance-reality and of intention-achievement; the reasons people give for stricter punishment of criminals are often not the real reasons they desire stricter punishment, and punishment intended to reform the criminal frequently leads to his becoming hardened in his criminal attitudes.

Frequently the recognition of irony takes you right to the central fallacy in a particular argument:

Argument: Censorship is necessary to prevent moral corruption.
Scene: Censor watching a movie prior to its release to the public.

Censor: Boy! Was that scene morally corrupting! Run it through again, Jack, while I'm writing up the demand that it be deleted to protect the public.

Exercise: Unconscious Needs and Fears

The following subjects evoke strong emotional reactions from most of us. These reactions derive much of their strength from unconscious needs and fears. State the "typical" attitude toward each subject. Do you find evidence of moral judgment? Do you find evidence of either–or thinking? Do you find evidence of the false application of the logic of mutual exclusiveness? If a particular subject (such as "incest" or "mother") evokes an immediate moral judgment, try to analyze the unconscious needs and fears that are responsible for this powerful aversion or approval. After analyzing these needs and fears, do you perceive any irony in the common response?

1. Nature of masculinity
2. Nature of femininity
3. Being "different"
4. Masturbation
5. Incest
6. Spiders
7. Pornography
8. Physical violence
9. Sexual deviants
10. Mother

Unconcretized
Abstractions

Parenthood can only . . .	*Tyranny* always . . .
If there is to be *freedom* . . .	Those who are *unfaithful* to . . .
Liberty demands . . .	*Selfishness* cannot be . . .
The only *honorable* action . . .	The goal of *communism* . . .
Justice will be done . . .	It is *un-American* to . . .
The nature of *capitalism* . . .	Only *cowardice* would . . .

Whenever you find yourself beginning statements of this sort, STOP!

The italicized words are unconcretized *abstractions,* and using an abstraction without *concretizing* it always involves an implied assertion. The implied assertion is always the same. It runs something like this: "_____ has one and only one acceptable meaning, and that meaning is the one I am using when I make my statement."

We can illustrate the way in which the use of unconcretized abstractions blocks logical thought by constructing a hypothetical scene between two undergraduate students. One is a typical Midwestern male student of twenty. The other is an African, a Zulu tribesman in America on a scholarship. They are sitting over coffee in the Student Union and the conversation turns to marriage.

☞ THE AMERICAN AND THE ZULU

AMERICAN: I tell you, if a man is going to sign the contract, he might as well get a good-looking package.

ZULU: I agree. There's nothing worse than the thought of trading fifty cows for a woman with no looks.

AMERICAN: You're right. When I marry, I'm going to marry a beautiful woman.

ZULU: Yes, for fifty cows a man has a right to demand beauty in his wife.

(*Both students sit back reflectively, sipping their coffee. Each pictures his absent fiancée, who, in each case, reflects his ideal of feminine beauty.*

The American recalls his love's little feet and dainty ankles, her slender calves and slim hips, her tiny waist, small breasts, and tapered neck, her fine sinuous arms and delicate fine-boned fingers. Ah! Beauty!

The Zulu, too, thinks of the beautiful woman tearfully tending her father's cows back in Bechuanaland, waiting for his return. He recalls her large, solid feet, amply calloused, ideal for following the grazing herd over the rocky land; her thick, stake-like ankles, a solid foundation; her well-muscled calves and spreading hips, perfectly functional for childbirth; her thick waist, plenty of room there; her large drooping breasts, no danger of her ever being short of milk; her sturdy neck merging solidly with her head, a fine support for carrying heavy loads; her fleshy, big-boned arms ending in thick-fingered, meaty hands full of strength. Ah! Beauty!

Both men gaze at each other across the table with misty eyes.)

AMERICAN: Say, I've got a picture of my girl. Would you like to see it? She's beautiful, all right.

ZULU: In exchange, I will show you a photograph of my fiancée. She, too, is beautiful.

(*Each removes a picture from his wallet and places it on the table.*)

AMERICAN (*trying to keep from vomiting into his coffee cup*): Uh, she's *beautiful!*

ZULU (*hiding a shudder of horror at the emaciated monstrosity the American dares compare with his lovely maiden*): Uh, yours too.

AMERICAN (*rising hastily*): Excuse me, I forgot about an appointment I have.

ZULU (*weakly, feeling too sick to move yet*): Yes . . . well . . . good-by.

The point, needless to say, is that "beauty" is an abstraction, not an absolute. "Beauty" is not a word that points to certain fixed, concrete, unchanging qualities. It is not a word with a concrete denotation as is, for example, the word "wolf" or "door." Beauty can have quite different meanings to different people. Yet all of these people like "beauty." Both the Zulu and the American, as we saw, want to marry a woman with beauty, and both intend to. But neither would be very happy if required to exchange his fiancée for the other's.

This is why an unconcretized abstract term is a block to logical thinking. It is *vague,* it is *imprecise,* it ignores the *complexity of the subject.* It thus *prevents* meaningful communication.

Consider, for example, the fact that both the Zulu and the American *agreed* that they wanted to marry a beautiful woman. This is the heart of the matter. The use of unconcretized abstract terms often creates *apparent agreement* where there is *no agreement at all.* The use of unconcretized abstract terms prevents what is really being talked about from becoming apparent.

It wasn't until the American and the Zulu got down to concretes, it wasn't until they showed what they meant by "beauty" (in this case through pictures) that they realized they profoundly *disagreed* on what constituted feminine beauty.

We must get a firm grasp of the nature of abstract terms if we are to avoid being suckers or fools, or both. So let's examine the matter a little further.

So far, we have seen that unconcretized abstract terms:

1. Apparently have a fixed and definite meaning (denotation), but really don't;
2. Are actually vague and imprecise;
3. Disguise the complexity of the subject;
4. Tend to create apparent agreement where there may be no agreement at all.

If you will recall the sampling of abstract terms at the beginning of this section, you will perceive that unconcretized abstract terms tend to have two other characteristics that also block logical thinking. They often:

5. Contain a built-in *moral judgment;*
6. Encourage *either–or* thinking.

We, as culturally conditioned twentieth-century Americans tend to react to the italicized abstractions in the left-hand column on page 199 as "good," "right," "desirable" and to react to those in the right-hand column as "bad," "wrong," "undesirable."

These six characteristics of unconcretized abstract terms that we have listed make them *very* powerful weapons in the hands of people who wish to influence us. These people may have what they consider our best interests at heart or they may be trying to gain control over us for their own ends. The motive is unimportant. What is important is that we, as citizens of a democracy in a complex age requiring intelligent decisions, should not become the mindless puppets of every skillful orator who wants to control our views.

IN GOD'S NAME

It has been said that the greatest sins in man's history have been committed in the name of God. What is meant by this apparently irreverent assertion is that when a reprehensible or unwise action is contemplated, an action for which *logical arguments* would be hard to find, the action can be made to seem good by committing it *in the name of* an abstraction considered "good."

In other words, one way to prevent logical, rational analysis of an action, a law, or a policy is to perform that action, pass the law, or form the policy in the name of some abstraction considered unquestionably "good," or in the name of opposition to some abstraction considered unquestionably "bad."

Thus, if our nation is following a certain policy, leaders may attempt (whether in good or bad faith) to win support for the policy and stifle criticism of it by claiming that our nation's "honor" is at stake. To oppose the policy becomes, then, to want our nation to "betray its honor," or behave "dishonorably." A person who exercises his intelligence will perceive that "honor" is an abstraction, not a thing. Hence to suggest that people who oppose a given policy want the nation to act dishonorably is a way of preventing a rational, logical analysis of the merits of the policy. It used to be thought that if a gentleman were insulted by another gentleman, the only honorable action for him to take was to challenge the other to a duel and attempt to kill him. A man who defends his honor in this way today may well find himself called not an honorable man, but a murderer.

Let's take another example, using the same abstract term. Many people believe that if a respectable girl (a rather nice distinction in itself) becomes pregnant while unmarried, the man responsible should "do right by her," should do the "honorable" thing—namely, marry her. If he doesn't, he's not an honorable man; he's a shirker from his duty, his responsibility (two other unconcretized abstractions, by the way).

Again, a hypothetical situation is in order. The way to deal with an abstraction is always to *concretize* it by searching for a specific situation or example which clearly makes the course of action advocated through appeal to the abstraction unwise or unsatisfactory. Remember, the exception does indeed prove the rule; it proves the rule *false*. What kind of logic is it that maintains:

Red-haired girls are always passionate.

I know a red-haired girl who is frigid.

This just goes to show that red-haired girls are always passionate.

If you can find or invent *one* reasonable case that makes a general rule absurd, you must kick out the general rule *entirely* and thereafter examine every case on its own merits.

So if it is stated that an honorable man will marry a girl who is pregnant by him, try to construct a hypothetical situation in which such an act would be unwise, undesirable. And, of course, such is not hard to do. Say, for instance, that the two people were only superficially acquainted, that their relationship was based on mutual desire rather than mutual respect or admiration; that neither loved the other; that to marry would mean that the man would have to abandon his education and take a job far below his potentialities; that he didn't want to marry the girl and felt resentful toward her; that she didn't want married life at the time and hated the idea of being tied down by a child. What is "honorable" about two people creating for themselves a little private hell in which to hate each other, their child, and themselves?

It would seem much more reasonable for the man or the woman or both to rationally and objectively analyze the relative merits of all courses of action open: marriage, admission of parentage by the man and financial support for the child, putting the child up for adoption, and (unless we want to kid ourselves here) abortion.

DENOTATION AND CONNOTATION

Abstractions derive much of their power from the feeling many have that words stand for *things*—that words point to specific objects or acts or characteristics. Some do: "cat," "house," "car," "run," "hike," for example. The specific object or act or characteristics that a word points to is called the word's *denotation*. Other words, however, have *no fixed denotation*. Abstractions are words of this type. However, an abstraction does tend to have a fixed and definite *connotation*. The *connotation* of an abstraction is the moral judgment built into it. And this connotation can generally be described as either "good" or "bad."

© 1966 *United Features Syndicate, Inc.*

This characteristic of the unconcretized abstract term, its lack of a fixed, definite denotation, is what makes its use in composition (and in any other context) so undesirable. You get the illusion that you are saying something, perhaps even something profound, when you are really saying *absolutely nothing.*

A woman in a play, admonished to think before she spoke, responded to this effect: "But how can I know what I think till I hear what I say?" This is rather amusing. Considerably less amusing, however, is the fact that many people don't know what they think even *after* they've *said* what they think.

The taxi driver you are going to meet in the dialogue that follows is a person of this sort. His fare is C. S. Rott, who is, if you recall, the analytically minded boyfriend of Yvonne.

☛ C. S. ROTT AND THE TAXI DRIVER

C. S. Rott has been visiting some friends in Chicago between semesters. When we focus in on him he is in a taxi on his way to O'Hare Field to catch a plane back to college. C. S. feels ill at ease because several times the taxi driver has turned around in his seat to sneer at him.

TAXI DRIVER (*watching* C. S. *through the rear-view mirror*): You're a college kid, aren't you?

C. S. ROTT (*nervously*): Eh . . . Yeah.

TAXI DRIVER (*smugly*): I knew it. I can spot 'em every time.

C. S. ROTT (*inching his hand toward the door handle in case he has to get out fast. "Roll when you hit the pavement," he remembers having read somewhere.*): Really? How interesting.

TAXI DRIVER (*grunts, shrugs his shoulders, picks up a folded newspaper lying on the front seat, and jabs it in the general direction of* C. S.): You see this?

C. S. ROTT (*ducking back to avoid being swatted by the newspaper*): Uh . . . what?

TAXI DRIVER (*waving the newspaper in front of* C. S.'s *face*): This!

(C. S. *takes the newspaper and makes out the item the driver means. It's about a college student of twenty-three who refused to be inducted into the armed services.*)

TAXI DRIVER (*who has been observing* C. S. *in the mirror again*): You finished reading it?

C. S. ROTT (*laying the paper on the seat*): Yes.

TAXI DRIVER: I hope he gets the full five years in the pen that he deserves.

C. S. ROTT: Why?

TAXI DRIVER (*getting more and more worked up as he talks*): Unpatriotic people like that *should be* locked up. He's shirking his responsibility. He refuses to serve his country. He's not willing to do his duty. He's a dirty un-American peacenik. In fact, he should lose his citizenship. He's a disgrace to our country. A lousy draft dodger!

Apparently the taxi driver has actually said something. *Apparently* he has said what he thinks about the young man. *Apparently* he has communicated his opinions to C. S.

Actually, he has communicated nothing except an *attitude,* a *moral judgment.* He has said nothing.

C. S. wants to pin him down, but he isn't going to have much luck.

C. S. ROTT: What do you mean when you say he's "unpatriotic"?

TAXI DRIVER (*with conviction*): He's un-American.

C. S. ROTT: Why?

TAXI DRIVER: He won't do his duty.

C. S. ROTT: What's his duty?

TAXI DRIVER (*decisively*): To support America.

C. S. ROTT: How should he support America?

TAXI DRIVER: By doing the honorable thing.

C. S. ROTT: What would be the honorable thing to do?

TAXI DRIVER (*glaring meaningfully at* C. S. *in the mirror*): Joining the Army.

C. S. ROTT: Why?

TAXI DRIVER: Because that's the patriotic thing to do.

C. S. ROTT: Why?

TAXI DRIVER (*banging the steering wheel with his fist*): Because a *real* American wants to support his country!

C. S. ROTT: Why?

TAXI DRIVER: Because he loves his country.

C. S. ROTT: How do you know this man doesn't love America?

TAXI DRIVER: Because he won't do his duty.

C. S. ROTT: What's his duty?

TAXI DRIVER (*waving his fist at* C. S.): I already told you! To support his country! If there's one thing I hate more than lousy draft dodgers, it's punk kids who think they know everything! In my day . . .

(*For the rest of the trip* C. S. *endures a lecture on punk kids.*)

CONCRETIZATION

The taxi driver is unable to concretize his abstraction "un-patriotic"; instead, he explains what he means by this abstraction through *other* abstractions ("un-American," "duty," "honorable," etc.), and finally his whole argument begins to run around in a circle like a dog chasing its tail. This man literally doesn't know what he thinks *or* what he means.

Often, like the taxi driver, a person will state his opinion on a subject *entirely* in terms of unconcretized abstractions. If you ask him to explain his meaning, he will do so in terms of additional unconcretized abstractions. No meaningful communication can occur, however, unless each of the abstractions is concretized. If you keep pushing such a person to explain what he means, he will often become quite threatened and may become defensive and angry. This is why "argument" has acquired the unfortunate but revealing connotation of dissension and ill will.

Such a person becomes threatened because *he doesn't really know what he means.* When a person can't concretize the abstractions he is using, it is almost always a sure sign that he quite literally doesn't know what he's talking about.

We noted earlier that the use of an unconcretized abstraction always involves an implied assertion that "_____ has one and only one acceptable meaning and that meaning is the one I am using when I make my statement." A person who can't concretize the abstraction he is using *doesn't know the meaning that he means.*

Such people are in the vast majority, simply because most men don't think. At best they record and play back to others a garbled version of what they themselves have heard from others.

Let's take just one of the taxi driver's statements about the young man who refused induction and examine the unconcretized abstraction it contains:

"Unpatriotic people like that should be locked up."

We look up *patriot* in the dictionary and find this definition:

Patriot: A person who *loves* his *country,* zealously *supporting* it and its *interests.* (Abstractions italicized.)

However, we now know no more than we did before. Since *patriot* is an abstraction, it has no fixed denotation, no one definite, concrete, universally agreed upon signification in the world of concrete instances. Therefore, all the dictionary can do is define it in terms of other abstractions. If we are going to use the term meaningfully, we have to do better than this.

Before we can judge whether or not a person "loves" America, whether or not he is "supporting it" by a certain action, we must formulate the possible meanings of "America." We must concretize the abstraction "America" before we can possibly tell whether a given action is or isn't a sign of love for America. (Of course, "America" in the sense of a nation consisting of a certain number of states in a certain area of the world, unified under one government, is not an abstraction. But "America," when it is used in such statements as "He is for America" or "He supports America" or "He loves America," is an abstraction. In these statements the term "America" signifies certain *qualities,* and all people don't agree on just what these qualities are.)

Concretization 1—"To me, the essence of 'America,' her unique nature and identity, is expressed in the principles set forth in the Declaration of Independence and in the Bill of Rights. Fidelity to these principles led the Founding Fathers to revolt from English rule. Any action taken by a particular administration which, to my mind, violates these principles is a betrayal of America. I feel that the present war is contrary to these principles. Therefore, I am showing my patriotism, my love for America, by refusing induction into the armed services."

Concretization 2—"To me the essence of 'America' consists of the policies of the administration in power at any given moment and the laws in force at any given moment. Therefore, if one is a patriot, if he loves America, he will praise and defend the policies of the administration in power, whatever they may be; and he will abide by and conform to all the laws, whatever they may be."

Possibly, the young man who refused induction would concretize "America" as in Concretization 1. If so, in his terms, he was a patriot.

If the taxi driver had been able to concretize what he meant by "America" he might have come up with a statement similar to Concretization 2. Judged against the latter concretization, the young man was behaving unpatriotically.

☞ NOTE: As in this instance, concretizing an abstraction seldom *resolves* an issue. But concretizing an abstraction *does* make clear what the issue *is* (in this case, two opposed views of what constitutes "America").

SUMMARY

Unconcretized abstractions subtly block logical thinking by giving an impression of meaning where none exists. They are sound and fury signifying nothing.

Whenever you come upon an abstraction, determine whether the writer or speaker is using it in a legitimate or an illegitimate fashion. He is using the abstraction in a *legitimate* fashion if he has clearly and calmly defined exactly what *he* is referring to in the world of concrete reality by the abstraction, if he has given some concrete and sufficiently detailed examples of what he has in mind when he refers to "liberty" or "tyranny" or "justice."

He is using the abstraction *illegitimately* if he has not indicated concretely and precisely what he means by the term. You can easily train yourself to recognize and to scorn this type of rhetoric. This illegitimate use of abstractions generally occurs in the context of other types of appeals to emotion. It usually appears in writing or speeches characterized by lots of high-sounding words, characterized by lots of words that are "sacred" ("motherhood," "God," "country") or "profane" ("communism," "decay," "injustice"), and characterized by a lack of concrete, specific, factual, and calmly presented instances.

Below are reprinted two brief examples of the illegitimate use of abstractions, so you can better learn to recognize this use. Following these illustrations of the illegitimate use of abstractions are two examples of their legitimate use.

Illegitimate Use of Abstract Words

I. "An informed citizenry, alert to guard our heritage, will guarantee strengthened sinews and heightened resolve that our flag on high will never be replaced with the butcher-red emblem of barbarous, godless communist slavery." (J. Edgar Hoover)

Blocks to logical thinking displayed in this passage:
A. Unconcretized abstractions ("heritage," "barbarous," "godless," "communist," "slavery")
B. Implied assertion (Communism is slavery.)
C. Moral judgment (Communism is evil.)
D. Either–or thinking (Communism is all bad.)
E. Figurative language ("sinews," "butcher-red")

II. "Movies are dirtier than ever.
Books are dirtier than ever.
The magazine stands are reeking.

We have come half-circle from the Victorianism of the past to the libertinism of the present. It's a little hard to see how we can get much lower. . . .

Even homosexuals seem to have their house publications. Have you seen the naked young man wearing gold bracelets in some of the so-called body-building magazines?" (Jenkin Lloyd Jones)

Blocks to logical thinking displayed in this passage:
A. Unconcretized abstractions ("Victorianism," "libertinism")
B. Implied assertions (Homosexuals should not have their own publications; a naked boy who wears a gold bracelet is a homosexual; the present is characterized by libertinism.)
C. Moral judgment (Sex is evil; homosexuality is bad.)
D. Either–or thinking (Victorianism versus libertinism, sex is bad, etc.)
E. Figurative language ("dirtier," "reeking," "lower")

☞ NOTE: The various blocks to logical thinking hang together. When you eliminate one, you will often find that you have eliminated several. For example, the single term "libertinism" in the second quotation above is an unconcretized abstraction, involves an implied assertion, reveals moral judgment, and indicates either–or thinking. Furthermore, the writer's whole hysterical condemnation of showing the nude human body or dealing with matters of sex in movies, books, and magazines is a result of cultural conditioning and unconscious needs and fears. (Actually, the writer probably doesn't believe one word of what he is saying but is trying to manipulate his audience by playing on *their* culturally conditioned attitudes, *their* unconscious fears, *their* irrational emotions. Don't let him or others like him manipulate you!)

Legitimate Use of Abstract Words

I. "Censorship, generally, falls into two significantly distinct classes, hidden and public. Of the two classes, the first is, of course, the more insidious because it is uncontrollable. Such hidden censorship is part and parcel of the system in accordance with which motion pictures are produced in the United States. All pictures that are to receive the approval of the Motion Picture Producers Code Administration must secure the approval *before* the pictures can be released. There is plenty of evidence that many of the specific stipulations of the Code are hopelessly outmoded. A specific ruling of the Code bans 'pointed profanity and every other profane or vulgar expression, however used.' It was this specific ruling that brought about the enforced elimination of three 'hell's' and one 'damn' from the picture showing actual battle conditions in Korea. Public censorship is that exercised by a legally constituted body such as the New York State Board of Regents, which may refuse to permit the showing of a picture anywhere within the limits of the sovereign state of New York. A more dangerous form of public censorship, however, occurs when private individuals or pressure-groups exert their influence to prevent the public sale of books or the public showing of moving pictures."*

☞ NOTE: The abstract term here is "censorship." However, before proceeding with his essay, the author states what he means by the term; he recognizes the complexity of the subject and gives concrete instances of the different forms of censorship. There is no appeal to emotion, either–or thinking, and so forth, in this passage. And notice the tone. It is calm, objective, reasonable. This author is addressing our minds, not our guts.

---

* Fred B. Millett, "The Vigilantes," *AAUP Bulletin* (Spring, 1954).

II. "To be blunt, our prisons are failures. This is obvious when we take note of the large number of recidivists among offenders who have been imprisoned. According to Sellin's study for the American Law Institute, 50.5 percent of males committed to prisons in certain selected areas had been institutionalized before in penal institutions. Then too, Glueck's study of 1,000 juvenile delinquents during the first five years after they were released from a penal institution indicated that 85.4 percent manifested recidivism. James V. Bennett, Director of the Federal Bureau of Prisons, made a statement in 1949 that approximately 60 percent of all the men released from prisons throughout the country returned again within a period of five years. Nathaniel Showstack stated that in 1955 84 percent of the men in California state prisons had been sentenced to prison or jail previously and that 70 percent of the men executed at San Quentin were recidivists.†

☞ NOTE: The abstract term here is "failures." And, once again, you will observe that the author *concretizes* the term. There is nothing wrong with using abstractions. Using them is necessary and desirable. But they must be *concretized* in a clear, calm, and objective fashion.

One final comment on abstractions. I have used throughout this chapter the phrase "unconcretized abstraction" to refer to a particular block to logical thinking. I have spoken of concretizing an abstraction as necessary. I have avoided stating that you should "define" an abstraction, because to do so might *erroneously* suggest that an abstraction can be defined, that its meaning can be stated, in the same way that words like "wolf" and "door" can be defined. There is no such thing as a definition of an abstraction. In other words, there is no one, single, generally accepted meaning. So the best you can do, and the most you can demand others to do, is to *concretize* the abstraction. If an abstraction is concretized, you can at least determine what the user of the term means by it. And you must know what he means by it before you can decide whether you agree with what he is saying or disagree, before you can determine, in fact, what it is he is saying.

---

† David Abrahamsen, *The Psychology of Crime* (New York: Columbia University Press, 1960).

Exercise: Unconcretized Abstractions

In the passages printed below, underline each unconcretized abstraction. Be able to state how each:

1. Apparently has a fixed and definite meaning (denotation), but really doesn't
2. Is actually vague and imprecise
3. Disguises the complexity of the subject
4. Tends to create apparent agreement where there may be no agreement at all
5. Contains a built-in moral judgment
6. Encourages either–or thinking.
   a. "The great, the good, the true, are inexhaustible for inspiration, example and strength." (S. L. De Love)
   b. "A spirit of national masochism prevails, encouraged by an effete corps of impudent snobs who characterize themselves as intellectuals." (Spiro Agnew)
   c. "Certainly, one can be too inhibited. This is one extreme. The solution, however, is in becoming *less* inhibited, not in becoming *totally* uninhibited. Reckless abandon is not the answer to rigidity." (James C. Cheatham)
   d. "Constructive criticism is one thing, sterile negativism something else."
   e. "True love is total acceptance of the loved one."

4

Uninformed Opinions

Mark each of the following statements "true" or "false."

	TRUE	FALSE
1. Marijuana is a habit-forming drug.	( )	( )
2. Husbands who beat their wives are generally the dominant spouse in the marital relationship.	( )	( )
3. Nudists tend to be sexually or socially abnormal.	( )	( )
4. Exhibitionists are often dangerous sex perverts.	( )	( )
5. Rapists are usually men with a strong sex drive.	( )	( )

The chances are that you judged some or even most of these statements "true," yet every one of them is false.

And if your opinions on some or most of these matters are false, it is virtually certain that many of your opinions on other controversial subjects are erroneous. But you are not to blame. You will be blameworthy, though, if you pass through college without revising your views on these and many other controversial subjects, if you go through college unaffected by new ideas, as if you had received a vaccination labeled "Immunization to New Ideas," with a guaranteed effective life of four years.

The cartoon reprinted below illustrates the fear many have that the vaccination may not work:

the small society   **by Brickman**

Washington Star Syndicate, Inc.

What are the ingredients that compose this vaccination? We can list a few of the probable ones:

1. Ignorance
2. Preconceptions
3. Misinformation
4. Middle-class attitudes

Now, obviously, these are not really four distinct and separate ingredients; they blend into and reinforce one another, but they all go into the creation of the vaccine we've spoken of. Preconceptions, misinformation, and middle-class attitudes result largely from cultural conditioning. We won't discuss them separately here. But ignorance, simple lack of accurate information, deserves special mention. However, before we turn to this matter, let me ask you candidly if you are offended? Do you feel angry? Do you feel I'm insulting you? Do you feel I'm telling you that you are an ignorant, stupid slob? It's quite possible that you do feel insulted, because almost all of us do tend to feel that if the worth and value of our ideas are challenged, it is really our value or worth as a person that is being called into question. We tend to perceive our ideas and opinions as the "children" of our mind. And we tend to feel just as angry when they are attacked or questioned as a parent feels when someone criticizes his "actual" children, his offspring.

THE MOTHER HEN SYNDROME

There is no easier way to make yourself hated than to criticize a person's children, because the person feels that you are indirectly telling him that *he* is an inferior, defective, worthless person. After all, a high-quality, valuable chicken lays high-quality, valuable eggs, and if the eggs are flawed there's obviously something wrong with the chicken.

In cultivating the ability to reason logically, the most important step of all is to train yourself not to react to ideas opposed to your own as if you were a mother hen whose eggs were being scornfully rejected.

The *accuracy* and *verifiability* of any given opinion which you may hold has not a damned thing to do with your worth and value as a human being. If you can force yourself to truly accept this fact, you will have freed yourself from that chain which binds most people, for their entire lives, to virtually every inaccurate, uninformed, and unverifiable prejudice that they picked up in their youth and young adulthood.

Ralph Waldo Emerson, the nineteenth-century American philosopher, noted that "A foolish consistency is the hobgoblin of little minds." By this statement he meant that it is the insecure, self-doubting person who feels that, having once formed an opinion about a subject, it is a sign of weakness or stupidity to change his opinion in the light of new facts, new knowledge. The larger mind says, "Do I contradict myself? Very well then, I contradict myself," because such a mind recognizes that to relinquish falsehood for truth is infinitely preferable to clinging stubbornly, like a mindless leech, to an inaccurate opinion.

With these observations in mind, with, hopefully, your recognition that I am not in any way attacking your worth as a person when I assert that many or most of your opinions on controversial subjects are probably either false or in part inaccurate, let's turn to this matter of ignorance—the state of being uninformed.

IGNORANCE

Among the many reasons for your coming to college, presumedly at least one was *to learn.* And if you came to learn, there is the implication that you don't know everything—that about many matters you are simply ignorant. (Not stupid, not a clod, not a hayseed or a hick or a bum, just *ignorant!* If it gives you any satisfaction, I cheerfully and honestly admit to being ignorant, too, about many subjects.)

But the danger is that while you find nothing threatening about admitting to yourself and others that you are ignorant about chemistry, biology, calculus, botany, zoology, art, literature (the list could go on and on), you do feel that there are many other subjects about which you *are not ignorant.* A supreme achievement is to recognize your ignorance about these subjects too, to recognize that though there are many subjects about which you have firm opinions, you are really relatively *uninformed* about these subjects. And an *uninformed opinion* is a *prejudice.*

Let's get down to some concrete examples, always a good idea after throwing out a bunch of generalizations.

FACTS, OPINIONS, AND PREJUDICES

People have a tendency to make a distinction, usually not even a conscious one, between subjects on which they feel there is only one correct opinion, and subjects on which they feel there are numerous accurate opinions. They usually call the former type of opinion a "fact." By this they mean that there is such overwhelming evidence of the accuracy of the opinion that no other opinion can be held by a reasonable person. Concerning the second type of subject, a subject on which they feel that more than one opinion may be reasonably held, their attitude might be described as:

It's a democracy, ain't it? So my opinion is just as good as your opinion. (And if you don't like it, let's step outside, and I'll show you whose opinion is right!)

Making this false distinction between two types of subjects is what allows people to retain their prejudices even when confronted with evidence which to an objective observer obviously discredits their view.

To take an obvious example, it is a widely held opinion today that the earth is spherical. Most people regard this opinion as a "fact" because it can be verified, or shown to be true, by appeal to such evidence as around-the-world voyages, photographs made from satellites, and scientific principles. Similarly, the opinions that man is mortal, that if you jump off a ten-story building you will fall, that lightning is an electrical discharge and not a thunderbolt hurled by Zeus are regarded as "facts" because of the evidence which can be amassed to verify them and prove them accurate.

But, all this agreement ends when we come to such controversial and in many ways more complex subjects as crime, censorship, religion, racial intermarriage, birth control, premarital sex, marijuana, communism. Here is where the blocks to logical thinking that we have discussed come into play; here is where the danger signals start flashing.

Asked to respond to subjects such as these, a person will generally react in one of two ways.

The first way we've already discussed. He will react by stating his opinion and maintaining that it's at least as valid as any other opinion. He makes the false distinction between *fact* and *opinion* which we mentioned earlier, and holds that since whatever one believes on the subject is "just an opinion" (that is, not a fact, not something that can be "proven"), his opinion is as "good" (meaning as "accurate") as any other.

A second way of reacting, however, is the more common

and leads to even more unfortunate results. The person will state as his *opinion* a view that is really a *prejudice,* while actually regarding it as a *fact!*

This is getting a bit complex, so let's take a hypothetical example, for it is of the utmost importance that you comprehend this process. Remember, what we want to show here is how a person, reacting to a controversial subject, states what he calls his *opinion* on the subject. Actually, though, his view is a *prejudice* because he is uninformed, in other words, ignorant of the subject. But though he calls his view an *opinion,* he really regards his view as a *fact* (and hence indisputable).

☛ C. S. ROTT AND M. ATBAR

TIME: *Thursday, 10:30* P.M.
PLACE: *The Rathskeller Bar.*
SETTING AND ATMOSPHERE: *A single long shoebox-shaped room. Red and blue spotlights vainly try to penetrate the smog of cigarette smoke. An electric band on a platform halfway along one side of the shoe box blares at full volume. Booths full of tittering coeds line both sides.* C. S. ROTT *fights his way toward the bar at the back end of the shoebox through scores of milling fraternity men leering at the coeds and bragging about their exploits.*

C. S. ROTT (*grabbing his stomach*): Ugh!
VOICE (*presumedly belonging to the elbow jabbed in his gut*): Oops.
C. S. ROTT (*wiping beer from the back of his neck*): Damn!
VOICE (*presumedly belonging to the hand holding aloft a tilted beer mug*): Hey! Watch it!
C. S. ROTT (*removing his toe from beneath the heel of someone's shoe*): Ahh!

VOICE (*presumedly belonging to the heel*): Sorry.

C. S. ROTT (*squeezing his way onto the only empty barstool, which is between a student and M. Atbar—a* Man at the Bar—*who has obviously had a few too many*): A schooner.

BARTENDER (*who looks like he may have enough fuzz in two or three years to justify shaving once a week*): Let's see your I.D.

C. S. ROTT (*shoving it across the bar*): Here.

BARTENDER (*staring from the I.D. to* ROTT): You don't look twenty-one to me. Let's see your driver's license.

C. S. ROTT (*shoving it across the bar*): Here.

BARTENDER (*comparing the I.D. and the driver's license*): It says here you weigh one hundred sixty, but the driver's license says one hundred fifty-five. Let's see your draft card.

C. S. ROTT: Here.

BARTENDER (*dropping all three cards in a puddle of stale beer*): Bourbon and water, huh?

C. S. ROTT (*wiping the cards on his pants*): A schooner.

M. ATBAR (*turning his bleary eyes on Rott*): Even'n' son.

C. S. ROTT (*to himself*): Oh, God.

M. ATBAR: What do you think about this latest outrage the Communists are trying to pull on us?

C. S. ROTT (*shrugging hopelessly*): Uh.

M. ATBAR (*firmly*): Communism has got to be stopped somewhere.

C. S. ROTT (*automatically*): Do you mean "communism" as a political system, as a social system, or as an economic system?

M. ATBAR (*indignantly*): I mean the world-wide, monolithic Communist conspiracy. It's got to be stopped.

C. S. ROTT: Well, there's Russian communism, Chinese communism, Algerian communism, East German communism, Cuban communism, Yugoslavian communism, Czechoslovakian communism . . .

M. ATBAR (*banging his first on the bar*): I mean *Communism!* The world-wide Communist conspiracy!

C. S. ROTT: There's Trotskyite communism, Stalinist communism, revisionist communism . . .

M. ATBAR: Look! Khrushchev said, "We will bury you." We've got to stop them.

C. S. ROTT: Who's "them"?

M. ATBAR: The Communists, before they bury us.

C. S. ROTT: Khrushchev was using a metaphor.

M. ATBAR: Huh?

C. S. ROTT: He was predicting that Russia would become economically superior to the United States and achieve economic victory over her.

M. ATBAR (*angrily*): Who says? He meant what he said. That the world-wide Communist conspiracy would conquer the United States and bury it in a pile of rubble.

C. S. ROTT: But, there is no world-wide Communist conspiracy. There are as many types of communism as there are communist nations. And . . .

M. ATBAR (*staring at* ROTT): What are you? Some sort of pinko? Some sort of Communist sympathizer?

C. S. ROTT: No.

M. ATBAR: Then what kind of rot are you talking? *Everybody* knows about the international Communist conspiracy.

C. S. ROTT: "Conspiracy" means "planning or acting together secretly"—how can you claim an international Communist conspiracy exists when Russia condemns China, when China accuses Russia of collaborating with the United States, when Castro accuses Russia of compromise with the capitalists, when the Chinese board a Russian ship to make the Russian crew members accept the doctrines of Chinese communism, when Yugoslavia institutes capitalism to stimulate production, when Albania refuses to send delegates to Russia. . . .

M. ATBAR: I don't know what you're talking about. A bunch of mumbo jumbo. *Everybody* knows there's an international Communist conspiracy.

C. S. ROTT (*sipping his beer*): No.

M. ATBAR: Listen. Will the sun rise tomorrow?

C. S. ROTT: Probably.

M. ATBAR: Look, son, don't try to put me on. I *know* the sun will rise tomorrow.

c. s. ROTT: You are an optimist.

M. ATBAR: Do fish swim in the ocean?

c. s. ROTT: Yes.

M. ATBAR: Do birds fly in the sky?

c. s. ROTT: Yes.

M. ATBAR: Good. You admit the facts. Then why don't you admit that we've got to stop the international Communist conspiracy?

c. s. ROTT: Because you haven't given any evidence that there *is* such a thing as the international Communist conspiracy.

M. ATBAR (*jumping up and waving his fist in front of* ROTT's *face*): *Everybody* knows about the international Communist conspiracy! It's a *fact!*

c. s. ROTT (*calmly*): The fact is that you are uninformed.

M. ATBAR: Oh yeah! I'll show you who's uninformed!

(M. ATBAR *swings wildly at* c. s. ROTT. c. s. *ducks and* M. ATBAR's *fist smashes into the face of the student sitting next to* c. s. *Barstools crash! Glasses smash! A coed screams! Students climb gleefully onto tables and throw beer mugs into the melee while yelling happily, "Fight! Fight!"*

c. s. ROTT, *clutching his drink, crawls carefully on his hands and knees until he is out of the brawl. He finds an empty table and sits down. "Rot," he says.*)

EVIDENCE

To return, we recall that M. Atbar's last semirational remarks were to the effect that the international communist conspiracy was a *fact*.

No. The fact is that many people in the United States believe in the existence of an international Communist conspiracy. But a belief in the existence of something, however widespread, is no proof of its existence and is no substitute for evidence of its existence. If it were, then the insane would be possessed by demons, and lightning would be a thunderbolt cast by an angry god.

Thinking back over this scene we can see that M. Atbar has what he claims to be an *opinion,* namely, that there exists a world-wide monolithic Communist conspiracy.

If this opinion is to be accurate and verifiable, M. Atbar must be able to show *at least* the following assertions to be true:

1. Communism is indivisible—that is, it cannot be broken down into an economic system, a political system, a social system, and so forth.
2. The various Communist nations are not divided among themselves as to the aims, means of implementation, or meaning of communism.
3. All the Communist nations have the same goal, and they are planning in secret together to achieve this goal.
4. This goal, held by all Communist nations, is the physical destruction of the United States.

However, as we have seen, M. Atbar is *uninformed.* He knows little, if anything, of the various points of view (economic, political, social, etc.) from which communism may be regarded; and he is not aware of the various forms that communism takes in different countries. Thus M. Atbar's "opinion" that there is an international Communist conspiracy is really a *prejudice (an uninformed opinion).*

Finally, as the last part of the dialogue makes clear, M. Atbar does not really believe at all that his view that there is an international Communist conspiracy is subject to question, for he actually believes that the existence of such a conspiracy is a *fact* as self-evident as the "fact" that birds fly in the sky and fish swim in the ocean and hence requires no supporting evidence.

But the difference is that M. Atbar can *verify* the *accuracy* of his opinion that birds fly in the sky, and so forth, by citing *evidence,* either the evidence of personal experience or the evidence of authority:

1. He can speak from his personal experience.
2. He can appeal to the personal experience of C. S. Rott.
3. He can (probably after sobering up) direct C. S. Rott to sources in the public library to support his opinion.

However, he is *ignorant* of the subject of communism and cannot cite acceptable evidence to support his opinion. The best he could manage would be a vague "They say" or "Everybody knows." But adding ignorance to ignorance does not add up to knowledge.

In order to arrive at an *accurate* and *verifiable* opinion on such controversial subjects as we have mentioned, you must first of all:

1. Recognize your ignorance.

Believe me, this is the hardest step to take. Once it is taken, the rest is relatively easy. The next three steps are to:

2. Achieve an open mind (suspend moral judgment and be objective).
3. Doubt your preconceptions (beware of primary certitude).
4. Inform yourself.

Your opinion, in other words, will be formed *after* you have informed yourself, *not before,* and it will be an informed opinion, one which you can verify and show to be accurate by citing qualified authority for your view.

☞ NOTE: One word of warning here. There is always plenty of money to be made and power to be gained by playing on the prejudices of large groups of people. When a large number of people hate and fear a minority race or religion, you will always find charlatans who will give "reasons" for hating and fearing the group. When a murderer is loose, there's money to be made selling locks. When a population needs a scapegoat to blame for its own frustration, there's money to be made selling imaginary witches. So, when you *inform yourself,* don't turn to the panders for prejudice any more than you would turn to a quack to learn the cure for a disease. Be sure that the writers whose articles or books you read are *authorities* on the subject they are writing about. Not just authorities on something, but authorities on the subject they are discussing. If you are not sure, ask your instructor.

And, as you read what they have to say, be alert for the appearance of any of the blocks to logical thinking we have examined. If you find more than one or two of these blocks in a given essay, you have no choice but to reject the essay, no matter how great an authority on the subject the author may be.

☛ ROCK NORMAL AND THE HORNY NUDISTS

Rock Normal, an ex-high-school football player, is a cleancut, blond-haired, broad-shouldered second-term freshman who stands six feet tall in his socks. In his first-term composition class he expressed his view of life when he wrote that "It's a doggy doggy world." Evidently, he meant a "dog eat dog" world, but anyway, he knows that in a doggy doggy world like this, there's no room for kooks. So when he was assigned a short theme on the subject of "Nudism," he knew that writing the theme would be simple.

When we focus in on Rock, it is 8 P.M. He is sitting at the desk in his dorm room.

ROCK (*over his shoulder to his roommate*): Hey, I'm talking to you.

ROOMMATE (*on the lower bunk, scratching his head*): Huh?

ROCK: I said, I'm talking to you.

ROOMMATE: I was sleeping.

ROCK: So, wake up.

ROOMMATE: Uh.

ROCK: I've got to write a theme.

ROOMMATE: Big deal.

ROCK: Listen, it's on sex.

ROOMMATE: Again? What's the matter with that instructor of yours, anyway?

ROCK: Not sex, exactly. Nudism.

ROOMMATE: What's the difference?

ROCK: That's what I mean. What a bunch of kooks.

ROOMMATE: Who?

ROCK: Nudists. Running around naked all day and pretending they're doing it to get a sun tan. Ha!

ROOMMATE: You're just jealous. (*He reaches under the bed.*) Hey, did you see this joke? (*He shows Rock a cartoon that depicts a scene in a nudist colony. A group of male nudists are inviting a group of girls to play "touch" football.*)

ROCK (*chuckling*): That just goes to show what they really have on their minds. A bunch of perverts, that's what they are.

ROOMMATE: Exhibitionists and voyeurs.

ROCK: Huh?

ROOMMATE: They must be half people who like to show it off, and half who like to look at it.

ROCK (*laughing*): Imagine two of the same kind meeting: One says, "Hey look!" and the other says, "No, you look!"

ROOMMATE: I bet there's plenty going on in those places. Those camps always have walls—keep people from finding out what they're really up to.

ROCK: Yeh. They've probably got plenty to hide.

ROOMMATE: Say. There's a new nudie film on at the art theatre, *Sin in the Sun*. Maybe you could get credit for going to see it. Part of your "research" and all that.

ROCK: That reminds me. Jim has a new "sunbathing" magazine. Some sunbathing. Maybe I could get credit for looking through that, too.

ROOMMATE: Oh yeah? (*He gets up.*) Think I'll take a look.

ROCK (*tossing down the pen he's been doodling with*): Wait, I'll go with you. I've got the idea for the stupid thing. I'll write it later.

Obviously, Rock doesn't know a thing about nudism. He is *ignorant* of the subject. He is not personally acquainted with any practicing nudists, much less a large enough number on which to base generalizations. Nor has he read any authoritative articles on the subject. But he doesn't recognize his ignorance because he has lots of "opinions" about nudism, opinions that are actually prejudices, since they are uninformed opinions.

How did he get these "opinions"?

He got them in the same way that M. Atbar got his views on communism: from his environment, his culture, his friends. His "opinions" are simply mindless, unquestioning reflections of the popular attitudes toward nudism. It is easy enough to understand how such attitudes could come into being, but understanding the probable causes of them doesn't make them any less false.

You will notice that Rock makes a virtually automatic connection between nudism and sex. Push the button "nudism" and out comes the association "sex." This reaction is understandable since most people associate being naked in the presence of another person with sexuality. But, just because the typical nonnudist makes such an association is no indication at all that the typical nudist makes the same connection. In other words, the uninformed person *projects* his own realization that he would be sexually excited by the presence of nude people around him onto the nudists themselves, and concludes that *they* must have sexual motivations for their behavior. And, of course, the fact that most people who look at "nudie" magazines or go to "nudie" pictures do so in order to be sexually stimulated reinforces this association of nudism and sex.

So, once again, the moral is to beware of the feeling of "primary certitude" about a subject, to doubt your preconceptions, and to avoid forming an opinion until you have *informed yourself*. If Rock had bothered to inform himself, he would have discovered evidence of the inaccuracy of his views on nudism, such as that reprinted below:

Nudists are much more normal than most of us, according to their scores on a famous Minnesota personality test, a University of Minnesota psychologist said Friday.

The Minnesota Multiphasic Personality Inventory (MMPI) was given to 159 members of nudist clubs in Southern California, reported Dr. John P. Brantner, and "they had twice the percentage of normal MMPIs that the average population has."

"They tend to be a healthy, well-adjusted group of people. I can't explain it, but nudists have been saying this for years. Maybe they're right."

Brantner said another surprising finding was that none of the single females in the study showed significant abnormalities.

His conclusion: "Most of the men and all of the women join nudist clubs for relatively healthy reasons. They're social nudists, but they're more social than nudists."*

Exercise: Uninformed Opinions

At the discretion of your instructor, choose one of the following topics as the subject for a short research project.

Before you begin your investigation, *write down* your major opinions on the subject. After you have completed your investigation, go back and mark each opinion: "accurate," "inaccurate," or "partially accurate." Which label predominates? Compare your markings with those of other students in the class. Is there enough agreement to warrant a tentative generalization about the prevalence of uninformed opinions?

1. Abortion	11. Middle-class delinquency
2. Air pollution	12. *Hell's Angels*
3. UFOs	13. Profile of a Negro rioter
4. Inflation	14. Computer dating
5. The inner city	15. Mutual funds
6. Racism	16. Selling stocks short
7. White backlash	17. Future of the big city
8. Alcoholism	18. Effects of the mass media
9. Drugs	19. Guerrilla war
10. Mafia	20. Black power

---

* Bob Lundegaard, "Expert Says Nudists Are More Normal Than Most of Us," *The Minneapolis Tribune* (March 18, 1967).

5

Figurative Language, False Analogies, Faulty Causation

FIGURATIVE LANGUAGE

Figurative language is a block to logical thinking very similar in its nature and effect to unconcretized abstractions. All we need to know about figurative language is that it is language that is *literally false.*

He doesn't have any *guts.*

Americans should be proud of their *flag.*

These are examples of figurative language. Every man has intestines. And the speaker in the second statement doesn't mean that we should unfold the American flag when company comes and brag about the stitching and the vividness of the colors.

At first glance, figurative language seems quite different from abstract words because it is *concrete,* it *appeals to the senses.* We can see "flag," picture and touch "guts." But since figurative language is *literally false,* it doesn't mean what it says. Therefore, in reasoned exposition it is *vague* and *imprecise* and *ignores the complexity of the subject* just as an unconcretized abstraction is vague and imprecise and ignores the complexity of a subject.

Another way figurative language is similar to abstract language is that while it *says* something concrete, it often *means* something abstract. Thus "He doesn't have any *guts*" (figurative

232

language) *means* "He doesn't have any *courage*" (unconcretized abstraction); "Americans should be proud of their *flag*" (figurative language) *means* "Americans should be proud of *America*" (unconcretized abstraction—recall "C. S. Rott and the Taxi Driver").

FALSE ANALOGIES

False analogies are one of the most powerful weapons in the hands of demagogues and are also responsible for some of the most brainless thinking around. "If you can't prove your point logically, use an analogy" is a rule all too many people follow, and all too many people are taken in by such use.

An *analogy,* when used in argumentation, is simply a *comparison* which argues that: (1) *two* situations are similar in *certain* respects; (2) they are, therefore, similar in *other* respects, also. Here are a couple of abbreviated analogies:

Leisure is like sugar. A little bit is sweet.

If a dog bites, club him! If a man commits a crime, imprison him!

If we were to trace out the argument implicit in the first analogy we would get something like this:

Leisure, like sugar, is pleasant only in small amounts. A lot of leisure is like too much sugar, unpleasant and cloying. So be content with your two weeks' vacation a year and don't envy the beautiful people. These people just *seem* happy; really, they feel as terrible as you would if I forced you to eat five pounds of sugar!

Generally, when used illegitimately in argument, analogies are employed to *reinforce* attitudes the audience already holds. (The analogy just examined plays on the so-called Protestant ethic that work is good and is the road to salvation, and on the quite understandable need of those people who *have* to work to feel that the "idle rich" aren't really happy anyway.)

A good rule of thumb is that analogies should *never* be used in argument as proof. If you use an analogy, use it to *clarify* an assertion that has already been supported by analysis or other means. In "Yvonne and the Dirty-Minded Instructor," if you recall, the analogy of looking at a mansion through various holes in a hedge was used to *clarify* the matter of looking at a subject from various points of view.

Use analogy only to clarify, and demand such restricted usage of another writer or speaker. If a writer is arguing a point by analogy, *be suspicious!* The reason you should be suspicious is that very few situations or predicaments are exactly the same. Generally, the *differences* are more significant than the *similarities*. Analogy *ignores* the differences and hence ignores the complexity of the subject.

FAULTY CAUSATION

CORRELATION IS NOT CAUSATION

Any effect is necessarily the product of a cause or causes:

The metal becomes fatigued $\rightarrow$ the wing of the plane gives way.

A man drinks ten highballs in an hour $\rightarrow$ he becomes intoxicated.

In all cause $\rightarrow$ effect relationships there is a *correlation* between cause and effect. When one occurs, the other occurs. They are mutually related.

But this principle cannot be reversed. A *correlation* between two events does not in itself establish a causal relationship between the two. Just because one event precedes or accompanies another does not mean that it necessarily *causes* that event.

Here is a perfectly serious statement by a pipe connoisseur:

So far as longevity is concerned it has been proved by statistics that the greater the smoker the longer he lives. A number of centenarians have been fiends for smoking. Statistics, again, prove that the expectation of life has been longer since the introduction of tobacco and its use by the ordinary man. Taking the example of France: in 1830 the average duration of life was no more than twenty-eight years; in 1953 it is forty-five years, the consumption of tobacco in proportion to the population having trebled in that period. This increase in the average duration of life is most marked among those people who beat the record for the consumption of tobacco, such as the Dutch and the Swiss.*

The author has mistaken a *correlation* (rise in consumption of tobacco—rise in life expectancy) for causation.

Whenever a cause → effect relationship is asserted, see if it can be explained as a correlation instead. Because some girls take the "pill" *and* are promiscuous does not mean that they are promiscuous *because* they take the "pill." Because "France, long famous for wine, women and truffles, folded up like a parasol in a tornado when the panzer divisions struck" does not mean, as the writer would have us believe, that France was defeated by Germany *because* many Frenchmen like wine, admire feminine beauty, and enjoy truffles.

HUMAN EVENTS HAVE MULTIPLE CAUSES

The same needs for certainty and simplicity that encourage either—or thinking encourage belief in simple-minded causal relationships.

Newspaper headlines such as these are common:

STUDENT KILLS SELF AFTER EXPULSION FROM COLLEGE

---

* Georges Herment, *The Pipe* (New York: Simon and Schuster, 1957).

HONOR STUDENT GOES ON RAMPAGE
Friends stated that John Bright had been depressed over the death of his girl friend.

Implicit in both these statements is an assertion of simple cause and effect: The student killed himself *because* he was expelled from college; John Bright rampaged *because* his girl friend had died.

But if expulsion from college really causes suicide, then every student who is expelled from college must commit suicide, which is absurd. The actions of both students were obviously the result of *multiple* causes.

Similarly, many scared, bewildered people today are crying for "get tough" police action to stamp out crime, for an end of welfare to encourage self-sufficiency, for "old-fashioned" discipline to teach kids respect for their elders. In each case they have fastened tenaciously on *one* action as the *one* cause of a complex phenomenon with multiple causes.

Exercises: Figurative Language

1. Turn back to "Yvonne and the Tender Trap," pages 23–24. List at least three instances of figurative language in Yvonne's paragraph on marriage and at least five from C. S. Rott's parody of her paragraph. How do these figurative terms reinforce the view of marriage each is trying to present?
2. Underline the figurative language in the statements below. Be able to explain how each figurative term is literally false.

   a. "Daily, news reports remind us of the rampaging reign of lawlessness." (J. Edgar Hoover)
   b. America is threatened by the "rapidly growing, menacing two-headed monster of subversion and lawlessness." (J. Edgar Hoover)
   c. "Ladies and gentlemen, I believe it is time for us, for the mad, rushing Twentieth Century American, to stop for a moment and think." (S. L. De Love)

d. "The indifference of most Americans to humiliation in Vietnam is evidence of cancerous patriotic decay."

e. "Criminals should not be coddled."

f. "Recent Supreme Court decisions have taken the teeth out of our laws and shackled our police."

g. "Crying 'Black is beautiful!' is simply a new form of whistling in the dark."

h. "*Adjustment* . . . is the theme of our swan song, the piper's tune to which we dance on the brink of the abyss, the siren's melody that destroys our senses and paralyzes our wills." (Robert Lindner)

i. "If the United States loses its appetite for struggle and cops out, those fighting to secure personal liberty are going to lose." (Carl T. Rowan)

j. "When it comes to physical desire, every individual—man or woman—has a different wavelength." (Hannah Lees, from *Reader's Digest*)

Exercise: False Analogies

State the two subjects being compared in each of the following analogies and explain how each analogy ignores significant differences between the subjects.

1. "To propose to punish and reform people by the same operation [imprisonment] is exactly as if you were to take a man suffering from pneumonia and attempt to combine punitive and curative treatment. To punish him and deter others you strip him naked and stand him in the snow all night, at the same time giving him cough drops to aid his recovery." (George Bernard Shaw)

2. "If we had stood up to Hitler when he first began to move in Europe, World War II could have been avoided. Now the Communists are on the move in Southeast Asia. Are we going to make the same tragic mistake again?"

3. Black militant: "The administration likes to say the reason for the bombing of North Vietnam is to force it to halt its

aggression against the south. White America has been committing aggression against the nation of the black man since 1619. If bombing cities halts aggression, I am willing to try Chicago and New York."

4. "To marry is to deliberately attach a leech to your body. Only a fool would be guilty of such folly."

5. "Spending too much money drains a bank account, pumping too much water drains a well, sleeping too often with a woman drains a man."

6. "If a boy is scared to stand up to a bully, his life will be hell. If we are scared to stand up to the Communists, we will have to live in a state of constant fear and dread."

7. The staff of the *Reader's Digest* carefully cuts and trims each article to be included in the *Digest,* so that, "after skillfully trimming away fat, bone and gristle, it emerges as a top-quality filet mignon." (*Reader's Digest*)

8. "The only way to deal with a malignant tumor is to cut it out. The ghettos are the malignant tumors of our cities. So burn, baby, burn!"

9. "Not everybody is allowed to drive a car. Not everybody is allowed to fly an airplane. Only those who have proved themselves competent, capable, and responsible are allowed to do so. Similarly, the sale and possession of firearms should be restricted to the competent, capable, and responsible."

10. "Interracial marriage is a repulsive violation of natural law. Does the fox breed with the chicken? Does the lion breed with the mule? Does the gentle dove breed with the vicious crow? Neither should the white breed with the black."

Exercise: Faulty Causation

The president and publisher of *The Detroit News,* addressing a gathering of corporation executives, listed as great improvements in America since World War II the nation's unequaled prosperity, huge college enrollments, growing respect for intellectuals, and improvements in the conditions of Negroes. But each improvement, he said, has caused certain unfortunate effects:

Prosperity has sapped economic incentive in young people, has stimulated a search for new values and motivations and has made it fashionable to ridicule a "materialistic" society.

The explosion in higher education and the exposure of intellectually restless young people to the teaching method of systematic criticism has led to a "rebellion in sheepskin clothing"—idealism without belief, philosophic anarchy, commitment to new causes, and cynicism about old causes.

The popularization of intellectuals and the increase in their power and influence has resulted in far more widely publicized criticism of American society.

The intellectual deals in new ideas, and "except in the physical sciences, it is unfortunately not always required that a man's ideas be rigorously tested in the crucible of experience."

"Just as James Bond was licensed to kill, everyone knows that the intellectual is licensed to criticize."

Betterment in the Negro's condition has led to a painful irony: "Improvements have replaced hopelessness with hope, hope has stimulated action, but some of that action has been directed against the very system that produced the improvements."*

Analyze the quality of this argument. Are the single causes the publisher gives the *only* causes of the effects he notes? If not, state other possible causes for each effect mentioned. Do you feel that he has, in one or more cases, mistaken correlation for causation?

---

* Chester Bulgier, "Help Solve U.S. Ills, Businessmen Urged," *The Detroit News.*

6

A Blockbuster

We can now, in concluding our discussion of "Clear Thinking for Composition," return to the matter of implied assertions with which we began it.

All of the logical fallacies which we have discussed by name —moral judgment, either–or thinking, condemnation by association, unconcretized abstractions, false analogy, figurative language, faulty causation—*all* of these fallacies and virtually all other significant logical fallacies (*ad hominem,* sampling, degree, *non sequitur, ignoratio elenchi,* etc.) involve as their central characteristic an *implied assertion* that, when *stated* and *concretized,* proves to be *false.*

A BLOCKBUSTER

Let us, then, state the three steps that you can take to correct virtually *all* reasoning errors that you will ever encounter, whether in your own reasoning or in that of others.

1. Discover the implied assertion.
2. State it as an assertion.
3. Concretize it to find an exception.

Examples

MORAL JUDGMENT AND EITHER—OR THINKING

"Premarital sex is wrong."

1. Discover the implied assertion.
2. State it as an assertion. "No situation in which premarital sex would be justified can be found."
3. Concretize it to find an exception. Recall "Yvonne and the Dirty-Minded Instructor."

CONDEMNATION BY ASSOCIATION

"Americans should not support the admission of Communist China to the United Nations. After all, Communist nations around the world want China admitted."

1. Discover the implied assertion.
2. State it as an assertion. "Americans should not support any cause advocated by Communist nations."
3. Concretize it to find an exception. "Americans should not support measures to reduce infant mortality rates because Communist nations advocate such measures. Americans should not support monogamy, because Communist nations advocate monogamy."

UNCONCRETIZED ABSTRACTION

"He doesn't love America."

1. Discover the implied assertion.
2. State it as an assertion. " 'America' has one and only one acceptable meaning and that meaning is the one I am using when I make my statement."

3. Concretize it to find an exception. Recall "C. S. Rott and the Taxi Driver."

FALSE ANALOGY

"If a dog bites, club him! If a man commits a crime, imprison him!"

1. Discover the implied assertion.
2. State it as an assertion. "Man reacts to physical punishment in exactly the same way that a domestic animal does."
3. Concretize it to find an exception: "When a man is struck he never attempts to strike back. Imprisonment makes a man fearful just as being clubbed makes a dog fearful."

FIGURATIVE LANGUAGE

Figurative language is *literally false*. It doesn't *say* what it *means*. Thus, though we could construct implied assertions for various uses of figurative language in argument on the basis of false analogy, it is best to simply reject outright any argument based on figurative language.

FAULTY CAUSATION

"The poem 'Richard Cory' isn't realistic. Cory had everything, so there was no reason for his suicide."

1. Discover the implied assertion.
2. State it as an assertion. "Happiness is a function of possessions. A person who possesses wealth and physical beauty is always happy."
3. Concretize it to find an exception: Think of novels you've read, friends of your parents, movie stars.

☞ NOTE: It is perfectly all right to use a statement containing an implied assertion *if,* when *stated* and *concretized,* there proves to be no exception to the assertion.

"John will die someday," contains an implied assertion that "Man is mortal." You concretize the assertion. You find no exceptions. Fine. You may go on. You don't need to state the implied assertion in your paper.

But "Don't vote for John, he favors trade with communist nations" contains an implied assertion to the effect that "All people who favor trade with communist nations are procommunist." When this assertion is concretized, it is revealed to be *false.* Therefore, you must modify your original statement.

Review: Clear Thinking for Composition

All of the statements that follow contain one or more implied assertions. Most of them also contain one or more of the specific logical fallacies we've discussed: moral judgment, either-or thinking, condemnation by association, unconcretized abstraction, false analogy, figurative language, faulty causation.

The statements in the first set are derived from essays of the sort you are probably required to read. The statements in the second set are from freshman themes. Those in the third set are from advertisements.

1. Discover and state the implied assertion(s) in each statement.
2. Identify the specific logical fallacies in each statement (M.J., E.-O., C.A., U.A., F.A., F.L., F.C.).
3. Many of the statements reflect the influence of cultural conditioning or unconscious needs and fears, or both. Be able to identify these forces and the role they play in the widespread acceptance or rejection of a particular statement.

S E T   I

1. "Imprisonment is at least partially effective as a means of reformation because 20 to 40 percent of offenders imprisoned never return to prison after being released."

2. "It seems to me that now more than ever before in our history, one is either *for* law enforcement—or he's *against* it. He's either *for* mob rule—or he's *for* the law. He either *loves* a cop—or he *hates* him." (George Putnam)

3. "There can be no liberty where there is no law."

4. "Our nation was unable to endure half slave and half free. Neither can it endure half law-abiding and half lawless."

5. "The right of the individual to choose the person to whom he sells his private property must be returned to the individual."

6. "If automation continues to increase, a large part of our labor force will be left unemployed."

7. "We must rededicate ourselves to the sacred values that our nation stands for."

8. "I do not believe that a true lover of children could write a book like *Lord of the Flies.*"

9. "The trouble with Holden Caulfield is that he doesn't like *anything* about the Establishment."

10. "Man is part angel, part animal."

11. "Many books today contain so many obscene words that you can't let your children read them."

12. "We must rededicate ourselves to decency and integrity."

13. "Must we conform? Must we fit ourselves into the pattern that molds Mass Man? Must we bend, submit, adjust, give in? Must we, finally, cease to be men?" (Robert Lindner)

14. "If kids are allowed to read pornography, they will get the wrong ideas about life."

15. "There is today a vicious movement to undermine the traditional spiritual and moral principles of our Nation. Freedom, divorced from authority and discipline, is a frightening thing and is the first step toward total moral degeneration." (J. Edgar Hoover)

16. "Liberty, not license."

17. "Let's win the war and get out."

18. "We must fight communism."

19. "He was too young to die."

20. "The trouble with kids today is that they lack respect for their elders."

S E T   I I

1. "If the mass media were not as highly developed in its advertising techniques as it has been shown to be, many people would not be informed of important discoveries or events."
2. "Agricultural surplus is a permanent feature of the American scene."
3. "The heritage of the American calls out his desire to re-create the life of the pioneer."
4. "Finding the answer to the true cause of alcoholism lies in the road ahead."
5. "Visits to a house of prostitution may be a kind of group male social activity, just as group consumption of alcoholic beverages is a social activity."
6. "Prostitution is an established fact of today's society. Therefore, controls should be set up for its legalization."
7. "The present system, which makes prostitution a crime, lends itself to the exploitation of prostitutes by panders, pimps, the police, and the underworld."
8. "Censorship of literature limits the possibility of a writer to express himself."
9. "One of the ways to keep the crime rate from increasing is to give the police the authority that the Supreme Court took away from them."
10. "The purpose of censorship makes it limiting to individual freedom."
11. "Unless poisons are kept out of the air, more people will be killed just because they breathe."
12. "My roommate is always borrowing my things without asking my permission first."
13. "Patients in mental hospitals should not be given jobs which make them necessary to the running of the institution. For example, a 'patient-worker' was discovered to be a homosexual taking care of his harem! When the situation was called to the attention of the superintendent, he agreed that it was a 'deplorable situation' but said, 'When you find some-

body else to do his work, let me know and I'll have him transferred.' "

14. "The best effect of the 'Pill' is that it has allowed women to enjoy sex as they never had before."

15. "If draft card burners and other protesters would only think of how great America really is, they would decide to become patriotic."

16. "The 'Pill' may be dangerous. A young girl taking the 'Pill' had trouble with vomiting, breathing, and a mysterious pain. She soon died."

17. "One drawback to sterilization is that, after sterilization, some women become overly attached to pets and their children."

18. "Marijuana is now being used by educated people, not just skid row types."

19. "One advantage of college is that it can lead to a better-paying job."

20. "With marijuana, there is no physical addiction to the drug as with alcohol and opium."

SET III

1. "What! You still don't own any mutual funds?"

2. "Not one of the nation's top twenty executives is fat."

3. "Successful businessmen have large vocabularies. This book will teach *you* to increase your vocabulary."

4. "Great Books—For people who are not ashamed of having brains."

5. "Today let these amazing shoes add inches to your height!"

6. "Cut out grease. Put your hair on a low calorie diet."

7. "Ninety-nine new homeowners out of 100 heat with gas."

8. "People who have everything always smoke Richman Cigars."

9. "Now. A contraceptive for the woman who *wants* children. Later."

10. "America. Love it or leave it."

Review: Themes for Analysis

That clear thinking is a prerequisite to effective composition is graphically illustrated by the following student essays.

1. Identify the *main* reasoning error in each essay.
2. Underline and label other blocks to logical thinking in each essay.

THE SHADOW OF DISASTER

The shadowy presence of disaster has changed the morality, religious beliefs, and even the dietary habits of many, many people in today's world.

The morality of today has changed sexually, ethically, and physically. Many people now hold the opinion that sex is enjoyable so why wait until marriage? These people feel that they will not be around that long and so they might as well enjoy sex while they can. When people start practicing free love, their ethical standards also decline. It is no longer necessary to follow tradition and many people develop their own standards or have their standards formed by the group they associate with. This wide range of standards has resulted in a "Do it to him before he gets you" type of ethics, which makes physical attacks on others acceptable.

The church of today is no longer the all powerful ruler God meant it to be. Many people have the belief no God exists, which makes it hard for the church to stay alive, much less be powerful. The church is definitely modifying its views and beginning to conform slightly to what the people want. But the basic problem is that the people are becoming more materialistic. They do not know when they are going to be dead or alive. People want something concrete that they can see or touch, not something akin to a dream. They want to see it before death.

Likewise, in a person's diet he wants something to eat *now*, not in half an hour or later in the afternoon. The demand for all these things is what causes our so-called "rat race life." In turn, our "rat race life" causes us to hurry a meal here and grab a snack later somewhere else. Because of this problem, we no longer sit down and enjoy meals like civilized people. No one ever has time, which makes people very nervous. Yes, our society is in the extreme, very nervous.

Our present day society is turning into a combination of hedonism and materialism, just like Sodom and Gomorrah. If the trend is not checked the shadow of disaster will not be a shadow much longer.

WORKING WIVES

Many young wives of today have been pushed into becoming the head of the family while their husbands are furthering their educations. The wife now has to assume the role of the provider, which takes pride away from her spouse. Her husband will probably develop a guilt complex. The complex he develops is one of guilt for he feels responsible for his mate; but since he is going to school, the ability to change the situation is not his.

As the provider for the family, the wife now takes on the responsibilities that the parents once had for their son. The wife now becomes a parent to her husband, supporting him and caring for his needs. When his education necessitates his wife's working, the husband becomes the little boy again. A guilt feeling of not being able to support his wife arises in him, which causes him to feel that his wife is dominating him.

Even after he has finished his education and
begins to work, he still experiences this feeling of guilt,
which draws him further away from his wife.
Instead of feeling pride in his accomplishments,
and in his wife, the husband's guilt feelings override
his sense, and he keeps drifting further and further
away from his wife. Often, it becomes easier for
him to leave his wife to escape his guilt, than
it is for him to stay and suffer shame.

Leaving the wife, just as a son would leave a
parent, becomes the only solution for the guilt-ridden
husband. The wife took the parents' position of
supporting the husband when she put him through
school. Now he leaves her much as he would
leave his parents after they put him through school.

INDIVIDUALITY VERSUS THE FAMILY

Throughout history it has been the individual
who stands out as the person with the initiative
and perseverance needed to become the famous leader
or the unexcelled inventor of the times. The type
of man with individualistic characteristics has the
strength and self-reliance to achieve. Along with
success, the individual has a true sense of
freedom, with nothing to tie him down.

What happens when the freedom is taken from
his existence? He becomes the family man, the
man with strong family ties. Family orientation will
simply not let a man be a free individual. He
is saddled with the responsibilities of a wife and
children. With the family as the center of his life, how
can a man even attempt to develop into a full individual? As an example, the person who is
dependent on parental support will not ever be alone
as a man. If he falls into trouble, the family will
be used as a crutch to fall back on. The person
who is alone will realize that, with no one to fall back

on, he will have to succeed. Therefore, the man
who is unmarried will be a true individual and will
have the tools needed to build and support his life.

The individual who stands alone is totally
responsible for his actions. He motivates his own
life pattern and thus assumes total responsibility for
the final reactions. Unlike him, the family man
does things for the good of the family and for the
needs of the family. He must answer to the family,
and then his center of life becomes the ball
and chain of his individualism.

Even though the man who is free of home bonds
does not have the responsibility of a family, it does
not mean he is irresponsible. He must be aware
of his owing it to himself to make a good life.
His actions will reflect directly back on him, and
no one else. The man of his own means can then say
with pride that he was self-made and stood alone
with the strength to come through as a freedom
loving individual. The individual proves also that
the only direction is forward and that, with family
bonds, he can only become a cocoon to the world, which
would deter him from that forward stride and
development.

THE IMMATURE MALE

What is Hugh Hefner's philosophy of women
doing to the American male? Hugh Hefner, the owner
of *Playboy* and the organizer of Playboy Clubs
all over the world, has made a fortune by using the
female as a sex symbol. He believes that the
bosom of a female should be emphasized in order
to catch the eye of the average American male.
Hefner has made his living by using "bunnies"
wearing obscene costumes as waitresses. But, because
of the immaturity of the American male, he
has become a millionaire.

The average man of forty-five does not consider himself immature, but he is. And using the bosom of the female as a sex symbol proves it. Only in America is the bosom used in this way. In other countries the hips, which are the normal portion of the body to associate with sex, are emphasized.

This immaturity goes back to what doctors call "momism." "Momism" is a difficult word to define, but essentially it means that men depend on women. Boys are brought up by their mothers; they have women school teachers; they are always surrounded by grandmothers instead of grandfathers. So they hardly see a male figure until they reach age twelve and enter high school. This is a little late. They have been around women too long.

This immaturity really goes even further back. It goes back to when the child was a baby. How is a child fed? By his mother's breast. The immature male remembers the pleasures of his "baby-hood" and associates them with the pleasures he wants now. This relates to the bosom. He thinks of the bosom as pleasure, because when he was a child the one thing that meant most to him was food. The food came from his mother's breast.

Is Hugh Hefner, by emphasizing the bosom, making the American male even more immature? Think about it.

UNMARRIED MOTHERS

Pornography on our movie screens, sex in our prisons, drug use among our youth! Immorality is rampant today. But I am most sickened by the aid given to unwed mothers. I cannot tolerate the fact that a woman without a husband gives birth, keeps the illegitimate child, and has only to sit back and collect money from the state for its support.

First of all, a woman has no human right to

bear a child from a man other than her husband.
The Bible states clearly that no woman shall lie
with another woman's husband or with any one other
than her true husband. This statement is found in
Exodus and throughout the entire Bible. God
has told us what is right and wrong. Adultery is
surely wrong.

In the second place the life of the child is at stake.
I have seen through friends that life without a
father is tough. Fatherly love is essential in becoming
a stable person. A mother's love is needed, but
a father's love is essential. I spent last summer in
West Berlin without a father. I never realized until
then how important his love was to me. Without
a father a part of life is gone; therefore the
child's life is at stake.

Thirdly, the woman collects money from the
state, supposedly to support her child, but does the state
know exactly what the money is used for? I know
a mother who actually lives for the paycheck for
her child. She does not, however, want it for
her child; she uses it to buy a new dress
to wear on her Friday night date.

The state is too easy on this type of woman.
If a woman has one illegitimate child, she will
probably sin again and have ten more. What kind
of life will these children live? What kind of
people will populate our world? We must not tolerate
unmarried mothers. To do so is to place a stamp
of approval on immorality!

Section Six

THE
RESEARCH
PAPER

"*Research Paper.*" *The term has a knell of deathly tedium about it. Despairing heroes have hurled themselves upon their swords at prospects far less bleak than those which the assignment of a "research paper" frequently conjures up before the mind's eye of the student. Yet the task need not be as formidable or neurosis inspiring as it is often allowed to become.*

Method Is the Name of the Game

The method presented in this section will not make the writing of a research paper easy or quick. But following it will make it easier and quicker and will ensure that you will end up with an acceptable paper rather than a pile of meaningless notes, an ashtray full of butts, a ballooning headache, and a drop slip.

It is important to recognize the significant difference between the research paper and the usual in- or out-of-class theme. When you are assigned or choose a subject on which to write a standard theme, you presumedly know enough about that subject to begin analysis of it immediately. The subject or aspect of a subject on which you write a library paper is fundamentally dif-

ferent. First, you must amass a fund of information on that subject. This you do through research and note-taking. Then you analyze not the subject, but the information about it which you have gathered. In other words, you determine the various points of view from which your sources have looked at the subject and classify these points of view.

Your originality manifests itself not in the content of the research paper, but in your classification and presentation of the views of diverse authorities.

Five Preliminaries

Put Yourself in a Positive Frame of Mind

If you can't approach the matter of writing a research paper with outright joyous excitement, don't approach it as if you were receiving a death sentence.

Choose a Subject That Interests You

You're going to have a lengthy affair with your subject. Choose one that has some charm.

Formulate a Question About Your Subject

It is answering this question that your research paper is all about. Your question should indicate clearly what *aspect* of the subject you are going to investigate. For example:

SUBJECT: Marital conflict
QUESTION: What are the primary causes of marital conflict?
ASPECT: Primary causes

SUBJECT: Marital conflict
QUESTION: What are the primary effects of marital conflict on children?
ASPECT: Effects on children

SUBJECT: LSD
QUESTION: What are the psychic effects of LSD?
ASPECT: Psychic effects

SUBJECT: LSD
QUESTION: How is LSD produced and distributed?
ASPECT: Production and distribution

Once you have formulated a question about your subject that clearly indicates the aspect of it which you are going to investigate, you should mutter this aspect to yourself every two minutes for at least an hour—"effects on children . . . effects on children . . . effects on children . . ." In your research you will be concerned *only* with that material on your subject which bears on the *aspect* you have chosen.

Get Your Instructor to Approve Your Question

This step is as important as any other. It may be that the aspect of the subject you've chosen is too broad, or too narrow. It may be that there is inadequate, easily available information on your subject or the aspect of it you've chosen. Your instructor will know.

Resolved: "I'd Rather Fight Than Switch!"

Once the question has been approved by your instructor, consider yourself a Catholic and your question the woman you've just married. Divorce is out of the question.

➋

Before You Go
to the Library

Most college libraries resemble cities that have been over-run, pillaged, and raped by hoards of barbarians. Faculty members invade and check out for eternity all books they think they may ever want to glance at; graduate students follow, filling their study carrels and sometimes maliciously misshelving crucial volumes to sabotage the efforts of fellow seminar students; and, close on their heels, comes a plague of noxious two-legged rodents that view a visit to the library as a chance to demonstrate their maturity by cutting, tearing, mutilating, and stealing.

To switch metaphors, the typical college library is a mining camp. You are a dogged prospector arriving well after the gold rush has begun. There's still gold in "them thar hills," but you're going to have to hunt for it. Resolve to have the patience of Job, the tenaciousness of a bulldog, the eternal optimism of a Colonel Sellers. Fill your mind with every half-baked "onward and upward" cliché you can scrounge up:

Winners never quit, and quitters never win!
Rome wasn't built in a day!
If at first you don't succeed, try, try, again!

"Forewarned is forearmed." You've just been forewarned. Now forearm yourself with a subject check list.

Prepare a Subject Checklist

A subject check list is a list of all subject headings under which, in the card catalog, *Readers' Guide,* etc., you might possibly find references to books or articles that might possibly have something in them on your subject.

Remember the gold prospector. Sure, he'd like to find a twelve-ounce nugget of pure gold, or even several. But he doesn't expect to. A book or an article directly on that particular aspect of your subject which you've chosen is such a nugget. Don't expect to find one, though you may find several. The best you can reasonably expect is to find, after a careful search, books and articles that have something, somewhere in them, to say about your subject.

The subject check list will allow you to locate these works.

☞ NOTE: Don't forget that you are concerned only with a particular *aspect* of your subject. But you must locate works on the subject before you can determine whether they deal with the aspect of the subject you are concerned with.

Say your subject is "Marital Conflict." Your question is: "What are the primary causes of marital conflict?" Think of all possible subject headings under which material on your subject might be classified.

Certainly, "Divorce" is the first that comes to mind, since conflict in the marriage is what, presumedly, leads to divorce. "Marriage" is another, since, obviously, people can't enjoy "marital" conflict unless they've first gotten married. "Marriage counseling" is another. Psychology is one, since conflicts are motivated, motives are mental, and Psychology deals with the mind. Sociology is such a related subject. It takes two to conflict and two to make a group, and groups are what Sociology is all about.

After you have written down every subject that you can think of that might bear on your subject, arrange them according to the *directness* with which they bear on your subject.

Your preliminary subject check list might look like this:

Marital conflict	Marriage counseling
Divorce	Psychology
Marriage	Sociology

Set a Date Limit on Your Research

Before going to the library, decide how far back you intend to go in your search for information on your subject. Almost all books and articles eventually become outdated. No iron-clad rule is possible, but, generally speaking, you should be able to find all the information you need in books and articles published within the last fifteen years. *Other considerations being equal,* the more recent a work, the better. If your subject is some contemporary phenomenon, such as LSD or Hippies or the Beatles, you will obviously move your date limit up to the year in which the phenomenon began to attract notice and comment.

Assemble Your Prospector's Kit

You will need a couple of pens, notebook paper, an ample supply of 3″ x 5″ lined note cards, some strong rubber bands, and an avid gleam in your eye.

3

In the Library:
Finding Gold-Bearing Ore

Assemble a Bibliography

A bibliography is a list of books and articles that may contain information relevant to your question.

You assemble your list of *books* by looking up each of the subjects on your subject checklist in the subject card catalog. You assemble your list of *articles* by looking up each of the subjects on your subject checklist in one or more of the indexes to periodicals.

The Subject Catalog

Start with the subject catalog. Look under the subject heading first on your list. Go through the cards one by one scanning the title and the list of "contents" that may appear at the bottom of the card. If either looks promising, even *faintly* promising, glance at the copyright date. If the book was originally published, or has been revised, within your date limit, jot down the call number, the last name of the author, and the title on a sheet of the notebook paper you have with you. Continue until you have looked at *every card* under that subject heading. At this point, put a check mark followed by the letters "cc" after the first subject on your subject check list, to indicate that you have gone through this subject heading in the card catalog:

Marital conflict/cc   Marriage counseling
Divorce   Psychology
Marriage   Sociology

Now go on to the next subject heading and repeat the process. Continue working through your subject check list in this manner until you have a list of twenty to thirty books or until you have exhausted your list of subjects, whichever comes first. Remember, out of thirty on your list, half may be unavailable. Out of the remaining fifteen, eight may be unusable for one or more of several reasons we'll discuss later. So out of a list of thirty you may, if you're lucky, come up with seven that contain material you can use.

Indexes to Periodicals

After you have assembled your book bibliography you are ready to assemble a bibliography of articles relevant to your question. Knowing how to assemble an extensive list of potentially relevant articles is especially important. Perhaps you will be unable to find enough material in books, or the books you want may be checked out, or most of the books available may be outdated. Furthermore, good articles tend to be highly focused, so you are more likely to find an in-depth answer to your specific question in an article than in a book that tries to cover all aspects of your subject. Finally, you are more likely to find the latest information or discoveries or views about a particular aspect of a subject in articles than in books.

In order to assemble a list of potentially relevant articles, you will use one or more of the standard *indexes to periodicals*. The two most comprehensive indexes to periodical literature are the *Readers' Guide* and the *Social Sciences and Humanities Index* (formerly *International Index to Periodicals*). The *Readers' Guide* indexes articles in popular magazines, the *Social Sciences and Humanities Index* articles in scholarly journals. Both of these indexes consist of a series of bound volumes covering a period of a year or more and soft-cover supplements that cover the period from the last bound volume to, roughly, the present.

Always use these indexes in a *systematic* fashion. Start with the first heading on your subject check list and work back from the most recent volume to your date limit. If, after you have reached your date limit, you do not have a bibliography of at least twenty to thirty promising articles, move on to your next subject heading or to the other index and repeat the process. Each time you follow a subject heading from the most recent volume back to your date limit, check it off on your subject check list with a /RG or /SSH. Never trust your memory.

Every time you find an article with a promising title, write out the citation *exactly as it appears* on a separate sheet of note paper entitled "Bibliography—Articles." But be selective. List only those articles with titles that indicate answers to your question. Assuming that our subject is "Marital Conflict" and our question is, "What are the primary causes of marital conflict?" which of the following articles indexed in the *Readers' Guide* would you list for investigation? Probably only three should appear in your bibliography (See highlighted passage taken from the *Readers' Guide.*):

Bibliography—Articles

Why marriages fail. S. Blum. il. Redbook 126:69 Ap '66

Marriage as a wretched institution. M. Cadwallader. il. Atlan 218: 57–61 N., '66

Stop divorces before they start. W. Hartley and E. Hartley. Good H 162:89 Ap '66

The titles of the other articles lack direct focus on your question.

DIVORCE

Early divorce warning system: Jewish community program. America 115:642 N 19 '66

Marriage, divorce and remarriage. F. R. Schreiber and M. Herman. il Sci Digest 60:24-7 N '66

New thinking on divorce: Catholic church. il Time 87:103-4 Mr 18 '66

Second thoughts on second marriages; views of Catholic theologians. Time 88:65 Jl 22 '66

Suggest new basis for divorce. Christian Cent 83:1023-4 Ag 24 '66

Why marriages fail. S. Blum. il Redbook 126: 69+ Ap '66

See also
Marriage

Great Britain

Divorce, English style. Newsweek 68:51 Ag 8 '66

Liabilities of being a lord; Earl of Harewood case. il Time 89:28 Ja 13 '67

Suggest new basis for divorce. Christian Cent 83:1023-4 Ag 24 '66

New York (state)

Catholic church opposes divorce reform. Christian Cent 83:197 F 16 '66

Catholics of New York; divorce issue. E. J. Hughes. Newsweek 67:23 Mr 21 '66

Century of progress; law revised. Newsweek 67:31-2 My 9 '66

Cutting the bonds of acrimony: New York may get new law. Life 60:4 F 11 '66

Divorce, New York style; Catholic church's stand. Newsweek 67:92 F 21 '66

Help wanted: divorce counselor. M. M. Hunt. il N Y Times Mag p 14-17 Ja 1 '67

In New York, new rules for easier divorces. U S News 60:12 My 9 '66

Liberalized divorce; New York state legislature studying 179-year-old law. Commonweal 83:524 F 4 '66

New York reforms divorce. Time 87:75 My 6 '66

New York reforms divorce statute. Christian Cent 83:610 My 11 '66

Sorry state of divorce law; Time essay. Time 87:26-7 F 11 '66

United States

Children at stake. K. D. Fishman. il N Y Times Mag p 146+ D 11 '66

Dearly unbeloved: Unitarian divorce rite. Newsweek 68:105 O 24 '66

Divorce American style. R. Hoffmann. Mlle 63:130-1+ S '66

Divorce and the family in America. C. Lasch. il Atlan 218:57-61 N '66

Marriage as a wretched institution. M. Cadwallader. il Atlan 218:62-6 N '66

Right of divorce. D. J. Cantor. il Atlan 218: 67-71 N '66

Stop divorces before they start. W. Hartley and E. Hartley. Good H 162:89+ Ap '66

Sunday daddy. B. Rollin. il Look 31:28-9 Ja 10 '67

Who speaks for Catholics? formation of Committee of Catholic citizens to support divorce reform. Commonweal 83:572 F 18 '66

DIVORCEES

Etiquette of divorce. A. Vanderbilt. Ladies
S '66

concern

Specialized Reference Works

In addition to the two general indexes we've mentioned, there are numerous specialized reference works.

BIOGRAPHY

Who's Who in America contains biographical details on important living Americans. *Who's Who* is the British counterpart.

The Dictionary of American Biography gives biographical sketches of important Americans no longer living. *Dictionary of National Biography* is the British counterpart.

The *Biography Index* indexes biographical material in books and periodicals.

CURRENT EVENTS

The New York Times Index indexes material published in *The New York Times.*

The *Monthly Catalog of the United States Government Publications* lists the publications of the various branches of the federal government. There is also an annual index to the *Catalog.*

MAJOR FIELDS

Art Index
Business Periodicals Index
Dramatic Index
Education Index
Engineering Index
Music Index

☞ NOTE: After you compile your book and article bibliographies, you will have a list of forty to sixty promising sources. But when you start searching for them, you're going to find many

of the books checked out or missing, many of the articles unavailable and others mutilated, and many of both irrelevant to
your question. What you've got to have, in a world in which
God is supposed to be dead, is *faith*. Don't get hung up on a
book that's checked out but *may* come back in a week; don't get
hung up on an article that you're sure was *just* what you needed
but which somebody cut out. Take these setbacks in stride and
keep searching.

4

In the Library:
Mining the Gold

TWO WARNINGS

Beware of Fool's Gold

As you know, in gold-mining areas of the West there is almost always abundant "fool's gold" which shines and glitters more than the real thing but which proves to be, on close inspection, little bits of absolutely worthless pyrite. Consider your instructor the county assayer. If you take him a bag of fool's gold, he's not going to place a very high value on it. In the cliffs and canyons of the library, too, you'll find fool's gold—*comment on your subject by people not qualified to write on it, or superficial comment, or illogically presented comment.*
These are the two tests for fool's gold.

1. Is the writer an authority *on the subject about which he is writing?*
2. Does the writer *avoid all "blocks to logical thinking" discussed in Section Five?*

Unless the answer to both these questions is "Yes," you should discard the work as fool's gold.

CONTROVERSIAL SUBJECTS ATTRACT FOOL'S GOLD

You are more likely to find fool's gold on the subject of "Pornography" than on the subject of "Photosynthesis."

POPULAR MAGAZINES ATTRACT FOOL'S GOLD

You are more likely to find fool's gold in *Reader's Digest* or *Look* than in *Saturday Review* or *Harper's*.

The surest test for fool's gold, however, is *internal* evidence. Here is where your experience in recognizing blocks to logical thinking can be fruitfully applied. Be especially alert for *either–or thinking, faulty causation,* and emotion-laden *moral judgment.* If the writer is relying on unacceptable implied assertions, or if he is not objective, or if his logic is fallacious, you must reject the work as fool's gold, *whoever* the author is.

Concentrate on longer articles. People who purchase fool's gold like it in small amounts. A three- or four-page article is less likely to be fool's gold than a one-page article.

Don't Be a Dirty Claim-Jumper

Most plagiarism occurs because the student doesn't have a firm grasp of just what constitutes it; but even if the instructor thinks it is probably accidental, rather than a deliberate attempt at deception, plagiarism, any plagiarism, makes your entire paper suspect.

You are, of course, plagiarizing when you quote a phrase, sentence, or series of sentences without enclosing them in quotation marks.

You are *also* plagiarizing when you go through a sentence or group of sentences and change words, rearrange, make deletions, etc. This is a strange situation. You now have a passage that is not as it was originally, so you can't put quotation marks at either end. Yet if you incorporate it in your paper, *even with a footnote at the end,* it is plagiarism, and will almost certainly be recognized as such.

There is only one sure way to avoid plagiarism:

Don't summarize or paraphrase a passage with the book or article open in front of you. Either *quote directly* or *close the book* and summarize the author's point.

MINING THE GOLD

Make a Bibliography Card

As soon as you see that a book or article contains answers to your question, make a bibliography card. When you make a bibliography card, you proceed like the prince who was searching for Cinderella. He had a slipper and sought the foot that fit it; you have some publishing data and must search for the bibliographical model that fits your data.

If your school does not issue its own style sheet, you can find all the information you need about footnote and bibliographical form in the standard *MLA Style Sheet.*

In the lower right-hand corner of your bibliography card, put a code letter, thus:

> Biblio—Bk
> Hollis, Florence. *Women in Marital Conflict: A Casework Study.* New York: Family Service Association of America, 1962.
>
> A

The code letter should be different for each bibliography card. We will discuss the use of this letter in a moment.

Take Notes

Efficient notes greatly simplify the process of writing the paper and help ensure that it will be of high quality.

TWO RULES OF NOTE-TAKING

1. Take notes *only* on material that answers your *question. Do not* take notes on material revelant to your *subject* but not relevant to your question about it.
2. Quote as *little as possible*. Combat the tendency to "copy out" material onto your note cards. "Copying out" may seem the quickest and easiest way. In the long run it's the longest and the hardest. The gold you're mining consists of facts and opinions, *not* phraseology. Summarize or paraphrase the author's opinion and the main reasons or facts he gives in support of it. Do not copy out his words.

Generally speaking, quotation in a research paper is best used for rhetorical purposes. When the author makes a point more succinctly and more memorably than you could possibly make it yourself, quotation is fully justified. But do not use quotation to communicate ideas or views that you can adequately express in your own words. Such misuse tends to weaken coherence and unity in your paper.

EXAMPLE: NOTE-TAKING

Our subject is "Marital Conflict," our question: "What are the primary causes of marital conflict?" Read the selection from *Women in Marital Conflict* that follows and study the nature of the notes derived from it.

Among the qualities most markedly interfering with satisfaction and comfort in marriage is an excessive degree of emotional dependence. What do we mean when we speak of excessive emotional dependence? Obviously there is a degree of dependence in all of us, young and old. Children, of necessity, depend on parents and others not only for physical care but also for love and affection. In early infancy they are completely receptive and unable to give anything in return for their parents' care. Before long, however, they begin to respond with returning love and affection. It is characteristic of the love of children that it comes in response to love given first by an older person. The child responds to affection but is usually not able to love if he is rejected. The slightest withdrawal of parental affection causes uncertainty and responding hostility on the part of the young child.

Adults are also emotionally dependent, or, perhaps we might better say, interdependent. The very need for love demands reliance on others. But the adult's dependence is not normally of the same degree as that of the child. He is usually able, at least part of the time, to extend love and affection even when he is not sure of a like response. Likewise, adults can stand periods of anger and withdrawal in love relationships without becoming excessively anxious, or retaliating by prolonged hostility and a retreat from the relationship. Rather, there is enough stability, warmth for the other person, and concern for him to enable the adult to endure with some equanimity the fluctuations that occur in all human relationships.

At times, to be sure, even the stable adult may retreat to a more childish type of relationship. This occurs most typically in illness, when people frequently become like children in expecting an excess of love and consideration from other people and, again like children, are able to give love themselves only when they are surrounded by affection.

When we speak of dependence in adults in the sense of an unusual degree of emotional dependence, we mean that the adult is characteristically reacting like a child in not carrying his fair share in the love relationship. For one reason or another he is demanding that others be more affectionate, more patient, more protective, than adults usually expect. If he is not given this sort of affection he becomes fearful, and hostile or depressed. He is too ready to believe that wife or husband is interested in another person, oversensitive to slights, demanding of attention, nagging and critical, or even openly abusive.

Excessive Emotional Dependence—Definition
Person is responding like a child. Can't give affection easily. Needs constant reassurance. Withdraws affection easily. Is suspicious and mistrusting.

A, 21–22

☞ COMMENT: Since the term "excessive emotional dependence" is not one for which there is a single generally accepted meaning (since it is, in other words, an unconcretized abstraction), you must concretize it before you can discuss it as a cause of marital conflict.

People vary in the amount of love they need and the amount they are able to give in return. Some, the most retarded of all, are able to give very little. Even with a good deal of affection, the best they can do is attain an equilibrium of nonhostility. Like the infant, their response is meager. More frequently, even unusually dependent people are able to respond with some love and warmth provided they are secure in the knowledge that they are loved by the other person.

Characteristically, excessively dependent people have not outgrown a childish type of attachment to their parents. Either consciously or unconsciously they cling to early love relationships, fearing to relinquish them for new attachments. We shall trace in Chapter IV the ways in which such unusually strong parental ties enter into marriage relationships. In this chapter we are more concerned with the quality of dependence itself.

The person who is dependent in his love relationships often shows other sorts of dependence. Such people are not self-reliant. They find it hard to make major decisions and prefer to be told what to do. Often they continue to rely on parental standards of conduct and seek advice in a way that is distasteful to the average adult.

☞ COMMENT: These three paragraphs *characterize* the emotionally dependent person. But since they do not explain why excessive dependence causes marital conflict, they are not relevant to our *question*. Hence you should take no notes from them.

What is the effect of such dependent patterns on marriage relationships? There is no such thing as a marriage completely devoid of hostility. Occasionally such hostile feelings are consistently repressed. But more frequently, and more naturally, they are expressed —sometimes mildly and sometimes with vigor. No two people can completely and exactly meet each other's needs. One likes to sleep late, the other is an early starter; one likes pies, the other prefers ice cream; one likes spectator sports, the other prefers a mystery story in a comfortable chair by the fire; one believes in saving for the future, the other thinks a bird in hand is worth two in the bush;

and on and on. Even the happiest marriage inevitably requires adjustments and compromises and brings frustration along with its satisfactions. We vary in mood from day to day. Disappointments and irritations in life outside the home as well as those inside contribute to black days and to even longer periods of discouragement and general grouchiness. This is one of the chief reasons why the dependent person finds it so hard to make a success of marriage. Normally each person must carry the other over the rough spots. Each must care enough for the other to be able to understand his distress or, if not to understand, at least to endure it without ceasing to love. This does not mean perpetual sweetness on both sides. It is perfectly possible to be furious at another person—and say so —and still to love and know that one is loved. Possible, that is, for the mature and stable person. For here is just where the dependent person falls down. He is not able to feel loved or to continue to give love during periods of hostility or temporary lapses in his partner's affection.

> Excessive Emotional Dependence—Effect
> Dependent person can't continue to give love and affection during periods of strife and hostility, or when partner's affection lapses.
>
> A, 28

☞ COMMENT: This inability of the excessively emotionally dependent (EED) person to "give" is one reason why excessive emotional dependence (EED) causes marital conflict.

When real evidence of infidelity exists, it is natural for a woman to be both jealous and angry but when there is only suspicion, the more secure and generous person refrains from jumping to conclusions and is able to discuss the matter. Even where there is actual infidelity, if the marriage as a whole has been satisfying, the wife's natural resentment and grief need not turn into complete and lasting denial of her affection for her husband and the values of her marriage. The dependent woman, however, often actually abets her husband's infidelity. If there really is another woman, by her immediate, strong hostility and withdrawal of love, she leaves the field clear for her rival. This behavior is in contrast to that observed, in our study, in several more mature women who showed an amazing amount of patience and, by continuing to be friendly with their husbands or looking in themselves for causes for dissatisfaction, were able to tide their families over a period of the husband's infatuation, returning to a better relationship later.

> Excessive Emotional Dependence—Effect
> Great suspiciousness. Especially of husband's supposed infidelity.
>
> A, 29

☞ COMMENT: Another reason why EED leads to marital conflict.

Another characteristic often found in dependent women, which can become very annoying to their husbands, is their excessive "need to be right." It is very difficult for them to admit that they might be wrong in a disagreement or in a course of action they have taken. When things go wrong, blame is constantly projected on someone else—all too frequently on the husband. One might speculatively suggest two roots for this. Both grow out of the fact that love in childhood is so often given as a reward for good behavior or on condition that the child will be good. Therefore: (1) The woman with an excessive need to be loved on a childish level will lay great store by being good. Within herself she feels that she must be good or she will not be loved. Hence she must insist that she *is* good. (2) The woman who feels that she has not been loved enough may have a strong need to believe that this is not her own fault, not a punishment for her own lacks and misdeeds, not something that she deserved. We caught a glimpse of this mechanism in Mrs. McCormick when she said that "wherever she stayed she felt she was only there on probation and could stay only if she were a good girl. She felt as though she had to hang up her clothes and be quiet or else she could not stay."

Excessive Emotional Dependence—Effect
The EED person has a great "need to be right." Therefore, such a person tends to blame her husband,
but never herself.

A, 30

☞ COMMENT: A third reason why EED causes marital conflict.

Despite the fact that dependent wives are quick to take offense and withdraw love easily, they tend to cling desperately to their husbands even though their lives may be a constant procession of disappointments and bickerings. Two factors, no doubt, contribute to this: (1) Their need for love is so very great that they hold on to even a meager and uncertain source of affection; half a cake is better than none. (2) Often they need someone on whom to lean and are afraid to take the responsibility for family leadership entirely upon their own shoulders.

☞ COMMENT: There is nothing relevant to our *question* in this paragraph. We are looking for reasons why EED causes marital conflict, not for reasons why the EED woman clings to her husband.

It is true that not infrequently a marriage between a very dependent woman and a man whose need to care protectively for his wife is unusually strong works out rather well. In our culture dependence is a quality that combines well with femininity; some men are glad to carry the kind of responsibility this type of marriage involves and are able to give their wives a kind of parental security. If we are right in seeing the dependent person as one who ordinarily is able to return love if he is assured of the affection of the other person, it is not surprising that these marriages work out satisfactorily, since the wife is able to respond warmly to her protecting husband.

Excessive Emotional Dependence—Qualification
An EED wife may not cause great conflict in the
marriage if the husband is emotionally secure and
likes a protective role.

A, 33

☞ COMMENT: You must *never* distort your source in order to bolster your point (or for any other reason). The author makes a significant qualification; you must make it too.

Unfortunately, all too often the husband is not able to bear his wife's dependence. One dependent person often attracts another and we find the husband as incapable of carrying this double responsibility as is the wife herself.

Excessive emotional dependence is indeed a hazard to marriage.*

Excessive Emotional Dependence—Effect
"hazard to marriage"

A, 35

☞ COMMENT: Like "need to be right," this is a succinct summarizing phrase you might want to use.

---

* Florence Hollis, *Women in Marital Conflict* (New York: Family Service Association of America, 1962).

SUMMARY: Note-Taking

1. Each note is *brief.*
2. Each note *condenses.*
3. Each note card contains only *one* fact or reason. (Each different reason why EED is a hazard to marriage is on a different card. This allows *you* to determine the order of presentation in your paper.)
4. Each note bears on the *question* about your subject. (No notes that, though relevant to the subject, do not answer the question about it, are taken.)
5. Each note avoids quotation. Only an occasional succinct *phrase* is quoted.

The Note Card

SUBJECT HEADINGS

Never put more than one opinion or fact on the same note card because you must be able to indicate the nature of the note by a brief subject heading on the top line of the note card. The subject heading should show the relation of the note to your *question.* If you can't come up with such a heading, the note is not relevant.

Given our question, "What are the primary causes of marital conflict?" your subject headings should reflect *causes*: "Changing interests," "jealousy," "boredom," "strife over children," "adultery," "Excessive emotional dependence," etc. Other questions about other subjects require different sorts of subject headings. For example:

Question: Is censorship desirable?

Possible headings: "No—Limits expression"
                             "Yes—Protects morals"
                             "No—Limits free choice"
                             "No—Has political dangers"

Question: In what areas does the Mafia operate?

Possible headings: Prostitution   Bribery
                             Murder   Blackmail
                             Extortion   Rackets

Question: Should abortion laws be liberalized?

Possible headings: Yes—Physical health
                             Yes—Mental health
                             No—Infant murder
                             Yes—Population control
                             Yes—Isn't murder

CODE LETTER AND PAGE NUMBER

CODE LETTER

This letter ("A" in our examples) corresponds to the letter on the relevant bibliography card. Using a code letter allows you to avoid writing out author and title on each note card and, as we will see, makes outlining and footnoting easier.

PAGE NUMBER

As soon as you have finished taking a note, *always* record the number of the page or pages from which it was taken.

REMINDER: If you have quoted, don't forget to put quotation marks around the quoted material. *Don't trust your memory.*

IN THE SALOON

—Three Diseases

The student research paper is especially susceptible to three diseases. Taking notes in the fashion that we have discussed is the best possible vaccination against all three of these diseases.

THE STRING-OF-BEADS DISEASE

The string-of-beads disease is caused by excessive quotation in your notes. The symptoms are a series of brief quotations strung together by words of your own. Here's an example from a student's paper:

Inflation is a "menace"[1] to the "economic security"[2] of Americans because it "eats away"[3] at savings and "reduces the value"[4] of life insurance and annuities. Inflation "steadily lowers"[5] the "purchasing power"[6] of the dollar. In some countries where "inflation is rampant"[7] the savings of the middle class have been "wiped out."[8]

THE CUT-AND-PASTE DISEASE

This disease is also caused by excessive quotation in your notes, especially that of the "copying-out" variety. Its symptoms are big blobs of quotation interspersed with a few lines of your own writing.

THE BOOK-REPORT DISEASE

The book-report disease is caused by overreliance on one or two sources, generally books. A paper suffering from this disease resembles a summary of one or two sources. The temptation, if you find a book that answers your question at great length and in detail, is to summarize page after page, chapter after chapter, and then use that author's order of presentation, and that author's classifications in your paper. The symptoms of the book-report disease are found in the footnotes of the finished paper. The footnotes refer almost exclusively to one or two sources, and as the paper progresses, the page numbers of the footnotes steadily rise.

All three of these diseases are themselves symptomatic. They reveal that the student, instead of dominating his sources, is being dominated by them. *You* properly *organize* and *write* a research paper. The points of view, the opinions, the reasons and facts that you present have been gathered from others; but *you* must present them in *your* own words, in an order and manner that *you* determine.

Exercise: Note-Taking

The excerpt that follows from "Why Couples Quarrel" describes another cause of marital conflict. Our subject is "marital conflict"; our question is, "What are the primary causes of marital conflict?" Read this material, taking as many notes as you feel appropriate. Make your notes display the five characteristics that we have discussed, and be sure to label each note card with an appropriate subject heading.

One out of every four women in our survey claimed that money was the main matter currently causing the most friction. Couples of every income group, including the highest, were fighting about it. But it turned up as the cause of serious fights in more than half the households with incomes between $5,000 and $7,500 a year. In comparison, only a quarter of the families in the lowest income group (under $5,000 a year) were fighting seriously about money, and in the income group between $7,500 and $10,000 a year, only one in eleven.

As one wife with a low income pointed out, below $5,000 a year there "simply isn't enough money to fight about. You spend for the necessities and there's nothing left over." When the family income mounts to the middle brackets, however, a few choices become possible. Since the extra cash isn't much, the choices must be discussed in detail; and if the couple can't agree, the discussion becomes louder—until they find they are fighting.

Accusations of complete economic incompetence are often hurled in such fights: "He claims I'm immature about money, that I don't understand it, I don't know how to budget, I don't put anything aside, I must be letting storekeepers cheat me. . . . I think he really did believe that two could live as cheaply as one." But in most cases it seemed likely that the problems arose because different backgrounds and different temperaments had given the couples completely opposed pictures of how money should be used. One wife, for example, came from a family that made a great fuss over Christmas, birthdays, anniversaries or any other occasion for gift-giving. What she saw as warmhearted generosity he saw as "simply crazy." She took to buying likely gifts whenever she had the extra cash and hiding them until she could find deserving recipients with something to celebrate. In time he discovered this drain on the family purse—and the result was a fight that to this day has not really been settled. Another story told by a young bride presents a classic vignette of two diametrically opposed attitudes. The couple had two bottles of Scotch, one expensive and the other low-priced. She brought out the cheaper one for company, "saving the good one for ourselves." He simply had not been brought up to treat company that way, and the resultant fight lasted two days.

The clash between borrowers and lenders, savers and spenders, hoarders and investors, can, of course, cause painful tensions all through married life. A North Carolina wife blames thirteen years of marital arguments on the fact that "I was brought up to be very careful with money, and his family always bought whatever they wanted, whether they could afford it or not." The wife of a Wyoming rancher wrote, "I go nuts worrying about bills. And he says, 'Why worry? It's only money!'" It is interesting that there was no apparent difference in the male and female attitudes toward the running up of bills. Neither sex can be said to take a truly liberal or truly conservative fiscal position. For every wife who fought to restrain her husband's freehandedness, another was struggling to liberate the treasury from what she took to be a tight tyranny. As the wife of a Wisconsin farmer wrote, "Money spent for anything is his bugaboo. I like to improve the farm. My worst argument with him occurred when I wanted to buy heavy rubber mats for under our fifteen cows. Our floor was made with a dip in front and their feet slipped, and they couldn't stand with their feet straight. I won —cost nearly $400."

In most households men tend to exercise greater power over the money than their wives—because in most cases they are earning the income. Generally, the more cash the husband supplies, the greater his fiscal authority. It is the husband whose income must be eked out by a working wife who is most likely to find himself in a fight over money—and losing it. One wife described two contrasting stages of her marriage. In the early years she and her husband fought seriously over money because "I was in creative work; he was entering a profession. My salary was greater than his, yet he demanded full control." Over the years her husband's annual income rose, until it is now well over $12,000. She continued, "We still tend to disagree about the spending of money, but I earn only bits for occasional work and he makes quite a lot, so today we seldom really fight at all."

In short, nothing seems so effective in ending fights over money as an increase in the supply of it.*

5

After You Leave
the Library:
Refining the Gold

After you have completed your note taking, you can bid farewell to the library. But don't stop too soon. You should have perhaps one hundred note cards for a 1,500-word research paper, twice that many for a 3,000-word paper. Be especially wary of stopping before you have fully mastered your subject. When you find yourself reading article after article relevant to your question without getting any new answers to your question *or* any new slants on answers that you have, that is the time to stop—only after, in other words, you have found all available answers to your question.

Analysis

Your job now is to analyze your notes in order to come up with a meaningful *order of presentation* and a *thesis.* To analyze your notes, you first determine the various *points of view* that they represent and you then *classify* these points of view.

1. DETERMINE THE POINTS OF VIEW

If you have given each note card an appropriate subject heading in the manner described in our discussion of note-taking, your points of view are already indicated. Simply "deal out" your note cards into separate piles according to the point of view (answer to your question) that each card represents. We can illustrate the process by examining some hypothetical questions and subject headings:

Question: What are the major causes of highway fatalities?

SUBJECT HEADINGS (POINTS OF VIEW)	Drinking Brake failure Inattention Blowouts Fatigue

Question: What are the various means of contraception?

SUBJECT HEADINGS (POINTS OF VIEW)	Estrogen and progesterone pills Plastic coil Morning-after pill Diaphragm Birth-control injection Sterilization of the woman Vaginal foam Sterilization of the man Vaginal suppositories

Question: What are the primary causes of marital conflict?

SUBJECT HEADINGS (POINTS OF VIEW)	Conflict over money Overcrowding in the home Excessive emotional dependence Conflict with wife's relatives Sexual incompatibility Conflict over discipline of children Adultery Conflict with husband's relatives Selfishness Mother-in-law living in the home

2. CLASSIFY THE POINTS OF VIEW

You must now, if you are to avoid the "Ten-Little-Indians Disease," find not more than three or four *major classifications* under which your various points of view can be grouped.

THE TEN-LITTLE-INDIANS DISEASE

A paper suffers from the Ten-Little-Indians Disease when the student has not clearly established *major* classifications. The first words of paragraphs in a paper suffering from the Ten-Little-Indians Disease read like this: "One cause of marital conflict is . . ./Another cause is . . ./A third cause is . . ./Still another reason for conflict in marriage is . . ./A fifth reason for such conflict is . . ." and so forth. Pity the reader. For all he knows, there may be fifty little Indians.

So analyze your points of view to determine the major classifications that they represent. We can illustrate this process with the three examples we used a moment ago:

Question: What are the major causes of highway fatalities?

POINTS OF VIEW	CLASSIFICATION
Drinking	Driver
Brake failure	Mechanical
Inattention	Driver
Blowouts	Mechanical
Fatigue	Driver

Question: What are the various means of contraception?

POINTS OF VIEW	CLASSIFICATION
Estrogen and progesterone pills	Chemical
Plastic coil	Mechanical
Morning-after pill	Chemical (experimental)
Diaphragm	Mechanical
Birth-control injection	Chemical (experimental)

Sterilization of the woman	Surgical
Vaginal foam	Chemical
Sterilization of the man	Surgical
Vaginal suppositories	Chemical

Question: What are the primary causes of marital conflict?

POINTS OF VIEW	CLASSIFICATION
Conflict over money	Money
Overcrowding in the home	Money
Excessive emotional dependence	Character
Conflict with wife's relatives	In-laws
Sexual incompatibility	Sex
Conflict over discipline of children	Children
Adultery	Sex
Conflict with husband's relatives	In-laws
Selfishness	Character
Mother-in-law living in the home	In-laws

The Topic Outline

You should now group your note cards in little stacks headed by your major classifications. Keep each point of view within a major classification separate. For example:

Stress resulting from inadequate income	Character deficiencies	Conflict over in-laws	Conflict over sex	Conflict over children
Conflict over money	Excessive emotional dependence	Conflict with wife's relatives	Sexual incompatibility	Conflict over discipline of children
Overcrowding in the home	Selfishness	Conflict with husband's relatives	Adultery	
		Mother-in-law living in the home		

1. Discard those major classifications for which you have only one point of view or only a few note cards (such as the "children" classification in the "marital conflict" example).
2. Rearrange your stacks of note cards to reflect:
   A. The order in which you wish to develop the major classifications.
   B. The order in which you wish to develop the various points of view within each major classification.
3. Mark each major classification with the appropriate Roman numeral; mark each point of view with the appropriate capital letter.

I. Stress resulting from inadequate income	II. Conflict over in-laws	III. Conflict over sex	IV. Character deficiencies
A. Overcrowding in the home	A. Conflict with husband's relatives	A. Sexual incompatibility	A. Excessive emotional dependence
B. Conflict over money	B. Conflict with wife's relatives	B. Adultery	B. Selfishness
	C. Mother-in-law living in the home		

Voila! A Topic Outline.

The Sentence Outline

This is the crucial step in the refining process. If you take your time and do it carefully, your paper will virtually write itself from the completed sentence outline.

A. You should first convert all Roman numeral and capital letter points of view into complete sentences in the form of assertions, and then formulate your *thesis statement*. Put your thesis at the top of your outline. It should *answer* the question that you used to guide your research. For example:

Subject: Marital conflict
Question: What are the primary causes of marital conflict?
Thesis: Inadequate income, interfering in-laws, sexual antagonisms, and character deficiencies in one or both of the marriage partners are the primary causes of marital conflict.

B. Next you should very carefully examine the note cards for each point of view within a particular classification and decide how and in what order you are going to use them to develop a paragraph or portion of a paragraph.

C. Then indicate that order in your sentence outline. This will enable you to write your paper directly from your sentence outline and your note cards.

Here is how that portion of your sentence outline concerning excessive emotional dependence might look:

IV. Character deficiencies in one or both of the marriage partners often cause conflict.
   A. Excessive emotional dependence threatens marital happiness.
      1. definition (A, 21–22)
      2. qualification (A, 33)
      3. eed is a "hazard to marriage" (A, 35)
         a. (A, 29)
         b. (A, 30)
         c. (A, 28)

Notice how you can write your first draft directly from your outline:

Excessive emotional dependence threatens marital happiness. A person who is excessively dependent is one who reacts, emotionally, in the manner of a child. Such a person is slow to give affection but quick to withdraw it. A person of this sort, most often the woman, is in need of constant reassurance from her husband, but is herself suspicious and mistrusting (A, 21–22). Of course, certain types of emotionally independent and protective men may not be seriously disturbed by this dependence, but most husbands have normal emotional needs themselves which the excessively dependent woman is unable to satisfy (A, 33). This sort of dependence is a major "hazard to marriage" (A, 35) for several reasons. The woman tends to be extremely suspicious, especially of infidelity (A, 29). She has a strong "need to be right" (A, 30) that causes her to blame her husband, but never herself, for any dissatisfaction she may feel. But most important of all, the wife who is excessively emotionally dependent endangers the marriage by her inability to support her husband in time of need. She is unable to continue to give her love and affection during inevitable periods of strife or hostility or during temporary lapses in her husband's affection (A, 28). The emotionally dependent wife, in short, is unable to make her husband feel either secure or accepted.

☞ NOTE:

A. *Order* of presentation is *entirely* the writer's own.
B. *Phraseology* is almost entirely so.
C. Quotes are *integrated* into the writer's own sentences.

Got it?
Let's be sure.

Exercise: Refining the Gold

The notes that you took in the previous exercise represent the point of view of "conflict over money" (B) within the major classification, "stress resulting from inadequate income" (I).

1. Construct a portion of a sentence outline, keying your note cards to that outline in the manner illustrated on page 289.
2. Write a paragraph from this outline in the manner illustrated on pages 289–290.

Parting Words

Well, that's it. The rest is just mechanics. This is not to say the mechanics aren't important. They should be *perfect*. But they don't require thinking, just technique.

After you've finished your rough draft, you should carefully revise your paper. Apply the various principles of effective writing that we have discussed and be sure your paragraphs and sentences conform to them. Then retype your paper:

1. Make a *title page*.
2. Put in *footnotes*.
3. Make a *bibliography*.
4. *Proofread*, and then have a friend proofread, the entire paper.

CORRECTION SYMBOLS

I. Paragraphs

AO: Acknowledge the opposition

TS: Topic sentence unclear, imprecise, or insufficiently limited

FD: Lacks full development

U: Lacks unity

Coh: Lacks coherence

T: Lacks transition

II. Sentences

ST: Fails sound test

BL: Be literal

W: Choose the exact word

NV: Noun into verb

VV: Verbal into verb

AE: Avoid exaggeration

PV: Avoid the passive voice

IS: Make the idea subject the grammatical subject

III. Reasoning

E-O: Either–or thinking

MJ: Hasty moral judgment

CA: Condemnation by association

CC: Culturally conditioned assumption

PC: Primary certitude

RF: Reaction formation

C: Compartmentalization

FL: Figurative language

FA: False analogy

FC: Faulty causation

IA: Implied assertion

UA: Unconcretized abstraction